Dear Reader:

The book you are about to [read] the St. Martin's True Cri[me Library, what the New] *York Times* calls "the leader in true crime!" Each month, we offer you a fascinating account of the latest, most sensational crime that has captured the national attention. St. Martin's is the publisher of John Glatt's riveting and horrifying SECRETS IN THE CELLAR, which shines a light on the man who shocked the world when it was revealed that he had kept his daughter locked in his hidden basement for 24 years. In the Edgar-nominated WRITTEN IN BLOOD, Diane Fanning looks at Michael Petersen, a Marine-turned-novelist found guilty of beating his wife to death and pushing her down the stairs of their home—only to reveal another similar death from his past. In the book you now hold, DYING FOR LOVE, legendary True Crime author Carlton Smith explores the twists and turns of a tale of love and marriage gone horribly wrong.

St. Martin's True Crime Library gives you the stories behind the headlines. Our authors take you right to the scene of the crime and into the minds of the most notorious murderers to show you what really makes them tick. St. Martin's True Crime Library paperbacks are better than the most terrifying thriller, because it's all true! The next time you want a crackling good read, make sure it's got the St. Martin's True Crime Library logo on the spine—you'll be up all night!

Charles E. Spicer, Jr.
Executive Editor, St. Martin's True Crime Library

THE TRUE CRIME TITLES OF

CARLTON SMITH

Available from the True Crime Library of
St. Martin's Paperbacks

DYING FOR LOVE

Carlton Smith

St. Martin's Paperbacks

DYING FOR LOVE

Copyright © 2011 by Carlton Smith.

Cover photograph of bride and groom by RK Studio / Kate Huisman / Getty Images. Cover photograph of window by Pelmof / Alamy.

For information address St. Martin's Press, 175 Fifth Avenue, New York, NY 10010.

ISBN: 978-0-312-38169-1

Printed in the United States of America

St. Martin's Paperbacks edition / December 2011

St. Martin's Paperbacks are published by St. Martin's Press, 175 Fifth Avenue, New York, NY 10010.

10 9 8 7 6 5 4 3 2

DYING FOR LOVE

I.

The Crime

Early Thursday Morning

April 13, 2006

Blairsville, Pennsylvania

1.

The killer drove through the narrow streets of the small town in west-central Pennsylvania. It was raining lightly, a midnight off-loading of warm, wet, windy, fat drops torpedoing down from the muggy darkness above. The intermittent spatter rendered the oily asphalt ahead shiny in his headlights. The atmosphere was pregnant with the sullenness of heavier thunderstorms that threatened from the northwest. It was the sort of edgy night that could make anyone sweat and wish it would just get it over with and pour.

The wipers slapped desultorily back and forth across the killer's windshield, beating a refrain of inevitability: the time *had come, had come, had come, had come,* in an almost maddening cadence. Something had to give, there had to be an end to it. The killer was more than ready to make sure it all stopped for the sake of peace, and maybe happiness.

The houses of the small town were older and the streets narrow, like many in this semirural stretch of Pennsylvania an hour or so east of Pittsburgh, before automobiles had been invented—well lived-in, yet well loved for more than a century, history in their front yards, their porches, their backyards, their sidewalks; in their Lions Club, Rotary club, Elks Lodge, and VFW, and in their churches; in the bandstand on the west end of town just before the Conemaugh River, the venerable high school recently converted to upscale office space, side by side with a local trade school, and especially the trees. In this town, moving from one economy to another, many generations had grown up, from toddlers to grandparents: almost everyone knew who everyone else was, if not by name, then by sight; and if not by sight, at least by reputation. This was the heartland of America, at least as the myth tells us it should be, and sometimes it really is.

By day, the large, well-branched trees provided comfort and shade for their small, welcoming neighborhoods. Elms and larches, mostly, where, under their protective umbrellas, children played in close-knit groups. But by night, in a sultry, threatening storm like this one, those same trees loomed dark and sinister, branches whipping violently in the warm gusts, their large trunks potential lightning rods, every one. And then a thunderclap followed three or four seconds later by the flash, and the smell of ozone. The unpredictable dance between the utter blackness above and the sudden lightning made it easy to think something demonic was hovering in the air. It was certainly safer to pull the covers over one's head and wait for a quieter, drier, cooler, saner dawn.

The killer turned off the small, two-lane highway, Route 217, then found his way into a narrow alley and parked. After some minutes he got out of his vehicle and made his silent way toward the rear of the darkened house, padding in his sneakers through the small puddles toward the back door, which he knew would be unlocked.

Sometime a little after 1:00 a.m., he slipped through the back, moved through the darkened kitchen and dining area, down the hall, and came upon his target dozing on a sofa in the small living room.

What happened next would become a matter of speculation. Did Dr. John Yelenic, a well-regarded thirty-nine year-old Blairsville dentist, awaken and recognize the intruder? Were harsh words exchanged? Was there an argument, then a struggle? Why had the killer come in the middle of the night? Only two people could say for sure, and within a very few minutes one of them would be dead.

Later, the neighbors would try to puzzle out what took place that night on South Spring Street in Blairsville. Some thought they heard two men shouting in the early morning hours, between 1:00 and 2:00 a.m. Several thought they'd heard screaming—horrible, bloodcurdling screams, as if a pig were being slaughtered, as one later put it. They said neighborhood dogs began barking. But at least one neighbor thought that the argument had taken place much later, say, around 3:00 or 3:30 a.m or even later than that.

So, had there been two arguments, two different confrontations? Or even two different intruders, but only one killer?

Whatever the time of the disturbance, by all accounts, by 4:00 a.m. the dogs quieted again and the neighborhood settled back to sleep. The volatile, thunderous storm drifted off to the east, giving way to a gray, uncertain mist in the ensuing, cooler dawn.

Sometime the following day—still April 13, 2006—a postal delivery person arrived at the old house at 233 South Spring Street, stashing letters in the box and magazines in the lower rack, right next to the front door. Whoever delivered the mail seemingly did not notice the narrow broken window next to the front door, or the broken glass underfoot, or the red streaks that cascaded all the way down the front wall to puddle on the wooden porch below. Nor did the mail carrier notice the unmoving sweat-suit-clad legs on the other side of the bloody window.

Around 3:00 p.m. that same afternoon, nine-year-old Zachary Uss, who lived with his family next door, came onto the front porch of the house owned by Dr. John Yelenic. He wanted to return a video game the dentist had loaned him a day or so earlier. Zachary saw that a small windowpane on the left side of the door had been knocked out. Broken glass was on the porch, and there were red streaks descending from the shattered frame and a red substance in a puddle below. He peered in through the broken window and saw the gray clad legs of a man lying on the floor in the entry hall. The upper torso was out of young Zachary's view, in the living room off to the left, and the legs weren't moving.

Zachary retreated to his own house and told his older brother, Craig, seventeen, that something seemed wrong at the Yelenic house. Craig decided to look for himself.

As Craig mounted the front porch, he, too, saw the broken glass and the red streaks running down from the broken window, and the red puddle on the porch. He looked through the shattered glass pane and saw the gray legs extending into the hallway. He called out to Yelenic but got no answer. Craig tried the front door but found it bolted from the inside. Reaching through the broken window frame, he slid back the dead bolt and, with his other hand, turned the doorknob from the front. He went in. Almost immediately Craig saw blood all over the entry hall on the floor, high up on the walls, even close to the entry hall light switch. He saw the curtains that normally hung over the door-side windows on the floor, crumpled with their rod, and splattered with a dark substance that looked like blood.

Stepping carefully, Craig made his way halfway down the foyer to the living room. There on the floor he saw John Yelenic lying faceup, surrounded by splotches of blood, evidence of what was surely a horrific crime. Craig looked to see if his friend the dentist was breathing, but Yelenic's chest wasn't moving.

Backing out of the house, Craig returned to his own home next door and called his grandfather, who lived a few

streets away. Then Craig returned to the front porch, where
he was soon joined by his grandfather, his grandfather's
neighbor, young Zachary, and another boy from the neighborhood, one of Zachary's friends. The grandfather went
inside the entry hall to make sure: yes, John Yelenic was
definitely dead. Then he reemerged and called 911.

Blairsville patrol officer Donald Isherwood got the radio call
just before 3:30 that afternoon. The dispatcher told him there
was a medical emergency at 233 South Spring Street, a possible heart attack; just where this particular information came
from, despite the bloody evidence, wasn't clear. Isherwood
drove to the address. Alighting from his unmarked patrol car,
he saw a gaggle of people milling around the porch in front of
the front door. As he approached the porch, Isherwood could
see a broken pane among three narrow windows along the left
side of the door, and what appeared to be a stream of dried
blood running down from the unbroken lower window to the
porch. Isherwood noticed that glass from the broken window
was *on* the porch, indicating that the breakage had come from
inside the house. As he approached, someone on the porch
opened the door for him. He told everyone to step back, then
went inside to see for himself.

There, lying faceup on the living room floor, was the horribly slashed body of the beloved dentist of Blairsville, John
Yelenic. Drying, tacky blood was everywhere, and Isherwood
could see at a glance that Yelenic was no longer of this world.
He noticed what appeared to be a shoe print in the blood on
the hardwood floor leading out of the living room into the
hallway. Given that Yelenic was barefoot—not to mention the
obvious wounds—Isherwood knew immediately that this had
to be a case of murderous assault: clearly a second person had
been present at or shortly after the time of death. Yelenic
could hardly have made the shoe print himself.

Besides the anomalous shoe print, the living room appeared

to be in a state of disarray, with papers and photographs strewn around the floor and the furniture disarranged. It looked to Isherwood that there might have been a deadly fight. The television was still on, droning mindlessly, tuned to the Nickelodeon channel for kids.

Isherwood backed out of the house and told the group on the porch to get away, to go home. Of course, the Uss contingent and everyone else present ignored him: Who could resist watching whatever was about to unfold, however gruesome? At least Isherwood was able to convince the growing crowd to get off the bloody porch. The rubberneckers reassembled in the narrow front yard, waiting to see what would happen next.

A minute or so later, several emergency medical technicians arrived, responding to the same 911 call that had summoned Isherwood. The EMTs made their way through the gathering crowd on the front lawn and went into the house, Isherwood following, watching as one EMT held her hand to Yelenic's pulseless carotid artery to confirm that the barefoot man inside was dead. Isherwood called 911 and asked the dispatcher to send his supervisor, Corporal Janelle Lydic. Lydic soon arrived and stayed with the body while Isherwood checked out the rest of the house. It wasn't clear whether anyone else was still in the house at that point—another victim, or even the killer.

After clearing the upstairs rooms and finding nothing unusual, Isherwood returned to the first floor. That was when he noticed what appeared to be more bloody shoe prints leading into the dining area, into the kitchen, and then to the back door, which was closed. Isherwood saw what looked like a blood smear on the handle of the back door. It seemed obvious that someone had slashed the dentist many times with a very sharp knife, left him to bleed to death on his own living room floor, and then exited by the back door, leaving the faint smear of blood on the knob. It was the only other way out of the house, given that the front door had been bolted from within.

It also appeared that whoever the killer was, he'd rammed the dentist's head through the narrow window next to the front door while Yelenic might have been trying to escape, and maybe—well, probably—the killer had pulled Yelenic's head back and forth a few times through the broken window frame, which accounted for all the bloody streaks and broken glass and the puddling on the porch, the bloody sprays on the foyer walls, as well as some of the ugly gashes on the dentist's neck. The whole scene was gruesome, to say the least.

A few minutes later Isherwood descended to the basement, where he found another puddle of tacky blood on the cement floor: the dentist's massive blood loss had seeped through the living room floor above, where it had dripped drop by drop, for many hours to make a large semi-coagulated puddle on the cement floor of the basement.

Yelenic had been viciously slashed, cut to pieces, and then left to bleed to death. From any perspective, this was a horrible, sadistic, heartless murder, certainly one committed by someone who hated the victim. The bodily destruction seemed to show that much: such a frenzied attack as to leave so many large wounds had to be the work of someone who knew Yelenic intimately—or so all the forensic psychologists agreed. An attack with so much frenzied slashing almost always indicated an intense, personal, emotional relationship between murderer and victim.

One could only imagine how the dentist must have felt in his final moments, knowing his life was about to end. The inevitable pain and panic would have made anyone scream in agony before his last breath. The killer was a sadistic brute—or out of his mind with rage.

A little more than an hour after the body of Dr. Yelenic was found in his living room at 233 South Spring Street in

Blairsville, the dentist's cousin, Mary Ann Clark, also in Blairsville, received a telephone call from a friend who resided at the end of Spring Street, a few blocks south of Yelenic's house. Something was going on, Mary Ann's friend told her, and it seemed to be happening right in front of John's house.

Like what? Mary Ann asked. She had not been particularly close to her cousin in earlier years. Although they were fairly close in age, their families had been slightly estranged when they had been growing up. Over the previous few years, though—ever since John's divorce and child custody fight with his former wife, Michele—Mary Ann had come to know her prosperous cousin slightly better. In that time, in their periodic encounters, John had often complained to Mary Ann and to other members of their numerous, extended family in the Blairsville area, that the Pennsylvania State Police—or at least a few officers who wore the badge of that organization, also known as the PSP—were harassing him. And, John had complained, some had even threatened him. It was all because his estranged wife, Michele, had taken a Pennsylvania State Police officer as a lover, John insisted.

State Trooper Kevin Foley was very big, very muscular, and very aggressive, and had friends in law enforcement who enjoyed giving Yelenic a hard time, John complained, all for the purpose of doing favors for their PSP buddy. Foley, John said, seemed to be acting as Michele Yelenic's "guided muscle," bent on intimidation.

To Yelenic, Foley and his PSP pals had taken his ex-wife's side in the Yelenics' increasingly bitter divorce, causing it to drag on for years, and had even made devastating allegations against him. These claims had prevented him from seeing the child he and Michele had adopted in 2000, Jamie.

To Yelenic, Foley and his fellow trooper, in the PSP were, for all practical purposes, a badge-toting goon squad, using their size, legal authority, and threats to intimidate him, all on behalf of Michele Yelenic, Foley's mistress. The worst of it, as far as Yelenic saw it, was the cops' tendency to sneer at him, flaunting their machismo. A state police badge, Yelenic thought, gave any bully carte blanche to do what they liked, no matter how amoral they were. State cops, he thought, could get away with anything, even murder.

Mary Ann, a conservative, law-and-order Republican, had always discounted her cousin's complaints of police harassment as paranoia. To her, it seemed outlandish that someone sworn to uphold the law, particularly state troopers, could so abuse their authority. To Mary Ann, John's claims about the PSP seemed some sort of emotional reaction to the fact that John's former wife was living with a state trooper—jealousy, probably, on her cousin's part.

And for some years, Mary Ann was fairly sure John would get over Michele if he ever found the right woman. Because, she knew, what her cousin wanted most in this world was to have a wife who loved him, children to call him Daddy, and a future that would allow him to say he had fulfilled the tragically unrealized desires of his own dead father.

Being a husband and father was all John Yelenic ever really wanted. He was, in a sense, dying for love; and when his first bite at this apple turned sour, John Yelenic was at turns amazed, then betrayed, and ultimately very bitter.

His family and friends tried to tell him: *This too shall pass*. But it wasn't easy for a thirty-something to see his lifetime's dreams crumble, his place in his bride's bed taken over by a hard-bodied, badge-carrying bully who seemed to sneer at him even as he also captured the affections of Yelenic's young adopted son, accompanied by obscene allegations against him. But to Mary Ann Clark, it was absurd to believe that the Pennsylvania State Police, of all people, could ever have done what John accused them of.

So when Mary Ann's friend telephoned, Mary Ann first

thought there must be some mistake. Why would all that emergency equipment be in front of John's house? It had to be a nearby dwelling, surely. But Mary Ann's friend was positive: all the activity was directly in front of the residence of John Yelenic, Mary Ann Clark's cousin.

That was when Mary Ann for the first time began to wonder at least faintly, whether John might have been telling it true from the start—that maybe someone really *had been* out to get her cousin, even a badge-carrying member of the Pennsylvania State Police. This was even before Mary Ann Clark learned that John Yelenic, the beloved dentist of Blairsville, had predicted to his divorce lawyer that he would be murdered; that his ex-wife and her cop lover and maybe even other members of the Pennsylvania State Police would be involved; and that, because of this foreboding, John had even tried to set aside a fund of $10,000 to help investigate the authors of his demise—as he thought, members of the Pennsylvania State Police—so that he would not die in vain. But that peculiar fact wouldn't emerge until more than a year later.

By then Mary Ann Clark had already made up her mind that the death of her cousin, whom she had doubted for so long, should not go unavenged. She wanted to make up for her earlier disbelief, even if she had to tear the Pennsylvania State Police apart piece by piece to do it. To Mary Ann, it was a debt that had to be paid, a debt of blood. And once Mary Ann Clark decided to do something, she wouldn't stop until the thing was finished. The Pennsylvania State Police would be in a world of trouble. Mary Ann Clark would see to that.

2.

Mary Ann had been expecting to see her cousin that same afternoon at her mother's house, a mile or so west of Blairsville. John had telephoned his aunt, Mary Ann's mother, the previous evening to tell her the good news: at long last, after four long years of bitter marital warfare, his divorce was about to become final. All he had to do was sign the papers and have them notarized, which he proposed to do the following morning in the nearby small city of Indiana, Pennsylvania. Mary Ann had told her mother that she would be there in the afternoon to help John celebrate his liberation.

At last, Mary Ann thought, her cousin's long, awful ordeal with the wife from hell was over. And maybe then his paranoia about Kevin Foley and the Pennsylvania State Police would finally fade away.

But now something seemed to be happening at John's house. Succumbing to a vague anxiety, Mary Ann drove to the neighborhood, where she discovered that police had already blocked off the street. Mary Ann parked well outside the barricade and began walking toward John's house.

Partway there, she encountered the local funeral director, a close relative. There were a lot of people in or near Blairsville who were related to one another, either by blood or marriage, and Mary Ann was not an exception. The funeral director tried to prevent Mary Ann from going toward her cousin's house. Looking ahead, she could see the red flashing lights of the ambulance, the patrol cars, the EMTs' trucks, the crowd of neighbors in the front yard. It was clear that all of this really *was* in front of her cousin's house, just as her friend down the block had insisted.

"What's wrong at John's?" Mary Ann asked. The funeral director wouldn't meet her eye.

"Well," he said, "something bad has happened." Mary Ann had the feeling he was being evasive for her sake.

"Well, I'm going to find out," Mary Ann said. But at that point the funeral director took her arm.

"No," he said, "I don't think you want to go there." He was insistent, which alarmed Mary Ann even more and made her even more determined. She shook his hand off and went forward. In front of the house she saw several uniformed Blairsville police and yellow crime scene tape. As she approached the front steps of John's house, the Blairsville police stopped her, telling her she couldn't go inside the house.

"Why not?" she demanded. "This is my cousin's house. What happened? Did he have a heart attack?"

The patrol officers shook their heads.

"No," one said, "it's worse than that. You can't go in."

Standing not far away was Melissa Uss, Craig and Zachary's mother and a longtime friend of John Yelenic—in fact, a former high school classmate of the dentist. Her son Craig had left the scene to collect her from her job at the local trade school after he'd found Yelenic's body that afternoon. Melissa was very distraught, weeping, as Mary Ann was to remember.

"So I'm standing there, knowing my mom's waiting for him," Mary Ann recalled several years later. Her brain was awash with conflicting thoughts: *What has happened to John? What am I going to tell my mother? Why had her dis-*

tant relative, the funeral director, been so adamant in tell-
ing her to stay away? Why were the Blairsville police so
close-mouthed about what had happened? What could be
worse than a heart attack?

"All these things are going through my head," she recalled. "Not knowing if he was shot, or—whatever happened." The police officer's remark came back to her mind:
that it was worse than a heart attack.

"So in the back of my mind, immediately," Mary Ann
recalled, she began to think of the possible murderous cul-
prits, and within seconds her thinking settled on the one
person Mary Ann knew had the most to gain by killing her
cousin. After all, if her cousin died before the awful divorce
was legally final, didn't that mean his estranged wife Michele would inherit his estate?

Michele! She's come down here and, finally, she's done
something to him. In the collision of shock and speculation
that so quickly assembles in the mind of any family survivor
after a horrific event, Mary Ann's brain quickly ran through
the direst of possibilities: Michele had to be the most likely
cause of whatever had happened to her cousin. But even
Mary Ann could not at that point imagine the abattoir her
cousin's house had become.

Overdosed on pills or something, Mary Ann thought,
wondering if Michele Yelenic had somehow contrived a sly,
nefarious way of doing in her estranged husband to get his
money. Had Michele employed some sort of drug to induce
a heart attack? Except it was "worse than that," according to
the police.

Then, on the sidewalk in front of the house, she encountered Melissa Uss, who was obviously even more distressed
than she was. The two women embraced and wept.

Almost at once Melissa Uss told Mary Ann: "You cannot—*cannot*—let the Pennsylvania State Police come down
here and have anything to with this case."

And in that moment Mary Ann Clark saw a state police vehicle parked in front of the house. Suddenly it all clicked together in her mind, almost unbelievably: John's long and often discounted litany of complaints about Michele, about Foley, about the PSP, especially the Indiana barracks of the state police, whom John had accused of harassing him for almost two years, ever since Foley had taken up with Michele.

Now Melissa Uss's intense warning, coupled with the sight of the state police car and the crime scene tape, gave John's paranoia a peculiar validity to Mary Ann Clark. The PSP cruiser parked at the curb suddenly seemed sinister to Mary Ann, an omen, or at least a sign of ominous forces that could be at work.

It now struck her: even if she wasn't sure exactly what had happened to her cousin, there was still way, way too much smoke to believe there was no fire underneath John's previous complaints of harassment. And Mary Ann Clark wasn't about to let the same people John blamed for all his troubles now investigate what had happened to him, whatever it was. Especially with John just about to finalize his divorce from his embittered, estranged wife Michele—the PSP officer Foley's girlfriend—and with several million dollars in possible assets in John's estate, all of which might go to Michele Yelenic, now the girlfriend of a PSP officer.

Everything that John had long claimed about Michele—her deceitfulness, her greed, her supposed manipulative nature—clicked into place in Mary Ann Clark's mind. There were Michele's allegations about John, scurrilous as they were, and repudiated again and again after official investigations, but which had still torn John's soul apart. "And I thought, *Yeah, I guess you're right*," Mary Ann recalled, after hearing the plea of Melissa Uss about the state police. Melissa's insistence that Mary Ann *had* to keep the PSP out of whatever had happened to her cousin suddenly seemed vitally important, given Kevin Foley's relationship with Michele and his position in the state police.

"So I got hold of one of our local police," Mary Ann said later. This was Blairsville police chief Donald Hess, who by then had come to the scene with most of the twelve-member Blairsville Police Department. Soon representatives of the west-central Pennsylvania news media were already setting up their cameras outside the yellow tape barricades and clamoring with unanswerable questions.

"I *do not* want anyone from the Pennsylvania State Police in that house," Mary Ann told Hess.

Normally the Indiana barracks of the Pennsylvania State Police would have taken the investigative lead over a fatal crime in a small town like Blairsville. But Hess knew Mary Ann Clark. He readily agreed that the investigation into whatever had happened to her cousin would be conducted by the Blairsville Police Department alone, even though his small force had neither the manpower nor the expertise to do the job. Like most small-town police chiefs in Pennsylvania and elsewhere, Hess understood that all politics is local, and Mary Ann Clark was a very big wheel, locally.

Then Mary Ann saw the one man she wanted most to talk to, Indiana County district attorney Robert Bell. Mary Ann had known Bell for years; in fact, he lived across the street from her. Mary Ann had supported him politically for more than a decade. If anyone could tell her what was going on inside her cousin's house, now blockaded by the police and their yellow crime scene tape, it had to be Bob Bell. As the top elected law enforcement official for the whole county, Bell had the power to tell the police what to do—maybe even let her in the house to see what the hell was going on.

Mary Ann quickly informed Bell in no uncertain terms that she had grave doubts about the capacity of the state police to honestly determine what had happened to her cousin, given the obvious conflict of interest.

* * *

As it happened, Bell had just arrived at his own house in Blairsville, across the street from Mary Ann Clark's house, just before she did when he heard of the death of John Yelenic from the county coroner. He had then driven the few blocks to South Spring Street and passed through the police barricade, and gone inside the house to see the awful sight of Yelenic's body when he saw Mary Ann on the sidewalk outside.

Although still a young man, Bell was a veteran prosecutor and in his third term as the district attorney for Indiana County. A stalwart Republican, he was somewhat taken aback to see his neighbor Mary Ann standing in front of him on the sidewalk, clearly agitated. What was she doing here at the scene of a gory murder? All Bell knew at that point was that a man had been found dead, supposedly a local dentist. He had no idea that the dead man was Mary Ann Clark's cousin.

But by this point, a bit after 4:30 p.m., Mary Ann had gone into full command mode, and after talking to Melissa Uss and Donald Hess and her near relative, the undertaker, her political radar was fully operational.

Once focused, Mary Ann could be formidable. She knew who was who, what was what, and how to get things done.

"Bob," she told her neighbor, "I don't know what's happened here, but I do not want, as his relative, the only one here on the scene, I do *not* want anyone from the Indiana barracks setting foot inside that house."

Bell asked her why not.

Mary Ann referred to the circumstances: John's impending divorce from Michele, the PSP trooper Kevin Foley's role as Michele's live-in lover, the divorce papers that were about to be signed—which, Mary Ann knew, would have cut Michele off from a very large potential estate, and which might benefit Foley as well, as Michele's paramour. It would be a gross conflict of interest to allow the Pennsylvania State

Police—or at least anyone from the Indiana barracks where Foley was stationed as a criminal investigator—to work on any case involving her cousin.

Bell appeared to be dubious.

"Well, I don't think we have anybody by that name working in the Indiana barracks," Bell told her, in Mary Ann Clark's recollection.

What was this? Foley had been assigned to the Indiana barracks for almost a decade, and had spent almost half that as a state police investigator in Indiana County. It seemed unlikely that a two-term district attorney would be unacquainted with Kevin Foley: there simply weren't that many PSP criminal investigators in Indiana County. Mary Ann thought Bell had to know Foley by sight, if not by name, or even personally.

"Oh, yes you do," Mary Ann recalled Melissa Uss piping up, glaring at Bell. And it was at this point that Mary Ann's doubts about her political ally and neighbor first took root. Already suspicious of the PSP, Mary Ann now became wary of Bell. How could he not know Foley?

If Mary Ann's recollection is correct, Bell may have been disingenuous with her and Melissa Uss. Bell later testified to receiving a telephone call from the local investigations supervisor for the Pennsylvania State Police at the Indiana barracks. The call, in which Foley figured prominently, was from Sergeant George Emigh, Kevin's Foley's immediate boss in the barracks' criminal investigation unit. A little before 4:30 p.m., Emigh had heard of the murder of John Yelenic, and it took him perhaps a millisecond to put one and two together: Yelenic, Michele, Foley. Emigh had quickly called Bell to tell the salient facts: the dead man, Yelenic, was the estranged husband of the girlfriend of one of his own investigators, Kevin Foley. This was the first of three telephone calls that evening between Emigh and Bell.

Not only that, Emigh told Bell, it was common knowledge in the barracks that Foley hated Yelenic, while Yelenic also hated Foley. If anyone was a prime suspect in Yelenic's murder, it had to be Foley. In addition, Emigh continued, it was Foley who had initiated two previous sex abuse complaints against Yelenic. Both of these had been investigated by another Emigh subordinate—PSP investigator Deana Kirkland, one of Foley's close friends—and each complaint by Foley involved the adopted Yelenic child, Jamie.

Both complaints had been dismissed as unfounded, but the question of Foley's involvement in Yelenic's murder divided the state police and created an awkward situation for nearly everyone involved in investigating and prosecuting the crime.

By the time the whole thing was sorted out years later, one man would be convicted, one would be voted out of office, five police officers would be retired or dismissed, five federal lawsuits would be filed, and the resulting mess would be a stink all over the Commonwealth of Pennsylvania, which would not go away anytime soon.

3.

By five that afternoon, the whole of South Spring Street was jammed with rubberneckers, with the patrol cars of the Blairsville Police Department, detectives of the Indiana County Sheriff's Department assigned to Bell's office, and soon a crime scene unit from the Pennsylvania State Police based in nearby Greensburg, Pennsylvania. There was also more discussion, out of Mary Ann Clark's earshot, of the fraught relationships between John Yelenic, the dead man; Michele Yelenic, his estranged wife; and Kevin Foley, the state trooper and criminal investigator from the nearest PSP barracks, who was also Michele Yelenic's lover.

And there was Mary Ann Clark, who knew Bell as well as all the other state politicians who counted, not to mention Emigh.

The nearest qualified crime scene experts for the PSP were based in the Greensburg barracks, some miles to the southwest, well away from the cliques and passions of the Indiana barracks, whatever they were. Because the Blairsville Police Department had nowhere near the expertise or the resources to scientifically document the evidence of the murder, and it was standard operating procedure in any homicide to call in the PSP's trained forensic personnel, with Hess's consent, Bell put in a call to Greensburg to ask for their assistance.

The task would have fallen to them in any case, since the Greensburg crime scene people had responsibility for covering Indiana County, among several others. Blairsville's department simply wasn't qualified to do that sort of work. The techs, at least, were scientists of sorts: it was their job to simply collect the damn evidence, no matter who was involved or who loved or hated whom.

Trooper Charles Gonglik and his associate Brian Kendgia arrived at just before 5:00 p.m. Over the next few hours, Gonglik exposed eleven rolls of 35 mm film of the death house and the eviscerated corpse of John Yelenic, while Kendgia first examined the outside of the house for signs of a break-in. Finding none, he then helped Gonglik take even more photographs inside the house. Gonglik paid particular attention to the bloody shoe prints, and the blood smear on the inside handle of the back door.

There was now yellow crime scene tape all around the yard. A near neighbor to the Yelenic house looked out her window and saw the yellow streamers and thought at first that the popular dentist must be holding an Easter egg hunt. She knew how much he loved children.

It was sometime late the same afternoon when Barbara Swasy heard the terrible news from a friend: a dentist had been found dead, murdered, on South Spring Street in Blairsville. Barbara was married to Roger Swasy, Mary Ann Clark's brother, and was also John Yelenic's cousin. Barbara realized almost immediately that the dentist had to be John; after all, there weren't that many dentists in Blairsville, and only one who lived on South Spring Street. She was also an acquaintance of Michele's: both women had children at the same parochial school, St. Bernard's, in Indiana, and had even seen each other on the previous Friday night. Kevin

Foley had been there, too, and had muttered dark imprecations about John, actually wishing that he were dead. Now it appeared that John *was* dead.

Barbara soon telephoned Michele Yelenic in Indiana.

"John is gone," Barbara told Michele.

"What do you mean, 'gone'?" Michele asked.

John was dead, Barbara said. He had died during the night.

Michele seemed remarkably muted in her reaction to the news. Barbara later said she'd then asked Michele to put Kevin on the line, although the timing of this request would later be disputed. In any event, she thought, because he was an investigator for the PSP, he might know more about what had happened.

"Can you find out what's going on?" she asked Kevin.

Kevin demurred. He told Barbara that he was off duty. And anyway, he added, it wasn't his jurisdiction. Barbara would have to get any information from the Blairsville police. (Later, some—including Mary Ann Clark and prosecutors— thought this was a curious evasion by Kevin.)

Ordinarily, homicide investigations in Pennsylvania were undertaken by investigators from the PSP—and in Blairsville, by Foley's own unit at the Indiana barracks. And when Barbara called Michele and Kevin—"between four and five p.m.," according to her later recollection—the jurisdiction question hadn't yet been determined. After all, this was only minutes after Mary Ann Clark had confronted Chief Hess and District Attorney Bell with her suspicions about Foley and the Indiana barracks.

Some saw this as a sign of guilt. Wouldn't an innocent person be much more likely to profess shock and hasten to add that he'd do what he could to find out what happened?

But on the day the crime was discovered, Foley seemed to be making an effort to distance himself.

On the other hand, Foley must have known he was quite likely to be the prime suspect in John Yelenic's death, and perhaps he chose to avoid future accusations of interference in the investigation. Nevertheless, one immediate effect of Barbara Swasy's telephone call to Michele and Kevin was to put both on notice that their bête noire, John Yelenic, had been murdered. This was more than six hours before anyone official even attempted to talk to them. Whether this was inadvertent or intentional would later become a matter of intense dispute.

Over the next few hours, a handful of Blairsville officers fanned out across the neighborhood, canvassing the residents of South Spring Street, trying to find out if anyone had seen or heard anything in the early morning darkness. Many told their stories: the storm, the barking dogs, the half-heard shouts of an argument, then the horrible screams, followed by silence. No one saw anything. But almost everyone remembered the screams—awful. Shortly after 6:00 p.m., the Uss boys, along with Melissa and her husband, Tom, a retired navy veteran, were taken to the Blairsville Police station to be interrogated by Bell's county detectives.

Almost at once it was apparent to the Uss family that the police were suspicious of them, or at least of Craig. In fact, some of the investigators had the idea that the bloody shoeprints found on the floor of the death house had been made by Craig Uss. The investigators made a point of collecting all the Uss family's shoes. Craig had previously been given permission by John to lift weights in John's basement, so didn't he have access to the Yelenic house? Young Zachary had borrowed the video game from the dead dentist. And hadn't two complaints had been made against John, accusing him of sexual molestation of a child?

From the outset, Bell's investigators wanted to know the nature of the relationship between the dead man and the Uss boys . . . and if there wasn't one, why had Melissa Uss just given Yelenic a check for $14,000? This had been found among the strewn papers on the Yelenic living room floor, along with photographs of the adopted son, Jamie. And why was the television tuned to Nickelodeon, the kids' channel? Was that significant?

The subtext was ominous. Here were two boys, both of whom readily admitted having friendly relationships with a single man, someone already twice accused—albeit exonerated—of homosexual child abuse by his former wife, one of whom had admittedly been inside the house of the deceased before any competent authority arrived, who might have left shoeprints before the body was actually discovered or even perhaps at the time of the murder—who could say *when* the shoeprints had been made, and by whom?—and one of whose parents had just signed a check to the deceased for $14,000.

On the surface, the circumstances seemed suspicious. Was the death of John Yelenic, the beloved dentist of Blairsville, a case of blackmail gone wrong?

The county detectives grilled the Uss family for hours on the night of April 13. But, try as they might, they could induce no breakthroughs; the fact was, there was nothing there, although it would take another year before this was finally revealed to be a dry hole. But by then a larger question would arise: just why were all these efforts directed at the Uss family, when a far more logical suspect—the PSP trooper Kevin Foley—had already been named at least three times, including by his own police supervisor, Emigh? The pursuit of the Uss family only made those doubtful of the authorities, like Mary Ann Clark, even more suspicious—as if those responsible for solving the crime were more interested in *looking* like they were on the job rather than actually doing something.

But why? Indeed, this would turn out to be one of the most intriguing questions stemming from the murder of John Yelenic. Mary Ann Clark, for one, would become convinced that the fix was in. And that, as Winston Churchill once said, was nonsense up with which she would not put.

As the events unfolded on South Spring Street that afternoon and evening of April 13, one of those who soon arrived at the death house was Blairsville police officer Jill Gaston. Gaston, in some ways, might have been unique among all the officials and onlookers there that afternoon: she was perhaps the only person to have actually known Bell, Foley, and John Yelenic, as well as Michele Yelenic—the principals in the unfolding drama. For a year prior to her appointment as a Blairsville police officer, Gaston had worked as an intern in District Attorney Bell's office, where she occasionally encountered Foley as a PSP officer. During the time she had worked there, she'd also met Michele Yelenic on occasion, knowing her as Foley's girlfriend. And then, in the fall of 2003, she'd actually arrested John Yelenic when Michele had filed a formal complaint accusing her estranged husband of violating a no-contact order issued from a nearby county, where Michele Yelenic had for a time taken up residence with another man before joining with Foley. Michele was hardly on good terms with her estranged husband, John, as Gaston well knew. They despised each other.

By the time Gaston arrived at the murder scene at 233 South Spring Street, the western Pennsylvania news media had assembled, having heard of the murder in Blairsville by monitoring over-the-air police communications. Besides the television stations and the radio people, there were reporters from the local newspapers: the *Indiana Gazette* and a regional office of the *Pittsburgh Tribune-Review*, out of Greensburg. By early evening, the gaggle of reporters had gathered in front of the death house. Hess assigned Gaston to brief them. She had little to say, other than confirming that a man had been killed inside the house and that an investigation was under way. But even as Gaston was saying very little, at least one of the neighbors was telling a very interesting story to the police.

Isaiah Brader was certainly a go-getter. He was just twenty-one and had grown up near Buffalo, New York, where he had established his own metal-fabrication business while still a teenager. Curiously, he had then branched out into ultrasonic cleaning devices often used in dentists' offices. He later found work in the food service industry while still attending high school. After a year or so at Jamestown Community College in New York, he decided to attend WyoTech, a Blairsville trade school, to learn metalwork for automobile chassis manufacture. In short, Brader was a very good potential witness: self-reliant, levelheaded, very disciplined, and precise, not at all the sort of person given to flights of imagination.

Noticing all the police activity in front of the Yelenic house on the evening of April 13, Brader contacted one of the police canvassers to tell what he knew. His story was simple and very clear. He'd heard shouting and breaking glass out on the street in the early morning hours of the night before. It was, he said, around 3:30 or 4:00 a.m. He wasn't sure, but he thought his information might be important. The canvassing officer dutifully wrote this down, and Brader returned to WyoTech for his evening class. The trade school ran both day and evening sessions.

Then, sometime around 9:00 and 10:00 that night, someone noticed the time discrepancy: while almost everyone else who lived on the street said the arguing, the breaking glass, and the screaming had occurred around 1:30 a.m. or so, Brader was claiming it actually had happened around two hours later, between 3:30 and 4:00 a.m. How was this possible? Sometime a little after 2:00 a.m. on April 14, Brader was contacted at WyoTech and asked to come to the Blairsville Police Department, where he again told his story.

He had, Brader said, come home from the school early in

the morning of April 13, around 3:00 a.m. He was absolutely sure of the time, because his class at WyoTech had finished around 2:00. He'd stopped at a local mini-mart, the Sheetz at Market and Walnut, off Highway 217 in Blairsville, to pick up something to eat and a video, and soon thereafter gone to bed. He had just drifted off to sleep when he heard breaking glass and what sounded like an argument.

"I'll never loan you money again," Brader told the detectives he thought he'd heard while lying in bed. And, he said, he'd heard screaming "back and forth." Around the same time or maybe a little after, he'd heard garbage trucks making their way up South Spring Street. Then he'd drifted off and thought no more about it until he'd seen the yellow crime scene tape blocking off part of the street and heard about the murder the following afternoon. That was when he'd first told his story: he had thought it might help.

No, he didn't know John Yelenic—had never met him.

So, if Brader was right, and if all the other neighbors were also right about the screams at 1:30 or so, what did that mean? Were there two different arguments, two different incidents involving broken glass and screaming?

And who, if anyone, had John Yelenic loaned money to?

Melissa Uss, for one: as even Melissa acknowledged, Yelenic had lent her $15,000 to help establish a local bakery business. That was the $14,000 check found on Yelenic's floor—Melissa's partial repayment of the loan. What else could the remark overheard by Brader—"I'll never loan you money again"—refer to?

Some of the police were sure the Uss family had to be involved in the murder of John Yelenic. Motive and opportunity were obvious. The means, a knife, was just a matter of searching, and once that was found, the case would be complete.

No one wanted to think that one of their own, Kevin Foley, could possibly be involved.

4.

At 11:30 that night, Blairsville police officer Jill Gaston drove with Indiana County deputy coroner Charles Conrad to the house of John Yelenic's estranged wife Michele, living on Susan Drive in the nearby city of Indiana, Pennsylvania. From her 2003 arrest of Yelenic, Gaston well knew that Michele, thirty-four, had long been engaged in tumultuous, bitter divorce proceedings with her husband, the now-deceased dentist. The marital battle had taken almost four years to near its legal conclusion, although it never would, now, with Yelenic slashed to death on his living room floor.

It was Gaston's job to help Deputy Coroner Conrad formally—legally—notify Michele that her almost ex-husband-to-be was now deceased. Exactly why this notice was taking place nearly eight hours after Yelenic's body had been found was somewhat peculiar. Gaston didn't know, and she didn't ask: as she saw it, her job was to do as she was told by Hess, or Lydic, or whoever else was ahead of her on the Blairsville Police Department chain of command. She knew Foley, and she knew Michele, at least slightly, and her observations that night would eventually become important evidence.

Of medium height, with dark hair and a very lean frame,

Michele Yelenic was extremely attractive to men, the sort of woman who exuded allure without even trying. During the course of the marital dispute, she had accused her estranged husband of physical and sexual abuse of their adopted son, Jamie. The allegations were as graphic as they were appalling, and attributed by Michele to Jamie himself, six years old at the time. After several investigations, the charges against John were deemed unfounded—that is, bogus, possibly made up by Michele and put into Jamie's mouth simply to squeeze her husband into a financial vise, perhaps to sweeten her portion of the marital dissolution pot. Or so John Yelenic was convinced, as were his divorce lawyers.

Being accused of molesting his adopted son had first infuriated John and then sent him into a horrific depression, despite having been legally cleared. The sheer shame of such an accusation hung over John like a dark cloud that might never go away, and fueled his anger toward his estranged wife. It was, of course, the H-bomb of any contested divorce case, and even after the claims were found to be a dud, John still felt radioactive.

Both before and after separating from Yelenic in 2002, and then initiating the divorce action, Michele had reportedly taken up with several others, including at least two men who were politically, socially, and economically prominent in west-central Pennsylvania. She had two children from her first marriage before John Yelenic, as well as Jamie, whom they had adopted from Russia in 2000.

As most people in Indiana, Pennsylvania, later recalled her, Michele was very, very smart—probably smarter than her estranged dentist husband, despite her lack of formal education and his advanced degree. But most of all Michele was a survivor. She knew how to take care of herself. And as Mary Ann Clark later came to see her, she could be utterly single-minded in doing so. By the spring of 2006, Michele and the three children lived in Indiana, in an upscale house on Susan Drive in the hills just west of the small city's downtown. Foley, the state trooper, had taken up residence with her there two years earlier, in 2004, much to John Yelenic's unhappiness.

As already noted, Kevin was big—about six-two, around 220 pounds, and extremely well built and conditioned. (Yelenic himself was about six-two and 230 pounds, although not nearly in the same sort of condition as his rival.) Foley later said he ran many miles every week: he wore out running shoes twice or even three times a year. Most of Foley's fellow troopers considered him a terrific athlete. A volunteer for the local Indiana Pennsylvania State Police SWAT squad, a prosecutor would eventually call Foley "a killing machine," although many of his best friends among the PSP would dispute that.

Some of Kevin's fellow troopers considered him something of a bully, especially with those he believed were breaking the law. Some later even called him a "Nazi," a Pennsylvania state senator would later say. Indeed, Foley's personality could be offensive. He always knew who was guilty: he could somehow sense it. Yet, he was "righteous," as some of the other cops like to say, in their peculiar vernacular: he stood for the weak, the abused, the dispossessed. A real hero. And if he despised and hated John Yelenic, it was only because he believed the dentist was some sort of sleaze.

Now, near midnight, it was Gaston's duty, with Deputy Coroner Conrad, to inform Michele Yelenic that her estranged husband, John Yelenic, was dead—murdered, cut to pieces in his own house in Blairsville. Some of the papers found scattered over the floor near his body had been the Yelenic's final divorce settlement, signed by Michele Yelenic only a few days before. Yelenic had not had the opportunity to sign them himself before the intruder, whoever he was, had fatally sliced him up. Which meant, although Gaston had no way of knowing it at this point, the divorce was not legally valid.

A few years later, Gaston recalled the scene: After driving from Blairsville to Indiana, she contacted Conrad at the county morgue. Together they drove to Michele's. At first it was hard to tell the right house: there were no streetlights, and no address signage was visible. They knocked on what they thought might be the right front door, of a fashionable two-story house set below the street's embankment, but no one answered. They retreated to the street, trying to decide what to do. A woman walking a dog appeared. Gaston and Conrad consulted her, and the woman confirmed the address: yes, that was the house where Michele and Kevin lived, with their children.

Gaston and Conrad returned to the front door they had already knocked on and tried again. The place seemed completely dark except for a light in an upstairs room. At length the front door opened.

Kevin let them in. Gaston could detect no surprise on Kevin's face; after all they knew one another from Gaston's stint as an intern in Bell's office. Michele appeared at the top of the stairs. Conrad explained who he was and introduced Gaston. Michele descended the stairs, and the quartet went through the living room into the kitchen. Kevin flicked on the kitchen light. Gaston noticed what looked like two bruises or abrasions above and below Kevin's left eye. He noticed her look.

"Hockey," he said, and Gaston nodded.

Michele sat at the kitchen table. Kevin remained by the doorway, watching Conrad kneel on the floor by Michele.

"As you are the next of kin, I'm here to advise you that we found Dr. Yelenic deceased," Conrad said. Michele told Conrad that she'd already heard the news: Barbara Swasy had called and told her John had died of a "heart attack."

Conrad looked at Gaston—not puzzled, exactly, but wondering how to put it.

"Well, no," he said, "it's a suspicious death."

Michele said nothing to this.

"Do you have any questions for us?" Conrad asked. Michele looked up at Kevin at the doorway. He silently shook his head no.

Conrad explained that the local funeral home would soon be contacting her about arrangements. Did she need to know anything about that? Again Kevin shook his head. Michele said she understood; no, she didn't need to know anything more.

"Is there anything else we can do for you?" Conrad asked. Michele again looked at Kevin, and again came the silent head shake: no.

But Kevin did have a question.

"Who's handling this?" he asked.

Gaston told him that it was her department, the Blairsville Police, but assisted by the Greensburg barracks of the Pennsylvania State Police and the Indiana County district attorney, Bell, and his county investigators. Kevin said nothing in reply.

Gaston and Conrad left Michele's house just before midnight. From the front seat of Conrad's car, she used her cell phone to call Chief Hess, who was still with Bell at the Blairsville police station. The Uss family was still being interviewed. Gaston described the demeanor of Kevin and Michele and reported the bruises or abrasions she'd seen near Kevin's left eye—which she thought suspicious, as it appeared to be fresh.

Both Hess and Bell told her to do nothing further, ask no more questions, just leave, go home, making sure she documented everything as completely as possible.

5.

The following morning, the mortal remains of John Yelenic lay on a stainless steel table at Carlow University's anatomical laboratory in Pittsburgh, for an autopsy by Dr. Cyril Wecht. Wecht was one of the more celebrated pathologists in America. Along with Dr. Michael Baden and, somewhat before their time, Dr. Thomas Noguchi, Wecht had often appeared on national television as a recognized expert in the forensics of murder.

The body had been brought to Wecht in the same clothing it had been found in: a gray T-shirt, gray sweat pants, white jockey shorts. Wecht noticed many tears in the fabric of the T-shirt, as well as extensive bloodstains. He and his assistant removed the clothing and packaged it for Gonglik, who was attending the autopsy, to take to the crime lab.

Looking down at John's eviscerated corpse, Wecht was immediately aware of an overwhelming reality: whoever had killed Yelenic had hatred in his heart. If anything, the wounds shouted this out: This was overkill, the result of a paroxysm of rage. And it was rage that had probably begun with a fistfight, then escalated into fatal bloodlust.

How did Wecht know this? Well, for one thing, he could see a number of small, superficial abrasions around the lips, as if Yelenic had been hit in the mouth by his assailant. Then there was a deep cut across the left side of the face, running across the left ear, partially severing it, and ending, or actually probably beginning, behind the ear at the scalp, as if John had had his head turned to the right. Wecht could envision the scene: The dead man had been facing his killer, standing nearly toe-to-toe, perhaps after being punched in the mouth several times. At some point after this the killer had flicked a very sharp knife at John's head while his face was turned away, cutting through the ear, then deeply across the left cheek. John had then likely thrown up his right hand in defense or possibly a counterpunch, and the killer had then slashed the inside of his upper right arm downward to his elbow, rendering the arm useless with the pain and the blood. Then, very quickly, two more slashes, downward across the chest, both also deep.

At that point, Wecht guessed, Yelenic had tried to get away, probably making the screams heard by the neighbors while being chased by the murderer. There were two more deep slashes down each side of his back as John had run for the front door; the blood on the entry floor and on the knob showed that. But the door had been dead-bolted from the inside, and while he was trying to turn it, the killer had shoved him from behind, causing John's head to smash through the narrow glass side window next to the door.

The killer had tried to pull him back inside the house, through the window. There were deep, jagged cuts on his throat from the broken window glass. It seemed likely that the killer wanted to shut John up at all costs: the last thing he wanted was some neighbor coming to investigate. Having pulled John back through the window—all the bloody spurts high up on the nearby walls seemed to show as much—the killer had dragged or somehow maneuvered John back into the living room a few feet away. And then had cut the carotid artery of his throat, severing his trachea and Adam's apple. John had finally shut up. He would have been dead within minutes, all his blood puddling on the living room floor, then soaking through to the basement below. The killer let himself out through the back door, leaving his running-shoe prints in blood on the floor and a red smudge on the doorknob.

Well, so much for the manner and means of death: homicide, and by extensive lacerations from very sharp instruments, a knife, and window glass, leading to a rapid and fatal blood loss. Wecht turned his attention to the finer detail. His autopsy assistant clipped the bloody fingernails of both of John's hands. It seemed possible that at some point in the life-and-death struggle, Yelenic had fought back. Any material under the nails might possibly include the skin cells or blood of the killer, assuming that John had been able to scratch his murderer at some point during the deadly struggle.

Wecht preserved the nails, and put them in an envelope for possible later analysis by the PSP crime laboratory's DNA experts in Greensburg.

Once the autopsy was finished, Wecht contacted the police. What was now to be done with the remains? No one was entirely sure. Someone with the PSP or the Blairsville Police Department called the local funeral director in Blairsville, Mary Ann Clark's close relative. The funeral director called Michele in Indiana. What plans had she made for a funeral for her husband? None, Michele told him.

The funeral director called Mary Ann and told her that John's estranged wife wanted nothing to do with his body. What should he do? Mary Ann was appalled: Michele's attitude toward the remains of her dead husband told her everything she needed to know. She was now convinced that her cousin had been murdered by Kevin Foley—egged on, she was sure, by Michele Yelenic, who stood to gain all the money, now that John was dead. Mary Ann made all the arrangements to bury her cousin. Michele didn't attend the funeral.

II.

John and Michele

"Come for fun, take home a memory . . ."
—Indiana County, Pennsylvania, tourist bureau

6.

Indiana, Pennsylvania. The home of Indiana University of Pennsylvania—IUP, the students proudly wear on their T-shirts and sweatshirts—the city and county of Indiana, Pennsylvania, was "Indiana" long before the state of the same name came into existence far to the west, and by almost a century, as almost anyone who lives in the original Indiana there will tell you (a bit like Washington, D.C., was Washington before Washington State).

As a place name, Indiana, Pennsylvania, reflected the seventeenth and eighteenth centuries' conception of the eastern frontier, a place where Native American tribes held mysterious, unlimited sway: *Indiana*, the place where the first Americans, characterized by some as "noble savages," ruled a sort of natural Utopia, an unspoiled Garden of Eden in some mythical land to the West, between the tidelands of Virginia and the French outpost Fort Duquesne, predecessor of today's Pittsburgh.

Well, that's the way it seemed to Romantics like James Fenimore Cooper in the early part of the nineteenth century; he hadn't spent much time in the woods with the mosquitoes of the West. It wasn't until the mid-1800s that land speculators began grabbing off the real estate of the

Tuscarora, the Cherokee, the Sauk, the Fox, the Shawnee, the Seneca, and other tribes, and began to strip away this romantic noble savage myth for the purpose of making money. Today we deplore these depredations practiced on the first Americans, but two hundred years ago our Anglo ancestors elbowed them aside to get rich quick by stealing their real estate. In some ways, America never changes.

In those colonial days, the country known as Indiana was a crossroads for tribes linking north to south and east to west, not only commercially advantageous in the early fur trade but very fertile in both soil and game. It is a land abundantly blessed by rivers, streams, trees, and gentle hills, along with a fruitful population of deer and especially groundhogs. A few miles to the north of Indiana is the burrowing ground of the nationally famous Punxsutawney Phil, the rodent celebrated for his shadow, or lack of it, and his February seasonal prediction known as Groundhog Day.

To the west of Indiana lies the big city of Pittsburgh, site of the former Fort Duquesne, with its three rivers and former steel mills. To the east lie the foothills of the western Appalachians, with scattered glens, glistening streams, and small villages dating back more than 150 years, land as beautiful as it is haunted by the ghosts of the Molly Maguires, the miner-revolutionaries portrayed by Sean Connery and Richard Harris in the film of the same name. This landscape today lies over the six-hundred-mile strata of rock know as the Marcellus Shale, where wildcatting companies drill down with "fractal fluids" to break up the rock to get at methane gas; most of the farmland in Indiana County is today the scene of drilling and fracturing, conducted by crews of roughnecks from all over. The social equilibrium of Indiana County has been in flux for the better part of a decade, as the subterranean rocks are fractured and the gas is piped out, with everyone focused on the bottom line: the money. But this is only the latest incarnation of west-central Pennsylvania, just another chapter in its long and bloody history.

By the early 1800s Indiana was a frontier town blessed with potential almost from its birth. By 1850 it was a bustling commercial center, a nexus of railroads and graveled turnpikes. By the 1890s its genteel streets would be fronted with many elegant Victorian-era homes, all testimony to its prosperity. Many of these still remain, a tourist draw for architectural students and others. Its eventual claim to fame would be as the hometown of Jimmy Stewart, the actor. It was in Indiana that James Stewart, the actor's grandfather, established a hardware store around the time of the Civil War, and where Jimmy's father, Alexander, raised his own family, supported by the hardware emporium.

Jimmy left Indiana in the 1920s for New York and eventually Hollywood, even though his father didn't approve, believing the theatrical arts to be unmanly. But by the 1930s, Jimmy was a big star, and after that, in the 1940s, a war hero. By the 1950s he was, along with John Wayne, the most bankable asset in the movie business, and certainly Indiana County's biggest claim to fame. In Indiana County, there is a Jimmy Stewart Boulevard, the Jimmy Stewart Airport, the Jimmy Stewart Museum, and a statue of Jimmy, in his costume as the star of *Harvey*, the tale of the man with the imaginary rabbit friend, adorning the Indiana County courthouse lawn. Anyone at a crosswalk on the town's main drag, Philadelphia Street, can hear Jimmy's recorded drawl instructing them as to when and where to walk. The town itself could double for Bedford Falls, the fictional setting of one of Jimmy Stewart's most memorable movies, *It's a Wonderful Life*. And indeed, that title has become Indiana's most ubiquitous slogan: "It's a Wonderful Life" is everywhere.

But by April 2006, when the lovable dentist John Yelenic's corpse lay on a stainless steel table in a morgue in

Pittsburgh, hours after his slashed-to-pieces body was found by his neighbors, it wasn't a wonderful life but rather a real-life tale more suitable to the noir of James M. Cain—perhaps *Double Indemnity* or *The Postman Always Rings Twice*. Because someone murdered John Yelenic—either for love or money. In either case, as in both of Cain's novels, the way the cops finally figured it out, there was a sucker involved—or, as Cain would have called him, a sap.

In this case, maybe even two.

If Indiana is a surrogate for Jimmy Stewart's Bedford Falls, Blairsville, a few miles to the south, might be a stand-in for one of Norman Rockwell's idealized middle-American small towns from the last century. Hard by the Conemaugh River, Blairsville is the sort of place where everyone knows everyone else. Its houses are generally older, and its streets are narrow. One can easily imagine a horse and buggy clip-clopping down the narrow streets; or even a Model T carrying men-about-town wearing top hats, cravats, and spats, and carrying fashionable canes; or, in a slightly later generation, bubble-gum chewing boys in a small barbershop queuing for their crew cuts, something from Rockwell's heyday. Its main drag, Market Street, lies in an east–west direction, chock-full of small businesses that give any small town its true character. There is a small park with a bandstand on the west end of the town, not far from the bridge over the river, and it isn't at all difficult to imagine the town volunteer orchestra tuning up on summer evenings for a free concert, fireworks, and hot dogs for the Fourth of July, and men with boaters and mustaches shouting hurrah for the U.S.A. in the early 1900s.

John Yelenic grew up in Blairsville, the son of John Yelenic Sr., a high school teacher, and his wife, Mary Lois, also a teacher. In 1967, when John junior was only three months old, his father was killed in a car wreck, smashed dead in a collision with a truck. Afterward, his mother raised him as a single parent in Blairsville, where John was surrounded by aunts, uncles, and cousins of an extended family, although Mary Lois tended to keep her distance from her siblings—for John's mother and father weren't married when John was conceived, a scarlet *A* for a place like Blairsville in that era. The extended family did not approve. Mary Lois didn't care.

And when her lover, eventually her husband, was killed three months after John junior was born, Mary Lois maintained that distance from those she had grown up with. She raised her only son by herself in a sort of protective cocoon, and even Mary Ann Clark, his cousin, Mary Lois's niece, would later admit that John junior was something of a "mama's boy," genial, well mannered, and rather naïve about the wicked ways of the real world.

One can only speculate: having had no father, no family other than his devoted mother, did John Yelenic look at all the other Blairsville children he had grown up with, gone to public school with, with envy? They had fathers, brothers, sisters, and lives that let them strive, challenge, and even fall down? Did he miss and yearn for something he never had? It appears so. For most of his life, up until the night he died, John Yelenic wanted more than anything else in the world to have a family of his own, to be the father he himself had so sorely missed.

Born February 27, 1967, John Joseph Yelenic Jr. was the only son of his namesake, who was almost a decade older than Mary Lois Swasy, born in 1944. Mary Lois was just twenty-two when she got pregnant with John junior, and in her first year as a teacher in her hometown. Her family was appalled.

"See, what happened was, Mary Lois got pregnant out of wedlock," John Yelenic's mentor and eventual dentistry partner, Dr. Thomas Riley, recalled. "In 1966, this just wasn't done." But Mary Lois told her family she didn't approve of their disapproval. "So she said, 'Wow, I don't want anything to do with you,'" Riley recalled, "and there were angry words spoken." When, only months after Mary Lois and John senior married, her bridegroom was killed when his car collided with a truck, Mary Lois resolved to raise her love child by herself, no matter what her relatives said or thought. Her son grew up never wanting for material things, and was always a generous soul.

But under the circumstances, probably the most formative male influence in his life was Dr. Riley. Mary Lois was, among other things, a zealous guardian of her only son's teeth, and regularly took young John for appointments with then-young Dr. Tom. "He was a patient of mine from the age of six," Riley said later, by then contemplating retirement. "Every six months, like clockwork."

Little John became fascinated by the equipment of dentistry: the drill, the pneumatic chair, the porcelain bowl with its continuous running water, the suction apparatus in the mouth, the X-ray machine. He was always asking Riley how something worked and what the purpose of it was.

"Why is that light so bright?" he might ask, and Riley would try to explain. He soon saw John as one of his more precocious patients, despite his young age, and clearly young John grew to admire Dr. Riley for his steady gentleness and humor, something perhaps missing in a single-parent home strained by disapproval from Mary Lois's well-connected extended family. Riley was as close to a father figure as John Yelenic Jr. ever had, but even he wasn't able to liberate his young patient.

"She kind of cloistered him," Riley recalled, of Mary Lois. "There was kind of a bubble over him, okay?" John's mother was by far the most powerful force in his life, as far as Riley could see. Yet, as young John grew up, he tended to view his schoolmates with some degree of wistfulness: for their larger families, their boisterousness, their freedom to try new things, and their obvious popularity among their peers. Most of his contemporaries saw John as something of a nerd—friendly, smart certainly, but hopelessly inept socially. Others might talk of DeLoreans or heavy metal, like Michael J. Fox in *Back to the Future*, but in many ways John was still a child of the decade before he was even born: he *was* back, and not of the future. His mother's son, he was hardly the sort of boy to score a surreptitious six-pack and go necking with the prom queen.

Then, in John's senior year in high school, during another dental appointment, while John was asking still more questions about teeth and dentistry, Riley finally asked him why he was so curious. "Why do you ask me so many questions?" Riley wanted to know.

Well, John told him, I'm thinking of becoming a dentist. Riley was floored: "Not a lot of people aspire to dentistry. Maybe they want to be a pilot, or maybe a doctor." But rarely a career of looking down into someone's straining mouth.

So Riley formed a bond of sorts with the boy he had treated since he was six years old, and helped guide him through college and then dental school, first Juniata College, then the University of Pennsylvania. When John graduated from dental school in 1992, Riley attended his graduation ceremony.

"I felt kind of bad," he recalled. "Because the only other person who showed up for his graduation was his mother."

Mary Lois had spent over twenty years as a teacher in Blairsville, living in the same house with her son, which she owned free and clear, without a mortgage. She was frugal, and if there had ever been any temptation to marry again, she had resisted it. She had an adequate income, supplemented long before by investments she had made from the insurance settlement resulting from John senior's tragic death. While not exactly wealthy, she was certainly very comfortable. Mary

Ann Clark, her niece, came to believe that there was a $1 million insurance policy on Mary Lois's life, although Indiana County probate records don't seem to show that. But there was money there, no doubt about it.

Just before graduating from dental school, John asked Riley if he had room in his practice for another dentist. Riley was noncommittal at first: "Let's give it a year," he told his protégé, "and we'll see how it works." But after a year, Riley was sold: John was not only a competent dentist, he seemed to have a way with the patients. In 1994, Riley and John formed a partnership, and from then on, the mentor and his student were tied together in a flourishing dental practice in Blairsville.

In Riley's recollection, John began to blossom, particularly socially. In the practice, the event of the year was the office Christmas party, and as Riley remembered, this was something that John enjoyed immensely. "He was the life of the party," Riley recalled. It was as if John had found his place at last: he was popular, witty, joyful and jocular, completely confident, no longer the nerd, but now the man-about-town.

Then came disaster: Mary Lois was diagnosed with terminal cancer at the age of fifty-two.

7.

The circumstances of exactly how John Joseph Yelenic Jr. first met Michele Magyar Kamler are murky. Riley heard one story, Mary Ann heard another, and there may be even other versions, or amalgamations of some or all of them. What does seem clear is that sometime in either late 1996 or early 1997, John was introduced to Michele, and soon found himself besotted. Although John had dated other women, none excited him the way Michele did. In his own mind, John was sure he had won the jackpot in the love sweepstakes.

Riley thought his young protégé had met Mrs. Kamler at some sort of promotional event for a beer distributor.

"She was a Coors Light girl," Riley recalled. Or maybe it was Budweiser, or Schlitz—who could remember, years later? John's friends and family were never sure when or where or how or who made the fateful introduction. Riley remembered that John had asked one of his patients if he knew any "single girls." Mary Ann remembered that this same friend of John's had taken him to some sort of outing sponsored by a beer parlor or possibly a distributor in Indiana. But later, when things got very bad, the same friend confessed to John that he regretted having put the two together.

"I wanted you to meet her, John. I never thought you'd marry her," or so the friend later confided to Mary Ann he'd told John as John's unhappiness over the demise of his marriage ensued.

Michele was by the time of their first encounter twenty-five, the mother of two children, a daughter, Nicole, then seven, and a son, Nathan, four. In a way, she came readily equipped for Yelenic: a beautiful woman with a ready-made family, in some ways desperate for stability. John was like a yearling stag caught in Michele's headlights, frozen by his own desire.

It wasn't hard for anyone who knew John to understand what he saw in Michele. Trim, vivacious, alluring, she represented a nerd's dream date. Or, as John put it to his cousin Mary Ann later, "I've won the homecoming queen."

At first, John's friends and relatives seemed delighted for him: he seemed so fulfilled, actually exalted. Whatever questions they had about the woman he so obviously adored were only the smallest of clouds on the horizon. If he was happy, they were happy. If some guessed that Michele was altogether much shrewder, or at least more worldly-wise than John, they kept that suspicion to themselves. John gave Michele a car, jewelry, and other expensive tokens of his esteem.

By March of 1997, John was so enamored of Michele that he financed a business for her in Blairsville. This was in a narrow storefront on Market Street, only a few feet from the intersection of Market and Walnut, also known as State Route 217—the heart of downtown Blairsville, so to speak. Ironically, only a few years later, John would sell the same lot to a prominent Pennsylvania convenience store corporation, Sheetz, which soon built a fast-food/gasoline emporium on a number of properties near the intersection, one of which included the one John had in 1997 provided for the sandwich shop to Michele. In what would be a macabre twist, video cameras at this Sheetz fast-food store would record crucial evidence in the murder of John Yelenic only a few years later.

But in the spring of 1997, a Sheetz store at the corner of Market and Walnut was only a gleam in the eye of some corporate marketing expert. The existing buildings at the intersection were old Blairsville—once thriving businesses in the days before discount supermarkets, a core now slowly withering if not vacant. John installed his new paramour in one of the narrow shops not far from the lucrative corner, and provided the cash to refurbish the place as a deli sandwich shop. Michele, her two children, and her mother occupied an apartment over the shop, some later recalled.

Between March and May of 1997, John put a little over $15,000 into Michele's sandwich shop endeavor, as records that Michele herself kept later showed. (These ledgers were discovered by Mary Ann Clark in John's basement at 233 South Spring Street years after John's murder.) At first, Michele kept very good records: how much was spent on meats, baked goods, payroll for her small staff (including her mother and herself), utilities, and taxes. Her meticulous record keeping seemed to show she was very organized, disciplined, efficient. The largest single expense for the sandwich shop was new flooring—altogether, almost $5,000. And the records showed the place was actually making a reasonable monthly profit, if one amortized the improvements—the flooring, mostly—over a longer period. The idea was sound: a sandwich shop at that location was a moneymaker.

But Michele wrapped up the sandwich emporium only two months later, by the middle of May 1997. By then, Mary Lois Yelenic was dying. Michele took up part-time residence in the Yelenic family home as Mary Lois's part-time caregiver. A few weeks later, in early June of 1997, Mary Lois died. As Mary Ann Clark recalled the scene, Mary

Lois's relatives came to the house at the end to visit her. Michele, according to Mary Ann, refused to let anyone see her. "She's sleeping," Mary Ann said her relatives were told. So Mary Lois Yelenic passed away in June of 1997, and her only son John was devastated by the loss of his firmest and wisest pillar.

Within a month, John had named Michele as his sole heir in case of his own death.

The "Last Will and Testament of John J. Yelenic, Jr." was a rather peculiar document. Signed on July 10, 1997, only a month after the death of his mother, it gave all rights in his estate—which would soon include the assets of his own mother's estate—to Michele Kamler, to whom John was not even related. At the time, few if any of John's relatives or friends were aware of this extraordinary decision on John's part. However, it was duly witnessed by John's personal lawyer, Matthew Kovacik, and a Blairsville woman, probably someone associated with the Kovacik law firm or the Riley/Yelenic dental practice, so there was never a shred of doubt as to its validity.

But why did John Yelenic, only a month after the death of his mother, agree to make his girlfriend of less than a year his heir?

There is little doubt that by July 1997, John was feeling particularly lonely. All of his life, a woman, his mother, had been his bulwark. Now, suddenly, she had been whisked away. In her stead stood another woman, seemingly as strong, as resolute, and just as dominating as Mary Lois: Michele.

Within a few months, John sold the Blairsville house he had grown up in and by the end of the year, in company with his cousin Roger Swasy and Roger's wife, Barbara, was in Las Vegas, Nevada. There, on the last day of 1997, New Year's Eve, he and Michele were married.

The rapid marriage of John and Michele left some people

in Blairsville aghast. Riley, for one, tried to caution his younger partner.

"We thought it was kind of quick," Riley said later. "I said, 'John, what's the hurry?' He said, 'I don't want to be alone at Christmas.' And that was not what I wanted to hear." His young partner's emotional vulnerability in the aftermath of his mother's death—his first Christmas alone—made Riley sense that John was about to go too far, too fast.

But John was adamant. If in earlier years he was diffident, deferential to Riley, the older man, when it came to Michele, he was insistent: Michele was the love of his life, the one and only. In a way, Michele was a prize—visible evidence that the high school turkey could attract a swan. John bought a house on South Spring Street in Blairsville and settled in with Michele and her two growing children. He had what he wanted; his mother might have died, but he had a loving wife, two children to care for, a neighborhood in which to raise a family. They began at once to try to conceive a child.

These initial efforts came to naught. Whether Michele's earlier tubal ligation or the attempted "reversal" of 1994 interfered with conception, or something else was involved, it soon appeared that in order for John to father a child, extraordinary measures would have to be undertaken. In the end, Riley would recall later, John and Michele spend a great deal of money in attempting to achieve in vitro fertilization. It didn't work, and it seems fairly clear that the effort to conceive a child took an emotional toll on the marriage.

Riley, among others, soon noticed something about Michele that John refused to discuss: when it came to the dental office and its small-town web of work and gossip, John was pulling away under the influence of his new wife, who seemed distant, disinterested in John's longtime friends and associates in his hometown. Riley guessed that Blairsville felt much too small for Michele, too closed in, too many wagging tongues. In a place where everyone knew everyone else—knew a lot about each other's lives—Michele felt uncomfortable, Riley guessed. People were curious about her, where she had come from, what the story was about the natural father of her children. Riley thought Michele felt people were talking about her, that she would never be accepted—or maybe it was that Michele was acutely aware that John's closest family and friends believed that she was some sort of gold digger. The reticence, whether from an unhappy past or a guilty conscience, convinced many of John's friends and family that Michele had something to hide.

"People in Blairsville like to know a lot about you," Riley said later. His years peering into the mouths of so many, young and old, had given him an innate sense of life in the small town. "There might have been questions about her children, where they came from. And her divorce. He would tell us, 'Michele doesn't like this, Michele doesn't like that.' Or 'Michele doesn't like this person, Michele doesn't like that person.' And I said to myself, 'This is bad. John's got himself into a bad deal now . . . she's got him going back and forth.' She took John out of our social life, okay? And didn't want him to attend anything. She didn't seem like the kind of person who would look you in the eye. You kind of felt there was something about her nature, there was some kind of agenda."

Riley concluded that Michele was very controlling of John, not least because of her penchant for criticizing him in front of others, even his subordinates in the dental office. John seemed to take this meekly, as if he was afraid to offend her. There was no balance to the marriage at all, at least as far as Riley could see: Michele had the whip hand. Which Riley thought was odd, in a way: just before John's mother, Mary Lois, died, Michele made a striking and, he thought, contemptuous remark about John:

"I don't believe it: his mother controls everything he

does," Michele had remarked. *Well, so what?* Riley thought at the time. *The man's mother is dying.* What son wouldn't, under those circumstances, do whatever his mother asked? But afterward, he realized that very soon John was doing everything *Michele* told him to do. "My initial take was that John could have done better." Riley said. "It didn't seem like a match to me."

Then, in early 2000, John and Michele decided to adopt a child.

8.

The way Riley recalled it, Michele "got on the Internet" and learned of babies up for adoption in Russia or maybe the Ukraine. The next thing Riley knew, in March 2000, John, Michele, her two children, and her mother were all off to Russia. John paid for the whole trip, according to Riley. There, John and Michele adopted Jamie, born in June 1998.

As far as Riley could tell, the months after the adoption of Jamie, both John and Michele seemed content. "Things were peachy," he recalled. But Mary Ann—who wasn't particularly close to her cousin at that point—remembered it somewhat differently, probably relying on John's own description of this period made later, during the traumatic divorce.

"She [Michele] didn't even want to take care of the child," Mary Ann said. "She put him in day care."

At some point in 1998, even before the adoption of Jamie, Michele convinced John to move the family from Blairsville to Indiana. If Blairsville was the Rockwellian small town where everyone knew one another, by comparison Indiana was the big city. Riley, for one, thought that Michele was unhappy in a place where people liked to know a lot about each other, where there might have been questions about Michele's children and her divorce. Indiana had more people, a university, many more restaurants and bars, and more social life, even if Jimmy Stewart in his own day didn't think so. But, of course, culture is relative.

"Maybe there was more social life in Indiana," Riley said. "People in Blairsville like to know a lot about you . . . and I think she kind of wanted to get away from that." Blairsville was far too small for Michele's true ambitions, Riley thought.

The couple soon bought a house in the somewhat upscale residential area of north Indiana on White Farm Road, perhaps a mile or so north of downtown and the Jimmy Stewart Museum. The house, a commodious two-story dwelling on a large lot with a swimming pool, cost $275,000. John began commuting from Indiana to his practice in Blairsville, at least a half-hour drive each way, depending on the traffic. For the first time in his life, John was out of his natural element, away from the protective cocoon of Riley and others.

This move from Blairsville to Indiana further estranged John from those in his hometown. John became increasingly reticent, seemingly morose, according to Riley. Attempts to draw him out were rebuffed. It was as if John was gloomy, alone, drifting in darkness toward an uncertain shore.

Sorting out just who did what to whom in the demise of the marriage of John and Michele Yelenic is almost impossible after so many years. Who first violated the oaths of matrimony was unclear. "There were issues of fidelity on both sides," Anthony Krastek, the Pennsylvania assistant attorney general who eventually prosecuted Kevin Foley for the murder of John Yelenic, would later say. But by all accounts, by late 2001 the marriage was in big trouble.

In some of these accounts, it was Michele who threw the first jealousy card. John had grown close to her son, Nathan, then a little over ten years old. Nathan played in a youth ice hockey league, and John often attended his practices and games. There John met the mother, a divorcée, of another player, and a relationship of sorts began. However innocent this might have been, Michele became jealous, or possibly nervous, at least according to John's later account to his cousin Mary Ann. According to John, Michele began following the other woman and sending her threatening letters. Mary Ann admitted that her cousin might have given Michele cause for complaint.

"I'm not saying John was a saint," she said later. But Michele's interaction with this other woman caused the woman to break off the relationship with John, according to Mary Ann. Who needed that kind of trouble? Whether this relationship began before or after John and Michele split their blankets isn't clear.

In any event, by February of 2002 the Yelenic marriage was on the rocks. John soon moved out of the White Farm Road house and back to the house on Spring Street in Blairsville. Michele was soon seen around town keeping company with a well-to-do Indiana businessman, an investor in the Marcellus Shale gas bonanza beguiling so many in west-central Pennsylvania at the time, and a man who also happened to be politically well connected.

The area's state senator, Don White, a friend of the shale gas entrepreneur as well as of Mary Ann Clark, recalled meeting Michele at a party in this period in early 2002. He first thought Michele might be a professional escort—in short, a highly paid hooker. Michele, he recalled, was dressed rather provocatively. He knew that the shale gas entrepreneur had recently separated from his wife and assumed that the woman's services had been arranged. It made no difference to White—it wasn't up to him to monitor his supporters' morality—but he wondered why the entrepreneur had taken the risk of getting involved with someone who seemed, as White later put it, "something of a wildflower."

But by April of 2002, the bloom of this romance had faded for Michele. The shale gas entrepreneur terminated the relationship to return to his wife. Within a short time, he reportedly complained about Michele to the state police and two state police investigators came to see Michele at the White Farm Road residence recently vacated by John. Reportedly, one of the investigators was Kevin Foley. Nothing came of the shale king's complaint—the investigation found no violation of any law and no criminal case was ever filed against Michele.

Afterward, according to Mary Ann Clark, the gas guy called John on the telephone, fuming about Michele.

"You can have her back," he told John.

"I don't want her," John replied.

This initial encounter between Michele Yelenic and Kevin Foley, in April or so of 2002, seems to have led nowhere—maybe. But the pair seemed matched in some ways: Michele, with a clear-eyed vision of how to take care of herself and her children, rather well accomplished at the age-old artistry of inducing men to help her get what she wanted; and Foley, a man who loved to do good, especially for women he believed abused by men. That a desire to take care of one's uncertain future eventually joined with another's desire to define oneself as someone who took care of others—to be a hero—is at the heart of the tragedy underlying the horrible death of John Yelenic. Sometimes evil isn't intended; it just happens, the result of the combustibility of the best of intentions, a confusion of motives, often two fatal misperceptions. It is all too human to see in someone else that which one most wants to see, whether it's there or not.

Kevin Foley, at thirty-seven years old, was a large man, almost six feet three inches tall and around 225 pounds, much of it muscle added through strenuous workouts and, some suspected, perhaps steroids. He had a raw-boned if well-muscled physicality; if he'd only been two or three steps faster afoot in his younger years, he certainly could have played strong safety in the National Football League. He had the size for it and, some said, also the native aggressiveness. Even without possible chemical enhancements, Kevin was a born athlete, gifted with size, strength, and agility, and most especially the love of competition. He regularly ran fifteen to twenty miles every week, keeping himself toned, and enjoyed playing football, softball, basketball, and ice hockey, usually on teams composed at least partly of other police officers. In short, if John was a born nerd, Kevin was a born jock. In fact, Kevin was designated the Indiana barracks' official physical fitness coordinator in 2001.

But Kevin also had some hidden, internal disabilities. One was his streak of self-righteousness, of moral certitude. As noted, White, the state senator, eventually observed that some of his contacts in the Pennsylvania State Police had told him some in the PSP considered Kevin a born bully, even something of a "Nazi." In short, Kevin was quick to judge those he deemed morally deficient, whether accurately or not. Regrettably, this is not an unusual fault in many young police officers, although most outgrow it in their later years, in the light of accumulated experience.

Still, this superficial view of Foley passed over a lot. In many ways, Kevin hardly saw himself as a "Nazi." In his own mind he was far more the man on the white horse, the chivalrous knight in shining armor, dedicated to the rescue of damsels in distress. He was far too streetwise to claim as much in words to his colleagues, who would certainly have laughed at such a self-description, given the cynicism of modern police work; but in his heart of hearts he still saw himself as something of a superhero, a Sir Galahad type. He might not have declaimed aloud, "Beware evildoers, wherever you are!" but that's what was in his heart and soul. And once Kevin made up his mind that you were bad, that was it: you *were* bad. Kevin knew bad: he'd been there, seen that, and even experienced it personally.

What a lot of people who later talked about Kevin didn't understand—probably never knew, even his closest friends in the Pennsylvania State Police—was what that this mentality, the desire to right wrongs, to even the moral scales, was the most dominating aspect of his personality.

Born in the suburbs of New York City, on May 30, 1965, Kevin and his sister Karen had allegedly been physically abused as children. This, at least, was the understanding of Tony Krastek, the man who later prosecuted Kevin for the murder of John Yelenic. In Krastek's opinion, Kevin's reaction to his early childhood was a key factor in what happened to Yelenic in the early morning hours of April 13, 2006.

"He had an absolute loathing for child molesters and abusers of women," Krastek would later say. If there was anything likely to set Foley off, it was the mistreatment of the weak and the defenseless, particularly children. This mind-set, almost a reflex in Kevin, would loom large as the events of the early 2000s unfolded, even before John Yelenic's murder.

Kevin and his sister were adopted, and when he was two, his adoptive parents bought a resort in upper New York State on Schroon Lake, north of Lake Placid, where the family moved. After his rough start in life, Kevin grew up in what would seem to have been a kind and bucolic environment, along with two other siblings in addition to his sister. Whether this upbringing between two extremes formed Kevin's most fundamental outlook on life—his penchant for seeing things in white and black, good and evil—is a matter of conjecture, but it surely acquainted him with the extreme ranges of human behavior. It certainly provided him with the parameters of his rather rigid sense of moral judgment: by his early adulthood, Kevin Foley was sure he knew what was right and what was wrong, as well as who was good and who was evil.

By his own account, after the age of five, Kevin had a rather normal life with his two adoptive parents, Ken and Gail Foley. When he was about twelve, the Foleys sold their interest in the Schroon Lake resort and eventually moved to Florida, in part because Ken Foley suffered from a heart condition, and it was thought he would enjoy better health in a warmer climate. From the late 1970s, the family lived on Florida's Gulf Coast, not far from the Tampa–St. Petersburg area. Kevin, after graduating from high school in the spring of 1983, joined the U.S. Army, taking training as a military policeman, then serving in Germany in the mid-1980s. Even in those years, Kevin was physically impressive: tall, raw-boned, powerful, capable of intimidation, just the sort of MP you never want to meet if you're a GI off on a toot: he could be scary.

After his discharge from the army, Kevin enrolled in a community college in St. Petersburg, obtaining an associate's degree in criminal justice. From 1990 to 1992, he attended the final two years of a four-year criminal justice program at South Florida University, graduating with a bachelor's degree in criminology in early 1992, the same year John Yelenic graduated from dental school. By then Foley had met his first wife, Barbara Ann Ray, while she was a pharmacist at a nearby Wal-Mart store; he served as a store manager for Wal-Mart when he wasn't attending classes at SFU. Barbara was from Pennsylvania—in fact, Armstrong County, just west of Indiana—and after graduation Kevin and his bride headed to the Keystone State. After passing an examination to qualify as a municipal police officer, Kevin was hired part-time by the town of Freeport in

Armstrong County in 1993. A few months later, Kevin applied for and was accepted into the Pennsylvania State Police training academy for the January class of 1994.

On June 1, 1994, Foley was assigned to the PSP barracks in Indiana as an over-the-road trooper, the usual entry-level work for a new recruit. His initial training officer was Trooper Brian Bono. Years later, Bono would be among the several PSP officers Mary Ann Clark would sue in federal court, alleging that Foley's closest friends among the PSP had helped facilitate Foley's harassment against her cousin, John Yelenic, prior to his murder.

On the last day of 1999, Kevin sued his wife Barbara Ann for divorce after almost a decade of marriage. There were no children, and Barbara Ann filed a petition to reassume her maiden name. A little over a year later, in early 2000, Kevin was transferred to the PSP's criminal investigations division—the plainclothes detectives of the PSP—and assigned to the Indiana barracks, the same place he had worked as an over-the-road trooper and where, as a result, he had many friends. There he soon ran afoul of Sergeant George Emigh, his ostensible supervisor in the Indiana PSP investigation unit. This probably wasn't entirely Foley's fault: by that point, or soon thereafter, Emigh had developed a deep-seated contempt for his own supervisor, a Lt. James Fulmer. As far as Emigh could see, Foley was an ally of Fulmer; worse, Emigh thought, Foley was an insubordinate smart-ass. The seeds of a long-running personality conflict were planted, and would eventually bear bitter fruit.

Whether there was objective validity to these conflicts wasn't as important as what it meant for the way the PSP would carry out its duties. These sorts of personality clashes and political schisms are rife in most police organizations; it's the nature of the work, no matter where or when. But years later, when the body of John Yelenic lay dead on his own living room floor, Emigh would come to believe that the PSP was conspiring to cover up Yelenic's death and to let their fair-haired boy, Foley, off the hook. As far as Emigh was concerned, the cover-up was all about politics and getting rid of *him*, one of Foley's longtime critics. He took it personally, and as with most things anyone takes personally, he wouldn't let it go.

9.

Kevin's divorce from Barbara Ann was completed by May 12, 2000. She moved back to Armstrong County and reassumed her maiden name of Ray—almost as if an entire decade, in some ways, had never happened. Almost eighteen months later, in September 2002, Foley married Susan Marie Smith, a bank employee in Indiana, who was a year older than he was. This marriage was also doomed to failure, although a lot faster than his alliance with Barbara Ann.

"Would it be fair to say that that marriage simply didn't work out from the outset?" Kevin was asked a few years later.

"That would be fair, yes," Kevin said.

Whether Kevin's September 7, 2002, marriage with Susan was conflicted from the start by his meeting with Michele in connection with the computer hacking case in April 2002, five months earlier, is a matter of conjecture. Both Kevin and Michele each formally filed for divorce from their respective spouses in June of 2003, thirteen days apart. In fact, Michele filed for her divorce from John exactly two days after Kevin said he had legally separated from his second wife, Susan. Kevin would later contend that he didn't begin dating Michele until the summer of 2004. Susan Smith has never publicly commented on her brief marriage to Kevin and their divorce, although Mary Ann Clark would later suggest that the demise of Kevin's second marriage was mostly a result of Michele's meeting with Foley in 2002 to 2003, during the investigation of the shale gas entrepreneur's complaint.

The specific dates involved with all of this aren't particularly important in and of themselves, except insofar as they reflect on Foley's later credibility as a sworn witness in the Yelenic murder trial. In short, if Foley was deceptive about one thing under oath, would he likely be deceptive about another more significant issue—say, where he was at the time Yelenic was being knifed to death? Was he lying then or was he lying later? Or was he lying at all? Contradictions are how lawyers earn their money, of course.

The fact was, while Mary Ann despised Foley for the murder of her cousin John, she despised Michele even more as the person who she believed had set the train of tragic events in motion, as she later alleged in a civil lawsuit she brought against Foley, Michele, and various colleagues of Foley in the PSP. Mary Ann claimed that Michele had manipulated Foley by intentionally fueling and encouraging Foley's hatred and jealousy of John Yelenic, and that she had conspired with Foley to kill Yelenic.

Whatever the truth of the timing of Foley's first intimate connection with Michele, by early 2002, just after John Yelenic vacated the White Farm Road house to return to Blairsville, Michele was already concerned with *other* legal troubles: her former husband, Jeff Kamler, then living in Westmoreland County, just southeast of Pittsburgh, was suing her to gain joint custody of their daughter, Nicole, then thirteen years old.

Thus, even as Yelenic was retreating to the Blairsville

house he had once purchased for his hoped-for family on South Spring Street as stepfather of Nicole and Nathan and then the Russian-born toddler Jamie—a dream dashed by the separation from Michele—and even as the PSP was investigating John's estranged wife in connection with the shale gas guy's complaint—Michele's former husband was suing her to establish joint custody of their daughter. Just why Jeff Kamler was trying this, so many years after divorcing Michele, or why his legal petition made no mention of their son, Nathan, wasn't clear, at least from the court records.

Michele fought back. She retained an Indiana lawyer, Nicholas Mikesic. Jeff Kamler retained Myron Hay Tomb, of Tomb, Mack & Kaufman, one of Indiana's more prestigious law firms. As it happened, Tomb, Mack & Kaufman would represent Kevin Foley in *his* divorce from Susan Smith the following year, and Mikesic would represent Susan Smith!

In any event, just how Jeff Kamler could have afforded the services of Tomb, Mack in the spring of 2002 and why he initiated these joint custody proceedings after so many years is another mystery, but it seems at least remotely possible that John Yelenic might well have financed this legal foray by Michele's first husband in an effort to rein in the wayward Michele and thus win back her favors, reasoning that Michele might well have concluded that John's arms were to be preferred to Kamler's claim on their thirteen-year-old daughter. Sometimes love weaves very tangled, sticky webs.

This custody case dragged on through the summer, fall, and winter and into early 2003. Eventually the lawsuit was settled between Michele and her former husband, or so it appears from the records. After mediation ordered by the court, Michele retained primary custody of Nicole.

By then, however, Michele had established yet another relationship, this time with the scion of a wealthy family in Johnstown—of legendary flood fame—some miles south of Indiana.

Michele's new boyfriend was a giant step up, at least in terms of house beautiful. From a rusty, leaky house trailer in Creekside, to a tiny apartment in Indiana, to a small flat over a sandwich shop in Blairsville, to John Yelenic's middle-class house on South Spring Street, to the large house on White Farm Road, the wealthy Johnstown scion's palatial brick dwelling in the hills overlooking Johnstown and the Conemaugh River illustrated Michele's social as well as material advancement.

Unsurprisingly, John was not happy to hear that the love of his life had moved in with a rich man's son in Johnstown. Spending most of his nights tossing and turning alone in the house on South Spring Street, the domicile of his dreams and nightmares, John alternated between anger and a desire to win back his still-yearned-for "homecoming queen." At one point he even agreed to pay for Michele's schooling as a dental hygienist in the fall of 2002: he probably had a fantasy that Michele would come to her senses and return to him, maybe even work as a tooth rinser in the Blairsville office!

But Michele, after taking up with the wealthy Johnstown scion, stopped attending the training classes. Flossing and rinsing the mouths of others, it seemed, wasn't her cup of tea. Then, on June 10, 2003, while still living with the scion, Michele filed for divorce from John. And in doing this, it seems, Michele went one step too far: she demanded sole custody of the Yelenics' adopted child, Jamie. It was the formal declaration of a war that would rage for almost three years, a conflict that would make a hostage of little Jamie, drive both John Yelenic and Kevin Foley nearly mad, eventually lead to Foley's conviction for murder, and cost John Yelenic his very life.

Michele would eventually walk free from the wreckage—
mostly.

In her petition for divorce from John, Michele claimed that
the marriage was "irretrievably broken" and that she, as
John's wife, had suffered "such indignities . . . as to render
her condition intolerable and life burdensome." Michele
claimed her residence was still at the house on White Farm
Road in Indiana, and wanted the divorce court to award her
occupancy of the dwelling, monthly alimony, and child support. John would later dispute that Michele was still living
with the children on White Farm Road: as far as he was
concerned, Michele had abandoned the place to move in
with the wealthy heir in Johnstown by July of 2003.

It would take another year and some negotiations, but on
June 24, 2004, John sold the White Farm Road house at a
significant loss. While he'd paid $275,000 for the property in
the fall of 1998, he'd sold it that year for $262,500—$12,500
worth of red ink, and in a real estate market that had sky-
rocketed during the five years between its initial purchase
and subsequent sale. But when John finally unloaded the
place, it was a wreck, according to Mary Ann Clark.

"She left the doors open," Mary Ann said, "[and] the
windows. It was trashed. Animals were living in it." According to Mary Ann, when it finally cleared escrow, the
buyers were astounded at its condition. It was, possibly, a
visual statement by Michele of her feelings for her former
husband. Of course, by the time Mary Ann made those assertions about the condition of the property in 2010, she was
not well-disposed toward Michele, to say the least: she was
convinced that Michele had somehow goaded Kevin Foley
into murdering her cousin.

The White Farm Road property debacle wasn't John's
only financial loss in the divorce battle, according to the

divorce court records. Somehow, between the time Michele sued him for divorce in June of 2003 and early 2006, John agreed to cede 60 percent of the couple's joint real estate holdings, although virtually all of these assets had been accumulated from either John's inheritance from his mother or his own income from the dental practice. These investment properties were both extensive and valuable, according to real estate records in Indiana County—maybe worth as much as a million dollars or more.

Just how and why John agreed to this uneven split was never made clear in the divorce record. Matthew Kovacik, John's initial lawyer in the divorce lawsuit, later said as far as he could recall, no division of property was made while he was officially on the case from July 2003 to June 2004. (The White Farm Road house was sold by John nine days after Kovacik was replaced by Pittsburgh divorce lawyer Effie G. Alexander, and after Michele had quitclaimed her interest in the property to John.) Yet, Kevin Foley later testified that as far as he knew, this agreement to divide the Yelenic real estate, so lucrative to Michele and injurious to John, had been made between John and Michele *before* Kovacik left the case, and before Kevin got involved with Michele: he claimed in the summer of 2004.

So either Kovacik was in error—not very likely—or Foley was either misinformed by Michele or deliberately deceptive in his testimony. The whole issue of the Yelenic property, land, money, and life insurance—that is, who got the dough—would turn out to be pivotal, at least as to a possible motive for John Yelenic's horrific murder in April 2006. Some thought the killing was *all* about money. Yet others thought it was actually all about revenge, whether real or imagined, past or present.

As the murder case unfolded after 2006 up until today, this question of motive would become one of its most enduring mysteries.

Of course, it's also possible that John voluntarily and informally agreed to give up more than half of his real estate assets, based on nothing more than Michele's considerable powers of persuasion, if not because she was making John's life so difficult. As Matthew Kovacik put it later, sometimes people agree to such unequal divorce settlements simply to get rid of the unwanted interspousal combat. But, given Yelenic's pining for his former wife, this seems unlikely; actually, given his unrequited yearning for Michele, it's more likely that John acceded to this uneven split in order to retain some glimmer of hope that someday, somehow, she might come back to his bed. Foley would later say he thought Michele got the bigger part of the pot because she had managed the real estate properties for John while they were married from 1998 on—a departure bonus, as it were.

This idea is slightly supported by something else a bit odd about the case of *Yelenic* v. *Yelenic*: although Michele had filed her divorce suit in June of 2003, it wasn't until June of the following year, 2004, that John finally responded to the action, at least in a substantive legal answer to the complaint, and this only with Effie Alexander's formal notice of appearance. It appears that for most of June 2003 to July 2004, John still retained the hope of regaining the affections if not marital relations with Michele, and so might have been amenable to a property settlement that was not equal. But by June of 2004, it must have been clear to John that it was really, truly over. Exit Kovacik, enter Alexander, well-known throughout Pennsylvania as one of the savviest domestic relations lawyers around. As far as Alexander could see, John Yelenic had become his estranged wife's goofy idiot—a sap. A lovable sap, maybe, but someone who was being carved up, emotionally and financially.

By then, as Alexander soon realized, Michele had already had John arrested and accused, for the first but not last time, of child abuse. This had happened nine months before she came into the case, and was in fact the first of the shadows that would haunt the murder of John Yelenic, both before and after his gruesome death. Even before Yelenic lay dying on his living room floor, things would get worse than a mere divorce—much, much worse. In fact, Michele would eventually accuse Yelenic of sexually molesting of their own adopted son.

10.

The first arrest of John Yelenic was the occasion that Jill Gaston of the Blairsville Police Department recalled so vividly, years after the murder.

By the late summer of 2003, with Michele and the children now living in the heir's three-story brick mansion in Johnstown, John's periodic custodial visits with his adopted son Jamie continued, with either John driving to Johnstown to pick Jamie up or Michele dropping the tyke off at the South Spring Street house or sometimes at the dental office. In late September of 2003, John had one such visit with Jamie, who was at that point five years old. Judging from photographs taken at the time, Jamie was a cheery, happy little child, despite all the turbulence that had so far marked his early years. Photographs showing Jamie at age three in the arms of John and Michele, before his parents' fall into matrimonial discord, are a joy to behold.

This visit of September 20–21, 2003, took place at John's Blairsville house, according to Michele. She said that when Jamie returned, the boy claimed John had hit him in the mouth with a closed fist, "which resulted in cuts on both his upper and lower lip," as an emergency room doctor noted almost four days later. But there were reasons to doubt the veracity of this account of abuse.

On September 25, 2003, when the doctor first examined little Jamie at Michele's behest, he referred the boy for further investigation by the county's Children and Youth Services department, CYS. A social worker then talked to both Michele and Jamie. Based on reports from these two interviews, a little over two weeks later, Michele's lawyer, Daniel R. Lovette of Johnstown, obtained a Cambria County judge's order barring John from further contact with either Jamie or Michele—in the argot of Pennsylvania law, a "PFA," for "protection from abuse."

A close analysis of these reports, and Lovette's subsequent legal filings, raises the possibility, however, that the whole thing might have been a put-up job by Michele in order to leverage a fatter financial settlement from John.

"Petitioner [Michele] avers that the petitioner and respondent [John] were having arguments concerning family law matters [presumably, the proposed financial settlement], and it is apparent that respondent became angry with his son based on the family law matters between mother and father," Lovette claimed to the Cambria County court on October 13, 2003, almost three weeks after the visitation.

To back up Michele's assertions about John's supposed "family law matters" attack on Jamie, Lovette incorporated as an exhibit the report of Bradley Callihan, apparently the emergency room physician who examined the little boy on September 25—as noted, four days after the conclusion of the regularly scheduled visitation with John.

In this report, Callihan noted:

"[Jamie] reports that his father punched him and choked him after he vomited. [Jamie] also states that his father swore at him."

Callihan noticed that Jamie had a swollen upper lip but went on to report that there was no visible evidence of any choking of Jamie's neck, although he did seem to have a sore throat, apparently from a swollen lymph node. Callihan referred Jamie and Michele to another physician, Regina T. Kupchella. Dr. Kupchella saw Jamie for the first and apparently only time five days after Callihan, on September 30.

"Patient is a pleasant [child] in no apparent distress," Dr. Kupchella wrote in her report.

Under an entry headed "Chief Complaint," Kupchella noted that Jamie had been referred for further examination by the Cambria County Children and Youth Services department: "Child allegedly hit in face by father; possible previous episodes of inappropriate physical contact. [Jamie] answers 'yes' when questioned if Dad had hit him before. [Jamie] denied any inappropriate sexual contact/injury."

And in fact, other than a sore throat and the slightly enlarged lymph node—and a possible minor ear infection—Kupchella could discern no injury at all to Jamie. Examination of Jamie's private parts, fore and aft, showed no sign of any "abnormalities," as Kupchella put it in her follow-up report. In short, on paper, there was nothing wrong with Jamie other than his slightly sore throat—not unusual in kids five years old.

As a result of Michele's complaint about her estranged husband's supposed smacking of their adopted child, a social worker began a log reflecting the investigation of the complaint of Michele against John with regard to the victim, Jamie, to the effect that John had whacked the five-year-old in the kisser after he had thrown up on the weekend of September 20–21, 2003. The paper record would long persist after the alleged event and cause no end of trouble over the next few years because of what it seemed to say about Yelenic.

In the social worker's log begun on September 25, four days after the complained-of visitation, a social worker identified as "TAC" noted: "The mother had the child examined due to him reporting to her that he had cuts on both his upper and lower lips and that his front tooth was loose from being hit by his father, John Yelenic . . . [T]he father also allegedly picked the child up by his throat and choked him to the point that the child vomited."

The phrasing of TAC's log suggests that TAC might have had some doubt as to the veracity of the claims of abuse: TAC noted that there were no obvious signs of injury, that the claim of abuse was through the mother, not initially from the child—"him reporting to her"—that "allegedly" Jamie had been picked up by the throat. It seems from this record that TAC had doubts as to the essential truthfulness as to this supposed abuse of Jamie on the part of John.

When TAC asked Jamie what day or what time of day his father had hurt him, Jamie couldn't remember—not a good sign for veracity. Even a five-year-old can distinguish between morning, noon, and night.

Jamie told the caseworker that he and John had been playing with water balloons in the driveway of the Blairsville house. (Perhaps significantly, there *is* no driveway in either the front or rear of the Blairsville house, although there was one at the house of the wealthy scion in Johnstown.)

"According to the child," the social worker's report continued, "the father got mad at him and pushed him to the ground. When the child recovered and got up, the father grabbed him with both hands by the neck and lifted him off the ground and choked him. The child said he was choked so hard he 'threw up' on his father. The child said that then the father also 'threw up.' Next the child said that the father got mad again and punched him in the mouth causing the previously mentioned facial injuries. The child does not know why his father was angry with him."

These interviews were conducted with Michele present, available to observe and possibly modify Jamie's responses.

* * *

Judging from the Cambria County records of Michele's 2003 complaint about John's supposed abuse of Jamie, no one ever bothered to follow up with John—that is, get *his* side of this tale of the vomiting water balloon battle in the nonexistent driveway in Blairsville. There is no record at all of either "TAC" or anyone else ever contacting Yelenic to see what was what. Nor did anyone in Cambria County discern that all this was going on at the same time that Michele was involved in an acrimonious divorce proceeding with John, which might have given her a motive to make things hot for her estranged husband by lodging a potentially spurious abuse complaint involving their adopted five-year-old child. It's not even clear from the records that John even knew about the allegation when Michele first made it. Still, the paper was pushed forward through the bureaucratic channels, and soon wound up on the desk of Cambria County judge F. Joseph Leahy.

Leahy, doubtless dealing with scores of these sorts of disputes every month, simply signed Lovette's requested protection-from-abuse order on October 13, 2003, temporarily forbidding John to have any contact with either Michele or Jamie. This went out by computer notification to law enforcement the same day, and without a substantive response from John or his lawyer, Kovacik, was permanently approved by the judge the following week. The PFA prohibited John from seeing either Jamie or Michele for the next six months, and barred him from coming anywhere near the scion's mansion in Johnstown.

A few days later, on October 23—after Judge Leahy's permanent order—John nevertheless drove from Blairsville to Johnstown. There he left a written notice on the front steps of the mansion saying that he would no longer assume financial responsibility for Jamie's health insurance premiums. Doubtless, this was John's way of striking back at Michele and her complaint—an unthoughtful response on his part, but understandably human. But in leaving the written notice, John technically violated the Cambria County court's protection-from-abuse order. He would soon go to jail, at least temporarily.

One of the peculiarities of legal proceedings in a few rural places in this country, like Cambria County, Pennsylvania, is the refusal of local magistrates to permit inspection of public records such as those produced in divorce cases. As judges in Cambria County later explained, they consider these records "private," not to be disclosed to the public, lest one or more of the parties be "embarrassed" by the possible publication of the contents of such legal files.

While this posture is definitely not in keeping with decisions of the U.S. Supreme Court as to public accessibility of court records, even in Pennsylvania, one can understand how the highest court's opinions might not yet have penetrated to the hinterlands of some localities, where legal practice for generations has been a matter for the good old boys there, whether judges or lawyers, to decide. They like it that way, especially when it comes to scions of prosperous families who are big wheels in the local economy—and politics.

In any event, the Cambria County court records of Jeff Kamler's divorce from Michele, or the mansion-dwelling scion's 1991 divorce from his own previous wife, remain mostly secret, because the facts might be "embarrassing," according to judges there. Still, an idea of what the 2003 beef between John and Michele was all about is nevertheless available in both Cambria and Indiana Counties. The records of Michele's complaint about John's supposed assault on his own child can be found in the Cambria County archives, and the records of John's arrest in connection with same are available in the Blairsville magistrate's court in Indiana County, and together they tell most of the tale, however embarrassing it might be to, well, whomever.

Michele's divorce lawyer, Daniel Lovette of Johnstown, obtained the temporary PFA banning John from contact with Michele and Jamie on October 13, and by the next day the court's order was disseminated across Pennsylvania and, quite specifically, to Indiana County law enforcement. Within two weeks John made his ill-advised drive to Johnstown, no doubt in a fit of anger after Michele's complaint about the allegation of the supposed smacking of Jamie's lip, and left on the scion's doorstep the written notice that he would no longer be responsible for paying little Jamie's health insurance premiums.

Michele collected this paper from the doorstep and, concluding this was a clear violation of the no-contact order of the Judge Leahy's PFA, immediately swore out a criminal complaint against her unhappily estranged husband. She called the Cambria County cops, and within a day or so a warrant was issued for John Yelenic's arrest. This was communicated to the Indiana County Sheriff's Office, which passed it on to the Blairsville Police Department, and at that point Jill Gaston, the former intern with the Indiana County district attorney's office, now wearing a uniform, a badge, and a gun as a Blairsville town cop, drove the two blocks from the police station to the Riley-Yelenic dental practice on Market Street in Blairsville with a legal order to put Dr. Yelenic in the local slammer.

Gaston, accompanied by an Indiana County deputy sheriff, knew Yelenic both by sight and reputation; after all, he was something of a bigwig in Blairsville. So Gaston was somewhat diffident in doing what the law required her to do: arrest John Yelenic, the beloved family dentist of Blairstown! But still, the law was the law, Gaston thought, and she had to do her duty.

Yelenic wasn't upset about the arrest—not visibly, anyway. "He was very pleasant," Gaston recalled later. "And as a matter of fact, when he came out, he stopped, and he said, 'You're not going to handcuff me?' And I'm, like, 'No.' And I knew Doctor Yelenic, he was a doctor in town." It would have embarrassed Gaston to handcuff the popular dentist right in front of his office, out in public. So she tried to give him an out:

"You're not going to give me any trouble, are you?" she asked. John shook his head no.

"But," he asked, "do you normally handcuff people for this?"

Gaston told him that usually the police *did* handcuff people when they arrested them, no matter who they were. It was standard operating procedure: in the stress of an arrest, who knew what someone might do?

"Well," he said, "you're going to treat me like a normal person."

"And he wouldn't take no for an answer," Gaston recalled. So she handcuffed Yelenic and brought him to the Blairsville police station, where he was booked, fingerprinted, photographed front and profile, and placed in a cell.

Within a few hours, John was brought before the Blairsville magistrate, who warned him not to violate the court order again. John agreed and was soon released.

This whole tale of the arrest of Dr. Yelenic on his estranged wife's complaint of the supposed assault of their five-year-old child, as well as Gaston's description of the pinch, seems to stand as clear evidence of Yelenic's essentially nonviolent nature as well as his haplessness—his very incapacity to lash out at the one he loved—despite the aggravation of being arrested; to somehow bring the relationship, no matter how badly had she mistreated him, back into some sort of psychological and economic equilibrium. In other words, his sappiness.

One wants to reach out to John Yelenic at this point, grab him by his dentist's smock, and smack him, yell at him, tell him to wake up and take care of himself, to fight back. But it's too late now: by the time the totality of this unhappy tale finally emerges, years later, Yelenic is already dead, mostly because he didn't know how to effectively fight back, either at this point in 2003 or three years later, when a killer confronted him in his home and sliced him up with a knife on his own living room floor in the early morning hours of April 13, 2006.

John Yelenic was not a fighter. His mother raised him in a bubble, and in the end it killed him, and there's nothing that anyone can do for him now. If he'd spent even one night down at the bandstand with a real homecoming queen and a six-pack of beer, he would have known a lot better. But John Yelenic was at heart a child.

11.

Having been barred by court order from having contact
with little Jamie from October of 2003 to April of 2004,
John soon sank into a deep depression. The winter was gray
indeed for John, as his mentor and paternal guide Riley noticed. It was bad enough that Michele had left John's bed for
other men, but being barred from contact with his adopted
child, his only son—and on grounds of supposed violent
abuse—seemed to take the heart out of him. How could Michele say such things? And especially the five-year-old Jamie? The betrayal was hard to take. Soon John concluded
that Michele had somehow induced the boy to say what Michele had told him to say; after all, Michele was with him
night and day and had complete control over his well-being.
Wouldn't any five-year-old say what his mother told him to
say if he really, really loved her?

But worse—much, much worse—was still to come.

By the winter or spring of 2004, the relationship between
Michele and the Johnstown scion had reached its own nadir.
Later, several stories emerged in connection with this development. In one, it was alleged that Michele—contemplating
marriage with the scion—had been asked at the insistence

of the heir's aged parents to sign a prenuptial agreement limiting her marital property rights and she refused to sign. In another similar story, Mary Ann Clark and Tom Riley later said they'd heard that the heir's parents had paid Michele money to leave their smitten son alone. Whether or not there is any truth to either of these stories, it is a fact that the relationship ended.

By April of 2004, Michele acquired a new house, a place at 10 Susan Drive, back in Indiana. This happened on April 23, 2004; about three weeks after, under the pending 60/40 divorce property settlement, the two Yelenics sold a valuable apartment building in downtown Indiana for, according to the Indiana County records, the fire-sale price of $190,000. It appears from the same real estate records that Michele bought the house on Susan Drive, in the hills east of town, for $200,000, paying $40,000 down. A forty-grand down payment only showed again how far Michele had come. Whether this down payment was her share of the apartment sale or a payoff from Johnstown, it didn't matter much: Michele had definitely moved on up.

And it also appears that sometime thereafter the PSP trooper, Kevin Foley, moved in with her and the children.

At the time, Kevin owned his own house in Indiana, at 275 Charles Street. He had retained this real estate in his divorce from Susan Smith, which, however, carried at least some financial cost to Kevin: alimony for one year of $622 a month, along with $9,550 for her share of the equity in the house, among a few other concessions, all of them agreed to by Kevin in July 2003. In some ways, Kevin seemed anxious to put his marriage to Susan Marie Smith behind him.

By this point, Kevin had been in plain clothes as a PSP investigator assigned to the Indiana barracks for almost four years, under the supervision of Sergeant George Emigh, whom Kevin seemed to despise. Emigh, of course, considered

Kevin a toady of the PSP lieutenant *he* despised, so he also despised Kevin. This internecine backbiting is not untypical of many police agencies, but while internal politics are often endemic in many organizations both large and small, even among civilians, they can have lethal consequences when practiced by those who carry badges and guns.

Kevin's track record as an investigator wasn't much to write home about—although, if he was no Sherlock Holmes, at least he wasn't Inspector Clouseau. The one thing that most people remembered about Kevin from these years was his difficulty in transitioning from a uniformed trooper to someone with a little more savoir faire, a detective capable of subtlety. The Thin Man he wasn't. Kevin still tended to rely on his physically intimidating presence, his glowering machismo, when, as an investigator, there were often more devious ways to get to the guilty party, and the usually prevalent shades of gray as to culpability. And what many remembered most vividly was Kevin's almost fetish-like attachment to his four-inch pocketknife.

As a number of state troopers later testified, many over-the-road troopers carried similar knives. These could be very useful tools in an emergency: if a motorist was trapped by his seat belt in a wreck, a sharp knife could be very useful in freeing him. Kevin seemed to have a number of knives, all flick-out blades, in which a quick snap of the wrist bared the sharpened steel from the haft of the knife. He often practiced his knife flicking, other troopers later recalled, almost as a nervous habit, the way some people chew gum. "Kevin played, always played, with a knife. He just flicked it, played with it, flicked it around and played with [it]," Trooper Daniel Zenisek recalled later. "You would see him at roll call or whatever and he would flick his knife and . . . just play with it."

Foley appeared to enjoy brandishing the naked blade; once, in fact, he had even accidentally sliced the groin area of the pants of a colleague, Trooper James Fry in a playful gesture, accompanied by a joke. The trooper wasn't happy, and Kevin was both embarrassed and apologetic. But Kevin still incessantly practiced snapping open his blade. For him, the knife was a security blanket of sorts, even after he'd left his road uniform behind, having donned the suit and tie of an investigator.

Thus emerged perhaps the most enduring image of Kevin Foley, vividly rendered by his fellow troopers a few years later at his murder trial: a tall, lean, seemingly angry, self-righteous man, constantly flicking open his knife, someone with a potentially deadly nervous tic, as if he was eager to cut someone's throat. It was an image that would resonate for many when John Yelenic's body was found sliced up on his living room floor, the victim of someone who had a propensity to fatally slash another human being with an acutely sharpened weapon.

Yelenic's formal if belated response to Michele's divorce suit in the summer of 2004 included one demand that set Michele off: *he* wanted sole custody of little Jamie. Whether this was simply some sort of bargaining position envisioned by Yelenic's new lawyer Effie Alexander—intended to make Michele back off from her property demands—isn't completely clear, but it certainly drove an even larger wedge between the warring couple.

In rapid order, the fate of the adopted child Jamie became the paramount issue between John and Michele, and soon came to occupy all of John's thinking, at least according to Tom Riley and John's cousin Mary Ann Clark. Getting little Jamie out of the clutches of Michele obsessed him. The more John tried to achieve this, the more strenuously Michele resisted. Later, Mary Ann ascribed the most venal of motives to Michele: John's estranged wife saw the child as her "meal ticket," Mary Ann came to believe, and would hang on to him with the tightest of claws, even using the struggle over custody to leverage still more material concessions from her unhappy estranged husband.

The clock on the judicial embargo of John seeing Jamie—imposed by the Cambria County court in October of 2003 in the wake of the water balloon allegations—ran out in April of 2004. Visitations between father and adopted son began again. Just why Michele permitted this isn't clear if she was so concerned that John might bash the child around once more. But at this point, negotiations for the Yelenic real estate split were well under way, and John had already agreed to give Michele proceeds from the sale of the lucrative Indiana apartment building and several other properties jointly owned by the couple. So the abandonment of the visitation proscription may have been an effort by Michele to keep her wealthy if unhappy husband at least semi-cooperative in the matter of the division of remaining property assets. Riley, for one, later recalled that Michele often called John at the dental office during this period, either demanding or wheedling money from John. John always took these calls, Riley remembered, and always acceded to Michele's importunities.

In any event, John and Jamie renewed their proximal relationship in the spring of 2004. This lasted, by most accounts, largely uninterrupted for the next year. Mary Ann Clark recalled that Jamie seemed happy to spend every other weekend at John's house in Blairsville, where John organized get-togethers with other children from the neighborhood to help entertain the by now six-year-old.

By this point, however, Kevin had begun his relationship with Michele. Doubtless the story of John's supposed abuse of Jamie was relayed to him by Michele. And while at least initially Kevin tried to avoid being drawn into the war between his new girlfriend and her estranged husband, the story of John's alleged behavior toward Jamie—the incident that had led to John's arrest by Jill Gaston—only tended to make his blood boil. Kevin hated—"loathed," in Anthony Krastek's later words—anyone who abused women and children. So, almost from the beginning of Kevin's relationship with Michele, he was ready to believe the worst about John Yelenic.

Kevin contended that there had only been "four or five times" he met John Yelenic before his death. Given what others, among them Tom Riley, said later, this seems hard to credit. Riley, for one, recalled Kevin coming into the dental office to pick up Jamie during this period. From his observation, Kevin seemed to swagger quite a bit. "I saw Foley one time when he came to pick up the child," Riley remembered. "He looked like he was cocky, on display, like he was in charge." He was, in a way, sneering at the cuckold John Yelenic.

If John had been besotted by Michele years earlier, Kevin was clearly enthralled by her in the summer of 2004.

And why not? Here was a beautiful woman in distress, the mother of three dependent children, apparently cast adrift by a man, a wealthy dentist, who seemed to care nothing for their fate but only for his money. Or so Kevin reasoned, based on the increasingly bitter relations between the two adult Yelenics. He, who had been adopted decades before, along with his sister, could not help but sympathize with Nicole, Nathan, and Jamie. Michele might well have been his *own* distressed natural mother back on Long Island in the late 1960s, before the adoption. And as the summer progressed, Kevin continued to flick the blade of his knife, and his contempt and anger toward John Yelenic grew, fueled by Michele's disgruntlement. It's likely that in Kevin's mind, standing up as Michele's protector, as the man she had never had, and taking care of these three abandoned children gave his life a meaning it had never had before—not with Barbara Ann, not with Susan Marie Smith. In a way, it might have been as wonderful as it was wish fulfilling: now he really *was* the white knight.

John's attempt to wrestle custody of Jamie away in the summer of 2004 with the filing of his first substantive response to Michele's suit for divorce soon resulted in a counterattack by Michele. Although the two battling Yelenics agreed in mid-September to a joint custody schedule for the boy—with regular visitations for John—and John agreed to provide $20,000 to Michele as a partial settlement of the community property, Michele, at least in John's view, tried to pull a fast one. After Jamie was enrolled in a public school in Indiana, and John had arranged with the same school to take the boy briefly out of school for a promised trip to Disney World in October, Michele pulled the boy out of that school and re-enrolled him in a parochial institution in Indiana without informing John. This would have the effect of making the trip to Orlando impossible: John had no permission from the new school's administrators to even see the boy, because Michele had kept John's name out of the school's records. As far as the administrators were concerned, John was a stranger. John learned of the school switch from Jamie, and immediately concluded that Michele was trying to prevent the trip to Disney World in order to further alienate the boy from him. John erupted with anger at Michele. His lawyer, Effie Alexander, quickly moved in court to negate Michele's maneuver, hauling Michele into court, asking for a contempt order against Michele, who was fined $1,000 by Indiana County judge Carol Hanna. John was provided with a court order to permit him to take Jamie to Disney World.

By then, apparently forewarned by Alexander, John arranged for another couple to accompany him and Jamie on the trip, along with the other couple's child, to make sure that nothing untoward was later claimed—another "water balloon" incident, so to speak. "To make sure she didn't pull anything, saying he did this, he did that," as Riley recalled.

After the visit to Disney World, John and Jamie resumed their court-ordered regular schedule of visitations for the next six months, until April 2005. There were arguments between the adult Yelenics: Michele frequently accused John of being late or absent for his scheduled visitations with the boy, while John often complained that Michele prevented him from seeing Jamie by claiming the child was ill or otherwise not available. All in all, this behavior of divorcing parents is not unusual when issues of marital fidelity are involved; sadly, the child becomes the piñata hoisted between the feuding parties' brickbats.

For John, the unhappiness grew much worse as the winter of 2004–5 unfolded. Soon he was hearing it straight from the lips of his six-year-old adopted son: "When Mommy marries Trooper, you won't be my daddy anymore." Jamie talked so often about "Trooper" that John began to believe that Michele was poisoning their son's mind against him.

And then, in early April 2005, Michele dropped the marital H-bomb on her estranged husband: she claimed that on Jamie's visitations with John, her estranged husband had sexually molested him.

12.

The first official suggestion of this actually came in late March of 2005, when Kevin approached a fellow trooper, Deana Kirkland, with a question: Was there any way to tell if a child was really being sexually abused or if the claim was made up? Kirkland, the Pennsylvania State Police Indiana barracks' expert on child molestation, told Foley that it was hard to tell. "Sometimes you can, sometimes you can't," Kirkland told him.

"He came to me and said that [Jamie] was making some strange remarks about his father and he didn't know what to think of them," Kirkland recalled. "And I think I asked him, 'Did he say these things to you?' And he said no, [Jamie] had said them to Michele." Foley's only knowledge of this supposed abuse, then, was from Michele, not Jamie, just like the driveway "water balloon" incident of September 2003.

Foley asked Kirkland if she wouldn't mind talking to Jamie to see what she thought, as the expert. Kirkland told Foley that the only way she'd get involved was if a responsible parent—in this case, it would have to be Michele—made a formal complaint.

"And he said he just wasn't sure about these comments that [Jamie] was making, but if he thought that something needed to be looked into, he would let me know," Kirkland remembered.

This conversation between Foley and Deana Kirkland apparently took place on March 28, 2005, a day after Jamie had returned from a scheduled visitation with John in Blairsville over the Easter weekend. What later became striking about Kevin's assertion to Kirkland on this day was that at least a portion of this visit by Jamie with his father was recorded on videotape by John—an Easter Sunday party hosted by John for his son and a number of neighborhood children on March 27, 2005. It appeared, at least from the video, that Jamie was having no problems with his adoptive father: visually, there was none of the behavior one might expect to see from a child being sexually molested by a parent—no fear, no avoidance, no stress discernible at all. In fact Jamie seemed to be having a wonderful time. Of course, this wasn't evidence of what might have happened later the same evening, but it seemed to contradict eventual assertions by Michele that Jamie had told her that he had been molested by John for more than a year before this.

This videotape was later offered by John as evidence of his innocence of Michele's claims of molestation to Indiana County judge Carol Hanna. According to Mary Ann Clark, the judge retained possession of it, even years after Yelenic's murder, despite its potential evidentiary value in later litigation. The judge's legal justification for retaining sole possession of this videotape, in light of the civil damage allegations that would later be made against the PSP, was unclear: Mary Ann's attempts to recover it from the judge were unavailing, she said later. In fact, it represented a record of one of the last happy encounters between John Yelenic and his son. Within a little over three weeks, they would never again be alone.

On April 13, 2005, Michele filed a formal complaint with the Pennsylvania State Police alleging that her estranged husband John had sexually molested their son Jamie on April 9. On the following day Kirkland opened a PSP formal investigation. Michele complained that John had routinely committed perversions with Jamie while having him in his custody over the previous year.

How did Michele know this? As Michele asserted in a new "PFA" petition filed by Daniel Lovette a little over two weeks after this, Jamie had telephoned her from John's Blairsville house on the evening of April 9, while he was on a regularly scheduled visitation with his father. The gist of what Michele claimed to know was related by Lovette in this petition:

"Sometime after telephone call ends," Lovette declared in the new PFA filing, "defendant [John] assisted [Jamie in] taking a bath. When bath had ended, [Jamie] was taken to his room, where defendant commenced to penetrate [Jamie's] anus with his tongue and to perform fellatio upon [Jamie]. Thereafter, defendant began to show [Jamie] defendant's penis, and thereafter, defendant requested that [Jamie] perform fellatio upon defendant. [Jamie] refused . . . whereupon defendant ceased his advances. On the following day, [Jamie] told his mother what had happened."

Nasty stuff, this—very, very nasty. But was it true? Of course, this was what Michele had told Kevin, and what Kevin had told Deana Kirkland. It appears that Kevin had told Michele that Kirkland needed a formal complaint to open an investigation, and thus, by early April of 2005, Michele had obviously talked to Kirkland, otherwise Kirkland would not have opened an investigation. And Michele had also told these things to Lovette, the former divorce lawyer for the scion of Johnstown, Lovette being the same attorney who had agreed to represent Michele against John Yelenic when Michele had first filed for divorce from John almost two years earlier. The sequence of events makes the claim of molestation appear possibly specious, nothing more than an effort by Yelenic's estranged wife to increase pressure on him for the purposes of obtaining a more lucrative property settlement, which was still being negotiated.

It is an intelligence rule of thumb that the provenance of information—where it comes from, and what the bias of the informant might be—is crucial to determining the information's credibility. But in this case, with John Yelenic labeled a child molester, provenance was shoved aside, at least initially. As far as the courts and social workers were concerned—they were doubtless influenced by Lovette's respectable imprimatur—their primary interest was to isolate the alleged molester, John, from his supposed victim, Jamie. Here the prevalent public policy was that it's always better to protect the child than the rights of the accused, even the wrongfully accused, at least in the near term. This might be correct as a public policy, but it demands a more thorough follow-up investigation. As social-work bureaucracies now usually deal with such complaints, nothing much is done after checking condemnatory boxes and pushing the paper onto the next two departments, the police and the courts. For most social workers, there is too little money, too much to do, and too little time.

Lovette, in his declaration, summarized the alleged perverted events: on April 13—rather bizarrely, a year to the day before John Yelenic was to be murdered—Michele contacted the PSP, as well as the Indiana Children and Youth Services agency, with the molestation complaint about John. The following day, the PSP's Kirkland interviewed John, no doubt acquainting him for the first time with these horrible allegations.

Kirkland later said she found John very cooperative in answering her questions, but also "arrogant" in his demeanor toward her. Just what the appropriate demeanor of a parent should be when being interviewed about sexual molestation charges made by one's estranged spouse, allegedly echoing one's own seven-year-old son, is difficult to imagine. Likely, however, there is usually a welter of emotions: outrage, denial, embarrassment, compassion for the child, as well as a desire to protect him or her from the consequences of being used by a possibly vengeful estranged spouse. And certainly, when innocent, fury: a conflagration of anger toward the estranged spouse that he or she might use the child for crass material advantage.

Besides this maelstrom of feelings, John would have had yet another thought: Kirkland was a coworker of Kevin, perhaps his witting ally—a co-conspirator in the effort to strip him of his money and his longed-for relationship with his adopted son. Was there anything he could say that might convince her that he was innocent—that this was all Michele's manipulation of Jamie for her own selfish, materialistic purposes? Was no to Kirkland really no? Wasn't she Kevin Foley's tool?

In John's mind, this seemed likely: this was simply, as he probably saw it, another awful escalation in his divorce battle with Michele. No wonder he was "arrogant": telling the truth meant nothing to Kirkland, in John's jaundiced view, if she was simply Foley's foil in his already agreed-upon destruction.

But Kirkland was made of sterner stuff than John had anticipated. Five days later, on April 20, 2005, she interviewed Jamie himself. It isn't clear from the available records whether Michele was present at this conversation: ordinarily, such an interview should be done privately between the investigator and the child, without the parent around to give cues. At the same time a Children and Youth Services investigation was opened, the social worker operating independently of Kirkland. The awful allegation hung in abeyance for almost two weeks as Judge Hanna issued a temporary order again barring John from contact with Jamie and Michele until a May 19, 2005, hearing on the allegations. After this hearing, Hanna extended the PFA for six months, while Kirkland and the CYS each continued what appear to have been rather haphazard investigations—despite John's denials and Michele's possible pecuniary motives, which should have been factored into the claims. But both of these investigations had the support of Kevin and Lovette behind them.

It appears that after being interviewed by Kirkland on April 14 and thus apprised of Jamie's supposed molestation assertions, John engaged Michele in a vitriolic argument over the telephone: John was irate and accused his estranged wife of "motherfucking" him—or so Kevin claimed later, attributing the off-color language to John.

"I could hear him on the phone yelling and screaming at her," Kevin said, "and swearing at her and cussing at her and calling her all kind of nasty names. And she just held the phone out and I could hear him yelling . . ." Well, in another way, this was understandable: the accusation of being a child molester might tend to make anyone angry.

The next week, when John arrived at the Susan Drive house to pick up the boy for the regular Wednesday visitation, Kevin said he decided to set John straight.

"I walked out to him and he put his window down and I said, 'John, I'd appreciate it if you wouldn't call here cussing and swearing at Michele. I don't have a problem with you calling her, and I will never interfere with you and [Jamie], or you and Michele . . . just don't call and cuss and swear at Michele, there's no reason for that.'

"And he responded with, 'Oh, just give me a ticket.' And I said, 'John, I don't write tickets, I don't do that anymore.'"

According to what Yelenic later told Riley, Mary Ann and others, almost from that point forward, Kevin went out of his way to try to intimidate him, to scare him away from Michele and Jamie, even to the point of accosting him at his office, his house, in the courtroom, and at Jamie's school, and even following him. And meanwhile, if Kevin's fellow state troopers were to be believed, Kevin had kept up a steady litany of complaints about John—even wishing he was dead. Once, in fact, Kevin suggested to another trooper that they collaborate in killing him, although Foley later swore he had been only joking.

Well, it was just a joke, dark cop humor, Kevin insisted years later. Of course, when Yelenic *was* killed, it was no laughing matter.

In retrospect there are a few interesting things about Kevin's recollection of this no-more-bad-words confrontation with the dead man, just after Michele's complaint that her estranged husband was a pedophile. One is that, in the way Kevin portrayed it—after John was no longer around to contradict him—*he* was the essence of politeness, although he later admitted that he'd used the "F-word" in the confrontation, as had John, he said. Another is Kevin's description of John's supposed taunting of him—"just give me a ticket"—and Kevin's reaction to this—"I don't do that anymore." From this it seems likely that Kevin believed that John was dismissing him as nothing more than a lowly traffic cop, a mere state-paid factotum, and Kevin's rejection of this seems to show his palpable desire to demonstrate to John that he had real authority as an elite criminal investigator, not just some meter maid. If Kevin in some way liked to sneer at John for his inability to keep Michele in his bed, John wasn't averse to dismissing Kevin as a public-salaried muscle head, a mere ticket writer, in much the same way that he had been "arrogant" in responding to Kirkland's questions. Whatever issues John and Kevin had over Michele soon became a matter of personal machismo. As Kevin's prosecutor Anthony Krastek later came to understand, Michele had both of them exactly where she wanted them: two males in rutting season, butting heads.

Possibly significantly, Kevin also made no mention of the how Michele's claims of molestation might have affected her divorce settlement claims against John. It was as if he had no idea of any of this when he told John to stop cussing his ex-wife.

In her investigation of the awful complaint against John Yelenic, Trooper Deana Kirkland had to have been torn in two different directions. On one side was her colleague Kevin, who seemed utterly and sincerely convinced that his cuckold, John, was a child molester. Kevin hated—"loathed," as Krastek put it—creeps who abused women and children. If the police were good for anything, it ought to be to stop that sort of thing. Kirkland couldn't help but feel some sort of loyalty to her fellow trooper, who seemed quite convinced that Michele's estranged husband was a pedophile.

On the other hand, all of Kirkland's instincts told her there was nothing there—no molestation, no pedophilia at all.

By September of 2005, Kirkland concluded her investigation, finding the molestation allegations meritless. Kirkland might not have liked Yelenic for his arrogance, and she *did* like Foley—they had known each other for years, and he seemed a paragon of virtue—but she had to go with her best judgment. John, at Kirkland's insistence, had passed a polygraph test. There had been no molestation. And soon the CYS came to the same determination. In fact, it's plausible that Michele had told Jamie what to say in order to damage her estranged husband John, to demoralize him, perhaps to get more in their settlement negotiations as their acrimonious divorce case proceeded. Although Kirkland never made such an allegation, she later testified that allegations of "coaching" become more relevant when the abuse allegations are made by one parent against another or during custody disputes.

But Judge Hanna's court order banning John from contact with either Jamie or Michele continued throughout the summer of 2005 as the Kirkland and CYS investigations proceeded to their null end. John scrupulously adhered to the order, doubtless under the influence of his lawyer, Effie Alexander, retreating to his dental practice, to his house in Blairsville, and to his few neighborhood friends, such as the Uss family.

By the end of the summer, John was no longer angry over the allegations, Tom Riley recalled.

"He was just depressed, overwhelmed," Riley remembered. "He didn't want to talk too much about it. And that [Jamie] was his blessed boy. [Michele] threw everything at him. To make up something like that! And he said, 'I'm not going to defend myself, I'm not going to defend myself.' So he took two lie detector tests and he passed them both with flying colors." And with that, John regained some hope, Riley said. "And he kept saying, 'Maybe something good is going to happen now. Maybe I'll be able to see him.'"

Meanwhile, Effie Alexander counseled John to put the child custody issue with the related molestation issue aside for the time being. The thing to do, she advised, was get the divorce finalized—get the property distributed fairly, get rid of the awful ex-wife, *then* address the thorny custody question. First things first.

Alexander later said she was surprised at how pliable John seemed to be in the face of his estranged wife's ongoing demands. Despite their separation, despite their antagonisms, she said—and Riley later agreed—Michele often called John at the dental office asking for more money. John always took those calls and almost always gave in to what Michele wanted.

"John was a very kind person and probably didn't have a

lot of, I would say, spine," Alexander said later. "He was very open to suggestions regarding money issues, and I think that he was far too generous with Michele, and he never held his ground. And at one point, I really didn't try to stop him from giving her more money for the child. I am always happy to have my clients make arrangements outside of attorneys for more money or—if it's for the kids, then so be it. That is the best spent money as far as I'm concerned . . ."

So John made no effort to contest Judge Hanna's protection order, and gave more money to Michele while spending the summer on the front porch of his house in Blairsville, never seeing the child he'd adopted and whom he had hoped would become his beloved son, the future Yelenic, his putative heir—the boy who would give his own dead father's life a chance for meaning.

As it happened, Tom Uss, John's next-door neighbor, retired from the navy that same summer and took a job at a steel manufacturing plant some distance away, which required him to rise early in the morning and often return fairly late in the evening. His wife, Melissa—who had attended high school with John in the 1980s—began to spend a few afternoons each week with John on his porch, sharing iced tea and old times. Soon a few nosy neighbors were sure that John and Melissa were up to something. After all, hadn't the rich dentist's wife left him? Wasn't Tom Uss away at work? And this was the same summer that Melissa Uss decided to open a bakery and asked John Yelenic to lend her $15,000 . . .

13.

As the fall of 2005 arrived and the expiration of the latest protection-from-abuse order barring John Yelenic from his son loomed, Kevin Foley became agitated once more at the prospect of renewed contact between John and Jamie. Although Kirkland had tried to convince Kevin there was no evidence to prove that John had molested the boy, Kevin did not believe it. Much of this perception on Kevin's part probably came from Michele rather than directly from Jamie, it appears. Certainly, Kevin was in a quandary. If he questioned Jamie directly and discovered Deana Kirkland was right—that Jamie wasn't telling the truth about John—that would mean that Michele *wasn't* telling the truth. Likely, this was not something Kevin wanted to confront.

According to both Kirkland and Krastek later, during this summer of 2005 Michele kept up a steady, agonized drumbeat to Kevin: John Yelenic was a child molester, a child molester, a child molester, and if he ever got his hands on Jamie again . . . well, who knew what might happen? Kevin's incessant flicking of his knife continued, a testament to his anxiety, according to other state troopers in the Indiana barracks. Kevin had always been tightly wound, but the stress of John's imminent reacquisition of custody of Jamie seemed to make him even more intense. The blade flicked out, was snapped back in, flicked out again, as if the mere appearance of the shiny steel could keep the devil at bay.

In late October of 2005, a new hearing on the April PFA order was scheduled by Judge Hanna, who had been assigned the Yelenic divorce case. A dismissal of the order would permit John to resume his weekly visitations with Jamie. John's lawyer, Effie Alexander, also asked Judge Hanna to order the Indiana County Sheriff's office to return two handguns belonging to John—weapons that had been seized from him in October of 2003 as part of his arrest by Officer Gaston. Moreover, Alexander wanted the judge to order both John and Michele to attend "family counseling." Alexander noted that although Michele had complained that her estranged husband had supposedly molested Jaime, neither Kirkland nor the CYS had been able to substantiate her claims.

"Father is troubled by the fact that the parties' minor child would make such statements and level such allegations to the investigators who interviewed the child," Alexander advised Hanna in her brief in support of the family counseling. "Father believes and therefore avers that the allegations leveled by the parties' minor child and subsequent investigation may result in long term damage to the child's relationship with his Father. Father denies any and all of the allegations and believes that the allegations were planted in the child's mind by Mother, who has embarked on an active agenda to alienate the child from his Father."

A hearing on these issues was set by Judge Hanna for November 3, 2005. By then, both John and Kevin were amped up, their machismos working overtime. John's previous experiences with Kevin had convinced him he needed his own posse, since Kevin had previously been backed by his own pals in the Pennsylvania State Police. He asked Tom Uss if he'd put on his navy uniform and accompany him to the courtroom. Uss suited up and accompanied John to the hearing. At over six feet and 250 pounds, Tom could be intimidating in his own right.

At this hearing, Hanna not only agreed to return John's guns to him, she also dismissed the April 2005 PFA. In light of the findings of Kirkland and the CYS—that there had never been any abuse of Jamie by John—she had little choice.

At a recess in the hearing, John, no doubt feeling he was about to be triumphant, turned to Kevin in the courthouse corridor. Fixing him with a stare and a small grin, John raised his hand and extended his forefinger at Kevin, cocking his thumb and making two noises that anyone would interpret as "Gotcha." It was, John said later, a *Seinfeld*—a gesture from the television show to make, in a nonverbal way, an exclamation of victory.

That wasn't how Kevin saw it, however. In his eyes, John's gesture was a threat to shoot him. When the hearing resumed, testimony was given to the effect that John had made a "terroristic threat" against Foley. Judge Hanna quickly ruled the claim out of order: it was ridiculous, she said. Nevertheless, Foley immediately filed a formal complaint with the PSP: Yelenic had threatened to kill a sworn police officer, he claimed. Given that Yelenic had just received his two handguns back from Judge Hanna, Foley said later, he was therefore in fear of his life. Foley made his report to another officer of the PSP, and an investigation of Yelenic's supposed threat to kill a police officer was initiated. Either Kevin had never watched *Seinfeld* or was using everything possible to make trouble for John. The complaint was eventually dismissed by the PSP as unfounded. For the next few weeks John began meeting Jamie under supervised conditions at a nonprofit family counseling center in Indiana, preparatory to resuming normal custody.

Then, as Thanksgiving loomed—under the custody agreement John was entitled to host Jamie for Thanksgiving that year—John, Michele, Jamie, and Kevin arrived at the Indiana police station for the final handoff, the day John could reestablish unsupervised custody with his adopted son after six months. But by that point Jamie had no desire to go anywhere with John, to say the least. Screaming, in a panic, he threw himself into Michele's arms. The Indiana police, some of them friends of Kevin, intervened. John was devastated. He could hardly take a child to a Thanksgiving dinner when the child was almost hysterical, obviously frantic to avoid him. John left the police station without Jamie, more resolved than ever to get the divorce from hell behind him and to find a way to reclaim his son from Michele and her hard-bodied, seemingly biased PSP lover, Kevin. This was, Kevin said later, the very last time he ever saw John Yelenic.

Sometimes civil litigation, and particularly divorce cases, can be like hacking one's way through a dismal swamp: the vigorous machete is the only way through the fetid undergrowth. Whacking and hacking through the primordial obstacles thrust up by the opposition requires constant exertion. If you ever stop, you're likely soon to be covered in opportunistic ancillary vines, slipslide into case-law mold, useless statutory mud holes, or maybe even declaratory quicksand. God help you if you ever sit down to rest: it may take years to emerge from the legal bog, if you ever do. Effie Alexander was resolved to push on through the watery wilderness, hacking and whacking, aiming for the high ground that would extricate her client from the stinking marital morass that threatened to devour him: Michele, Kevin, Jamie, the PSP, all of them seemingly ready to eat him alive, human Venus flytraps all. Or so Alexander saw matters.

By January of 2006, Alexander had hacked away enough of the underbrush to see daylight ahead. She induced Lovette to agree to a tentative financial settlement. Lovette also agreed to produce his client, Michele, to approve it.

Alexander said her client, John, would be there, too. By that point, after several years of struggle, both Alexander and Lovette were equally tired of the fight and anxious for their respective clients to finish things off, even if they were hardly prepared to kiss and make up.

The meet was set for a coffee shop in north Blairsville, just off Route 22. Alexander arrived with a yellow legal pad and John. Lovette arrived with Michele. The two soon-to-be ex-spouses sparred for a while, each of them scoring off each other for earlier slights. Eventually Alexander and Lovette got their clients under control and each side settled down to business. Alexander ticked off the particulars of the proposed agreement. Lovette nodded; so did Michele. As outlined by Alexander and agreed to by Lovette and Michele, John would continue to pay Michele child support for Jamie of $1,300 each month. In addition, Michele would get $30,000 in cash upon signing the agreement and another $24,000 some weeks later. Altogether, including fourteen separate pieces of real estate that had already been divided between the two Yelenics, Michele would receive nearly $300,000 in total assets from John. The spousal support John had been paying of another $2,500 each month would cease, now that Michele was living with Kevin. Alexander began writing these points down on her legal pad; her idea was to get Michele to sign this paper, on the spot, just to be sure. But Lovette soon told her it wasn't necessary: Michele had already agreed to everything, he said, and all Alexander had to do was have the formal agreement typed up and sent to his office for Michele's signature. Alexander put away her legal pad. Everyone shook hands. The lawyer seemingly forgot, or perhaps never knew about, the will John had signed in July of 1997, which gave all of John's assets to Michele in case of his death, which would include a $1 million insurance policy on his life.

*   *   *

But as December turned into January, Kevin was becoming increasingly agitated about John. Even before the aborted Thanksgiving one-day change of custody, and this sit-down between the parties, he had told his mother, then still living in Florida that he prayed that John would die; that would solve everything, he said. But his own mother wasn't the only person Kevin told of his desire to wish Yelenic off the face of the earth: several other troopers in the Indiana barracks were later to recall that Kevin had habitually wished for the demise of Yelenic. Deana Kirkland, for one, remembered that in January of 2006, Kevin had told her what he'd told his mother about Yelenic the month before.

"Kevin," Kirkland told him, "you can't say that." Foley admitted that he knew it was wrong. It was just the frustration of not being able to deny John's legal custody of Jamie.

Clearly, despite Kirkland's findings and Judge Hanna's conclusions and even Michele's refusal to take a polygraph test regarding to Jamie's claims, Foley still believed that John Yelenic was a child molester. (Michele's refusal to take the polygraph, which Foley's attorney later claimed was due to "vaginal bleeding," is part of the trial record, but Kirkland was not permitted to testify to it at trial.) And if anything, the failure of officials to do anything to stop Yelenic—even, God almighty, granting him permanent custody of the boy— would likely have made Kevin's blood boil. The Thanksgiving eve episode in the Indiana police station told Kevin everything he needed to know about the dentist. Jamie's hysteria about being in John's sole company convinced him that everything the boy had said about his father was true. (In fact, the Indiana police had surreptitiously videotaped the horrid encounter, which Kirkland had used as part of her justification for her renewed investigation—one that she soon closed after Michele's refusal to take the lie detector test, and after Judge Hanna's tête-à-tête with Jamie in her chambers in early December.)

Of course, the other side of this pre-Thanksgiving coin is that Jamie might well have been reacting somewhat unwittingly as a result of "Trooper's" advice, in order to help Michele make a better financial settlement with John—not that Jamie would have understood this at the time. Perhaps even Kevin himself was oblivious to what Michele stood to gain, although not everyone agreed that he was that naïve as to the financial stakes involved.

Pennsylvania State Police sergeant George Emigh, for one, would later become convinced that Michele and Kevin together were intent on leveraging as much money from Yelenic as possible to support what Emigh was convinced was a "lavish lifestyle" Michele and Kevin had adopted, based in part on the $2,500 each month in spousal support that John was providing to Michele before the finalization of the divorce. But then, Emigh never believed that Foley was the white knight that he'd always claimed to be: he was sure the whole thing had to do with money from the start. After all, once the divorce was finalized, the Kevin Foley–Michele Yelenic household would be $30,000 a year poorer.

One other thing was clear, though: by November, Jamie appears to have believed his foster father, John Yelenic, was a dire threat. Jamie's hysteria at the police station in late November suggests as much. And it might lead one to wonder just how far a parent might go to influence an impressionable child, given sufficient stakes.

As the spring of 2006 emerged, Kevin's animus toward John only grew, and in a way obsessively. Kevin knew in his heart that Yelenic was a pervert; he could tell just by looking at him. John was sure that Kevin had some of his PSP friends keeping him under surveillance. He complained about this "harassment" to his cousin, Mary Ann Clark. If this really happened, there seems to be no official record of it: neither Emigh nor Kirkland could validate these claims. Of course, if John really was a pedophile, sooner or later he was bound to "go off the reservation," Kevin knew from his training as a police investigator. All Kevin needed was some firm evidence that John had been "grooming" little boys somewhere. A pedophile couldn't help himself: it was an obsession. But this suspicion owed at least as much to Kevin's own intense desire to see John Yelenic in the worst possible light—two obsessions, actually: one imagined, one real.

In any case, there were two saps, both in love with the same woman.

Late in March of 2006, Foley and Kirkland were assigned to transport a prisoner from another barracks to court in Indiana. As they drove, somehow the conversation between the two troopers turned once more to Yelenic, Michele, and Jamie, an obsessive topic for Kevin. Kirkland later testified that he had told her in January (about the time of the Yelenics' settlement negotiation in the Blairsville coffee shop) that he'd told his mother after the Thanksgiving episode that he prayed John would just die—that his death would solve everything. But it now seemed to Kirkland that Foley was even more serious about wishing Yelenic out of the way. On the way to get the prisoner, Kevin told Kirkland that he hoped that John would be killed in a car wreck. Clearly, Kevin had no knowledge of how Yelenic's own father had died.

"I am not sure who brought it up," Kirkland testified. "[But] Kevin had said, made a comment that 'I just wish he would die in a car accident.' And I said, 'You can't, you shouldn't say that,' or something to that effect. And he said, 'I know,' and I told him, 'Whatever you are going through, God understands your frustration, but, you know, you shouldn't say things like that.'" At trial, Kevin testified that he didn't recall saying that, although he remembered expressing anger about Yelenic.

By this point, Michele had still not signed the final divorce agreement. Instead, she seemed to be stalling. It turned out that John had stopped sending the $2,500 monthly spousal support to Michele in January of 2006, reasoning that she had agreed to the cessation of the payments at the coffee shop meeting. But Michele wanted the money due until she actually signed the document, so John's last payment had been in December of 2005. Now Michele wanted John arrested for his failure to pay alimony for January, February, and March. Michele swore out a complaint for failure to pay the spousal support, another jailable offense. Alexander soon filed a motion asking the judge to compel Michele to sign the agreement, as Lovette had promised she would do back in January. Alexander called Lovette, trying to find out what the holdup was. Lovette said he wasn't sure, that he'd try to find out. It appears that Michele and Lovette had words; apparently Lovette had run out of patience with Michele.

Then, on either Monday, April 3, or Tuesday, April 4, Michele called the dental office again, demanding to speak to John. Georgette Johnson, the office receptionist, later said that when she told Michele that John wouldn't speak to her unless she signed the final divorce agreement, Michele became angry. She needed some of the money John had agreed to pay her on signing, she said, to pay for some expenses of Jamie's. If John didn't send her the money, Michele said she'd have to apply for food stamps. She threatened to "go to the media," Johnson recalled. Still John refused to speak to Michele or provide the money: no signature, no money, he insisted.

A few days later, on April 8, 2006, Kevin and Michele found themselves at a Friday-night fish fry sponsored by the parochial school attended by Jamie in Indiana. Also present was Barbara Swasy, John's cousin Roger's wife. Barbara, who also had children in the school, had been a witness with her husband when John and Michele married in Las Vegas

on New Year's Eve 1997. After John and Michele had separated in 2002, Barbara had maintained contact with Michele, even after she took up with Kevin in 2004. So Barbara
knew Foley as well.

As Barbara encountered Michele and Kevin that night,
she realized that Kevin was talking about John. She well
knew that there was bad blood between John and Kevin, and
that much of it had to do with Jamie. She later testified that
Foley said he wished John was dead.

Barbara was serving the fish, and the first thing she knew,
Michele was also complaining about John; somehow John
had learned that Michele and Kevin had just adopted another
small child, from Guatemala. (Later, a number of friends of
Kevin, some in the PSP, said that Kevin's desire to have children of his own had animated this decision to adopt.)

How John learned of this adoption by Michele and Kevin
isn't clear. Barbara Swasy assured Michele and Kevin that
the information hadn't come from her, and because John
hadn't seen Jamie since the prior November, it couldn't have
come from Jamie. Perhaps he'd heard this from Nathan, who
by some accounts had kept in contact with John over the
years. Nevertheless, John somehow knew about the recent
adoption—Michele's fourth child. Why Michele wanted to
keep this a secret from John is obscure.

In any event, on this particular Friday night, as Barbara
Swasy was helping to serve the fish at the school, Michele
was complaining that John had somehow heard of the adoption. She asked Barbara if she had let this slip to her husband's cousin. Barbara denied this. At that point, according
to Barbara, Kevin piped up:

"I wish that guy was dead," Kevin said, according to Barbara.

"No, no," Barbara told him. "You don't wish that."

But Barbara was pretty sure from Kevin's attitude that he really did wish John was dead. He was, she indicated later, very serious—dead serious.

Michele finally did sign the divorce agreement—a day or so before her estranged husband was murdered, and before he could sign it himself. Lovette had insisted she sign—Alexander was pressing him—and according to the Johnstown lawyer, Michele wasn't very happy to do it. He sent the signed copy to Alexander, who sent it to John. John called his aunt, Mary Ann's mother, and told her that the light at the end of the horrible divorce tunnel was in sight and that he would celebrate the end of the ordeal at her house on the afternoon of Thursday, April 13. This was where Mary Ann Clark had agreed to be on the fateful afternoon when she received the terrible telephone call from her friend.

Meanwhile, on the same Wednesday evening, April 12, 2006, Kevin got off his shift at the Indiana barracks and drove to Delmont, midway between Pittsburgh and Indiana, where he suited up for a recreational ice hockey game. Half of his team was composed of PSP officers. A little after midnight, the game over, Foley opened the rear door of his tan Ford Explorer to stash his hockey gear for the trip back to Indiana on Route 22, which led through Blairsville. He claimed not to have changed out of his uniform after the game. Placing his hockey stick in the rear of the Bronco, he said later, the stick somehow got hung up on one of the seat belts. Trying to force it into the truck, it sprang back and hit him in the face, leaving him with the two small abrasions above and below his left eye. That was Kevin's claim. But sometime early that same morning, only an hour or so later, someone with a very sharp knife went through the unlocked back door of John Yelenic's house in Blairsville and slashed him to death in a murderous frenzy.

It wasn't him, Kevin later insisted. By the time Yelenic died, he was home in Indiana, on Susan Drive, with Michele, Nicole, Nathan, Jamie, and the newly adopted baby from Guatemala, an all-American family. They could all testify to that, Kevin insisted.

III.
The Investigations

14.

If the aftermath of the death of John Yelenic demonstrated anything, it was that the Commonwealth of Pennsylvania was ill prepared to deal with a case in which one of its own state troopers was the likeliest suspect. Indeed, almost from the time that Mary Ann Clark first confronted the Indiana district attorney Bell on the sidewalk in front of John Yelenic's house on the afternoon of April 13, 2006, an effort to shift suspicion away from Foley seemed to be under way. Sergeant Emigh had tried to flag Kevin as the most logical suspect; Mary Ann Clark and Melissa Uss had said much the same thing. Even Jill Gaston had her suspicions, from her encounter with Foley and Michele later that night, after noting the abrasion on Foley's face. But almost from the beginning, it seemed that efforts were made by Bell, Indiana County detectives under his supervision, and even the Blairsville Police to find someone else to blame.

As Blairsville police corporal Janelle Lydic later said—she, after all, was soon in charge of the investigation, after Mary Ann Clark had told Blairsville police chief Donald Hess in no uncertain terms that she did *not* want the Indiana barracks of the PSP involved—she wanted to make sure that there were no other possibilities before turning the glare of suspicion on the one man who clearly hated Yelenic, the man who liked to flick open his knife, and who had even been known to wish Yelenic was dead: Kevin Foley, of course. At least the PSP had the sense to respect the proprieties of the circumstances, however: the department relieved Kevin of his badge and his gun and assigned him to desk duty in a different barracks.

There was plenty of circumstantial evidence: all the bad feeling between the two men, as almost everyone knew, as well as the pending divorce between John and Michele, with the unsigned final divorce papers scattered about the floor, flecked with Yelenic blood spatter. And Michele's peculiar behavior at the formal notice of the demise of John: not a tear shed, and looking to Foley for advice as to how to respond to Deputy Coroner Conrad's gentle questions. And Michele's refusal to have anything to do with John's body after the autopsy.

The rest of the evidence was physical: Gonglik's voluminous photographic documentation of the bloody shoe prints; the blood smears on the rear door handle; and perhaps most important, the scrapings of tissue taken from beneath the dead dentist's fingernails, possibly containing DNA.

But at least at first, this was not to be a PSP case: Mary Ann Clark had insisted on that. And so, the day after the Yelenic autopsy by Dr. Wecht, a police officer from Blairsville, John Brant, drove to the Pennsylvania State Police forensic services unit headed by Trooper Gonglik in Greensburg to take possession of all the physical evidence associated with the murder of John Yelenic, including the clothes John had been wearing, as well as the potentially incriminating fingernail scrapings. Brant then provided some of these—John's clothing and blood samples, mainly—to the PSP crime lab, located across the street from Gonglik's office in Greensburg. The fingernail scrapings, however, were taken by Brant back to Blairsville, where they were placed in a small refrigerator normally used for DUI blood draws by the Blairsville police headquarters on Market Street, and basically ignored for months while Corporal Lydic tried to conduct an investigation that she had neither the resources nor the expertise to successfully conclude.

Meanwhile, Mary Ann Clark was hearing things. One was that if a state trooper had committed the murder of her cousin, the case would never be solved: the state troopers would certainly cover it up.

"Because they're a big brotherhood, they cover for each other," Mary Ann said later. But Mary Ann wasn't going to let the "brotherhood" get away with that. "I was, like, I'll be damned, this is not going away. I knew what they did to John in life, and I was the person who should have done something in life, when he was here. I should have done something, and I didn't, because I defended the state police. When John would say the things that were happening to him, how they treated him in court, how, when he'd go to pick up [Jamie], they were pushing him around, or they'd be waiting for him at his house to intimidate him . . ."

Well, Mary Ann admitted, she just hadn't believed him at the time. But after John was found dead, people suggested to Mary Ann that if a state trooper had murdered John, nothing would ever happen: the guilty would never be exposed and punished. Some of these people were news reporters, who clearly had their suspicions about the PSP and probably also Foley. It seemed likely that word had leaked to the news media somehow as to Foley's long-standing feud with John.

But in those early days, Mary Ann mostly kept her suspicions to herself. She didn't want people thinking she was hysterical—"rushing to judgment," as she put it later.

"I was afraid someone might think I probably watched too much TV . . . But deep down I knew, because John didn't have any enemies," she said. "Nobody hated John. So

I wouldn't say who I thought did it, but they would say, 'If it's a state trooper, nothing will happen.'"

Mary Ann first put her faith in Hess, who assured her he would keep the local PSP barracks out of the case.

"He did not want the Indiana State Police," she recalled. In fact, Mary Ann was sure, Hess soon began to have doubts even about Bob Bell, the Indiana district attorney and Mary Ann's own neighbor. "He very early on wanted the attorney general involved, which Bob Bell did not," she said. "And Chief Hess—and I'm not saying he did everything perfect in this case—but had he [first] turned everything over to the state police, I think this was going away. It was going to be covered up if he had given them sole control of the case." As it turned out, Mary Ann was thinking mostly of the scrapings from under her cousin's fingernails, which would prove to be critical. Hess and Lydic, through Brant, took possession of this vital evidence and therefore saved it from possible destruction.

It was only later that Mary Ann heard of George Emigh, Kevin's supervisor in the PSP's Indiana barracks, who believed from the beginning that Kevin had committed the murder but who was soon commanded by higher-ups to keep his nose out of the investigation. In the first months after the murder, Mary Ann knew nothing of Emigh's suspicions about Foley: the PSP essentially kept Emigh out of the loop, and he kept his mouth shut. Instead, it was eventually Hess, the Blairsville police chief, who eventually convinced the Pennsylvania attorney general, Tom Corbett, to insist that the PSP do a real investigation, and with the Federal Bureau of Investigation looking over their shoulder.

But this was only after nearly four months had elapsed and most of the leads were cold. By then, Emigh, in part because of his suspicion of Foley, was already in trouble with the PSP brass.

"So I think that if Chief Hess had let Bob Bell or the state police take the case [in the beginning], they were willing to cover it up," Mary Ann Clark said. At first she couldn't say why: she just had a creepy feeling that some people higher up the law enforcement food chain might have been willing to look the other way, including her neighbor Bell. She wondered whether there might be secrets that some in law enforcement wanted to keep suppressed at all costs, maybe some having nothing to do with John's murder.

"I don't know what goes on in that courthouse," she said, referring to Indiana County, "who's loyal to whom, or who defends you. But I know he [Bell] was very—he put me off, at every step of the way." (In 2010, Bell, by then out of office, declined an invitation to be interviewed for this book.)

While Mary Ann was musing about the possible politics behind the investigation of her cousin's murder, the county detectives reporting to Bell fanned out, looking for other leads. After letting the Uss family go on the night of the day the murder was discovered, they weren't entirely ready to abandon them as prime suspects. That $14,000 check from Melissa to John bugged them. They had possession of the uncashed check, and Melissa Uss soon stopped payment on it, apparently having some doubts about whose account the funds might end up in. The detectives thought that the stop-payment order might be suspicious, too. Soon they began to collect gossip from the neighborhood to the effect that John and Melissa were lovers. Of course, this was completely contrary to their first theory, that John was sexually abusing the Uss boys. Either John was a pedophile or he was a Don Juan.

The fact was, neither notion was true, and it only seems to show how anxious investigators were to keep the spotlight off Foley, which of course only made Mary Ann and other friends of John suspicious that the "brotherhood" really did have the fix in.

As noted, the county detectives did collect a number of alternative theories. In one, a former patient of John's, an admitted drug user, was said to have claimed to have done the deed while in search of controlled substances. In another, a well-known jailhouse snitch in Pittsburgh claimed that gang-bangers from the big city had cut the dentist's throat during a home invasion robbery gone wrong. But the local detectives still favored big Tom Uss as the most likely culprit. There were puzzling pieces there: the $14,000 stopped-payment check from Melissa, the gossip from some of the neighbors about John and Tom's wife. All one had to do was arrange the pieces so they fit. Maybe Uss had killed John in a jealous rage. Or John was blackmailing the Usses. Or the Usses were blackmailing John. Or . . . well, the pieces were ragged, it was true. One of the nosy neighbors noticed Tom mowing the grass in the backyard of John's house a few days after the murder and doing something to the rear door. What did that mean?

But no matter how much the detectives may have longed for the pieces to mesh, they didn't seem to fit. And behind all this there was that nagging reality: the most likely suspect was really none other than Kevin Foley, the state trooper, the same man who had often wished Yelenic dead—whose mistress, Michele, stood to gain all the money, now that Yelenic was no longer among the living. The same man well-known for wearing running shoes; the man with the abrasion under his eye the day after the murder; the man who, after Yelenic was dead, put his pocketknife away and never flicked it again, according to his fellow state troopers.

Trooper Charles Gonglik was certainly a professional. He'd been processing crime scenes for the PSP for years. He'd looked at his own photographs of the bloody shoe prints and had some notion that if he ever got a suspect's shoes, he could very likely match the soles to the images he had made with his camera. The killer of Yelenic had been sloppy, in a panic, or possibly arrogant to leave such prints behind. Maybe all three.

A shoe print, to Gonglik, was almost the same as a fingerprint because of wear patterns on the sole of a shoe. Because no human being walks exactly the same way, the wear pattern on a shoe was distinctive, and a shoe print was for all practical purposes unique. Find the shoe, find the killer, Gonglik knew. But within a few days the Blairsville Police Department had taken all the evidence, including all eleven rolls of his shoe print photographs. Whatever doubts and suspicions Gonglik had about this development, he kept to himself.

Blairsville police officer Brant obtained this evidence from Gonglik in Greensburg on April 15, 2006. He turned the Yelenic clothing and blood samples over to the PSP crime lab, which was across the street from the Greensburg barracks where Gonglik's crime scene unit was based. The crucial fingernail clippings from the autopsy, however, went back to Blairsville. That wasn't actually the end of Gonglik's involvement in the Yelenic murder case, however. Not content with his first gleanings from the crime scene on April 13, he returned a few days later with a solution of luminol in an effort of develop more shoe prints. Gonglik sprayed the floors and walls with the chemical, which reacts to the presence of human blood, and soon took more photographs, which revealed still more faint shoe prints also traced in blood. Altogether, Gonglik claimed he could identify nearly a dozen shoe prints, most rather indistinct, as they exited the South Spring Street rear door after the murder was committed. He was absolutely sure that if someone brought him a suspect's shoe, he could identify the killer.

Meanwhile, Mary Ann Clark had gone to court, asking a judge to appoint her the personal representative of her dead cousin's estate, and seeking to be named guardian of Jamie. By then Mary Ann was convinced that Foley had murdered John at the behest of Michele. She wanted to make sure not only that Kevin answered for the crime but that Michele never got a penny of John's money.

15.

By early May of 2006, Lydic had gone just about as far as she could with the limited resources of the Blairsville Police Department. There were higher-ups on the law enforcement totem pole who could stymie whatever she did simply by giving her the freeze-out. Hess had promised Mary Ann the investigation would be handled by Blairsville, and if the PSP decided not to cooperate for whatever reason, Lydic had no hope of solving the crime.

Lydic did have one notion that was to prove out, however. She sent a Blairsville officer to the security offices of the Sheetz stores. The stores were wired for video: anytime a driver pulled in for gas, a camera recorded them. The same was true inside the convenience stores adjacent to the pumps. Lydic had the idea that if the killer had come into Blairsville around midnight and then left around 2:00 a.m., there was a chance that the Sheetz video camera at Market and Walnut—where John had once bankrolled Michele with her sandwich shop in 1997—might have captured an image of the killer's vehicle passing by. And, in fact, if Foley was the culprit—he'd said he'd been in Delmont at the hockey game until after midnight—the Sheetz store at the main corner of downtown Blairsville might have captured an image of his vehicle if it passed by.

After consultation with the Sheetz security expert, Russell States, Lydic assigned a Blairsville officer to collect a DVD video for the hours in question. This Lydic placed in the Blairsville police evidence room. The fingernail clippings remained in the small refrigerator, which was not in the locked evidence room but in the department's small coffee break room next to a larger appliance used by the Blairsville officers to store food items and cold drinks, and therefore essentially unguarded. It was, however, marked with a piece of red tape reading "Evidence."

Lydic did not collect similar Sheetz surveillance DVDs from the video recorders of three other Sheetz stores, two of these on the highway heading north, Route 119, from Blairsville to Indiana, one at Black Lick, another at Homer City just before Indiana, and a third at the street in Indiana where Kevin Foley would have turned right on his way home to Susan Drive. If the two videos from Delmont to Blairsville might show Foley's vehicle heading east on Route 22, might they also show him heading north on Route 119 and into Indiana proper? And if so, at what time? If Foley's vehicle could be shown going north on Route 119 at, say, 12:40 a.m., he would likely be in the clear for the murder of Yelenic. But if the videos showed his vehicle heading north at, say, 2:00 a.m. or later, he would definitely be in the soup.

In fact, no one ever collected those videos, and by the time that was realized, it was too late. The videos had been erased.

As April edged into June of 2006, Sergeant Emigh's suspicions of Foley as Yelenic's possible murderer became a big issue among the troopers in the Indiana barracks. Some of the troopers in the barracks believed Emigh; others were sure that Emigh's well-known antipathy toward Foley had colored his judgment. E-mails flew back and forth among the troopers. Emigh later claimed to have obtained copies of these, which he said showed that higher-ups in the PSP were trying to cover up for Foley. These e-mails would later become evidence in Emigh's federal lawsuit against the commonwealth, in which he claimed that he was improperly demoted and forced to retire, at least partly due to his criticism of how the agency handled the Yelenic murder.

In the fallout after Yelenic's death, Emigh was tagged with a reputation of sorts among the PSP as less than a team player, certainly not one of the "brotherhood." He laid accusations of improper conduct against a variety of PSP higher-ups, and seemed to find it hard to distinguish between technical violations of the regulations by officers and serious misconduct: to Emigh, they were all violations, and if the PSP brass were going to find fault with him, he'd return the favor, with interest.

In any event, on June 8, 2006, almost two months after the Yelenic murder, Emigh was accused of sexual harassment by district court judge Susanne Steffee, a friend of a female trooper under Emigh's supervision, Allison Jacobs, who also was, by her own admission, a workout friend of Kevin Foley. The harassment complaint was filed two days after Emigh had given Jacobs a negative performance evaluation. The harassment, according to Steffee, had taken place more than eighteen months earlier at a party. Emigh, Steffee contended, had kissed her and "grabbed her buttocks." Just why Steffee had waited so long to file the complaint against her friend's superior officer wasn't clear, but Emigh, at least, came to believe it had a lot to do with his insistence that Kevin Foley had to be responsible for the Yelenic murder. Whatever, the complaint, denied by Emigh, illustrated the intense internecine personality conflicts that afflicted the Indiana barracks of the PSP around this time. It also had the effect of damaging Emigh's credibility as Foley's principal doubter within the PSP. One has to wonder, under the circumstances, whether the harassment complaint against Emigh was only made to cast doubt on Emigh's believability.

Emigh actually had an interesting take on the Yelenic murder. As he recalled, he was just about to leave the Indiana barracks on April 13 when he heard about the death of Yelenic. This, he said, was about 4:30 p.m. Almost his first thought was of Foley, given what he already knew of the fraught relationships among Foley, Michele, and Yelenic. As it happened, Foley had left the barracks, just west of the town, about a half hour earlier, making his way through downtown Indiana to the house he shared with Michele on Susan Drive. According to Emigh, after having heard of the murder of Yelenic, he at once called his supervisor, Lieutenant James Fulmer, based in Greensburg, and quickly sketched in the relationships: Foley, Michele, John. Fulmer was the same man Emigh was convinced was Foley's "rabbi," or protector in the PSP. Many of Emigh's later claims of misfeasance on the part of PSP ranking officers might be traced to his disagreements with Fulmer, and Fulmer's loyalty to officers Emigh disapproved of, such as Foley.

In any event, at that point, a little after Yelenic's body had been found, Emigh later claimed, he was told to stay away from the murder scene, although this was a case he would ordinarily supervise. Agitated by this instruction as well as by his knowledge of the ongoing feud between Foley and Yelenic, Emigh then called Indiana district attorney Bell directly and quickly acquainted him with the unhappy backstory.

"He hadn't put two and two together," Emigh recalled. In his telephone call, Emigh said, he asked Bell: "You realize who this is?" Bell seemed not to know who was involved, according to Emigh. He said he told Bell that the case required a full-court press by the PSP. "I'd rather send you everything we have than put Band-Aids on this later," Emigh said he told Bell. He still hoped to take over the case.

But shortly after this, Bell allegedly had talked with Mary Ann Clark, who had told him, "Bob, I do not want the Indiana State Police involved in this case." The "Indiana State Police"—the PSP's Indiana barracks—meant Emigh as well as Foley. Crediting Mary Ann's account, this would have placed Bell in a pickle. Yelenic, Foley, Michele, Mary Ann, Emigh—the whole thing was a headache.

Emigh soon called Fulmer back, in Greensburg. He didn't have to summarize the problems for Fulmer: "Anybody who had any knowledge of these people," Emigh said later, "thought there was a potential for Foley to be involved."

But if that was the case, why didn't Bell, or the Blairsville police, or even the Indiana County sheriff's detectives who worked for Bell, drive at once to Indiana, to the Susan Drive house of Michele and Foley, and conduct an immediate search and interrogation of both Foley and Michele? After all, it was always possible that some sort of forensic evidence implicating Foley in the murder might be found there—perhaps blood in Kevin's Ford Explorer, or bloody clothes or shoes, or even a bloodstained knife. Certainly, given the amount of blood shed by Yelenic in the hallway of his house, there was every chance that crucial blood evidence might be discovered in an immediate search of Foley and his truck.

Or it was always possible that Foley and Michele would tell significantly different stories. In any situation in which a logical suspect is quickly identified, as Foley was, it's always imperative to obtain separate statements from all the principals—who, in this case, would include Michele, Nathan, Nicole, and even young Jamie—as soon as possible, before alibis can harden. Discrepancies as to times can be a powerful wedge to crack open a case.

But according to Emigh, Bell resisted such suggestions, claiming there simply wasn't enough probable cause to justify a search of Foley or to question Michele. To Emigh, this seemed laughable: had Foley been just Joe Six-pack instead of a Pennsylvania State Police investigator, PSP officers would have been all over him.

Emigh recalled discussing the situation with Lieutenant Fulmer that evening—well before Jill Gaston was sent to the Susan Drive house to accompany Deputy Coroner Conrad to the house for the formal death notification, and before Gaston had noticed the abrasion on Foley's face—and at that point, according to Emigh, Fulmer had agreed: someone from the PSP had to interview Foley as soon as possible. A Pennsylvania state trooper was standing by, ready to conduct the critical interview around 10:30 or 11:00 p.m., Emigh later said, noting that Fulmer agreed "there was sufficient probable cause for an arrest warrant" of Foley.

Well, that was probably going a bit too far—but there were certainly grounds to ask Foley to come into the PSP barracks to answer questions, and to ask Foley to consent to a search based on "reasonable suspicion." And, depending on the answers received, possibly legal grounds for a formal search warrant as well. At the same time, there was also certainly enough reasonable suspicion, under legal standards, to bring Michele, Nicole, Nathan, and maybe even young Jamie in for questioning, just as the Uss family had been brought in.

Instead, almost an hour later, the relatively inexperienced Gaston was sent, with the instruction to ask no questions; and after making her observation of Foley's facial abrasions and hearing his explanation—"hockey"—Gaston told Hess and Bell of her observations and was then told to go straight home but "document everything." Nothing further was done that night. The way this initial contact with Foley was orchestrated does tend to support Mary Ann Clark's suspicion that the fix was in, almost from the start, even if it was not. Sometimes appearances can seem more condemnatory than the actual deed.

Afterward, Emigh would also become convinced that someone powerful had intervened on Foley's behalf. "Something happened between the time he [Fulmer] agreed and later," Emigh subsequently contended.

Well, what could have happened?

This was the central enigma of the Yelenic murder. Why would superiors in the PSP be so anxious to put the kibosh on a murder investigation in which Foley was the prime suspect? It hardly seems credible that higher-ups in the Pennsylvania State Police would do this simply to preserve the reputation of the PSP and its leadership, despite Emigh's jaundiced suspicions. Foley was a respected state trooper, and if he was a murderer, certainly this would be something of a black eye for the force. But it was hardly the end of the world. Under intense emotional circumstances, people often did emotional, even criminal things—even cops, who are human, after all. But it would be far, far worse for the department to be seen as trying to cover up a murder because one of their own was the killer: that sort of scandal might last for months if not years.

Admitting that Foley had simply lost it in a spasm of anger at the supposed "pedophile," Yelenic's murder might be explained as an understandable if deplorable, horribly regrettable aberration by one of the finest.

On the surface, there was no need for anyone in the PSP to try to short-circuit any investigation. So, to Emigh and later Mary Ann Clark, there had to be more to the story: why the apparent cover-up, the investigative slowdown, the attempts to find another explanation, even including the Uss family? For Emigh it was all about politics, both within the PSP and among local and state officials.

In either case, for both Emigh and Mary Ann Clark, the behavior of higher officials of the PSP in the immediate aftermath of John Yelenic's murder suggested that there had to be some sort of shadowy suppression of the real facts.

Yet, there is another possibility, albeit one that almost no one, except for Tom Riley, seemed ready to consider. Given the horrific violence visited on the body of John Yelenic— the frenzied, obviously emotional attack—something else might have been going on that dark, stormy night on South Spring Street in Blairsville.

Based on Wecht's description of the injuries in his autopsy, it was possible that the killer was under the influence of steroids—"roid rage," as the vernacular has it. True, neither Anthony Krastek nor even Emigh ever advanced this notion as a possible explanation for what might have happened between Foley and Yelenic in the early morning hours of April 13, but still, it has to be considered.

Riley, the dentist and John's friend, thought of it almost right away. The killer, whoever he was, seemed out of control, someone whose rage and aggression was almost inhuman. In retrospect, the savagery of the assault with the knife seems to belie Emigh's notion that Foley killed Yelenic for money. Why so many cuts? Why the thrust of the head through the narrow glass window? This seemed to shriek rage and hatred beyond reason. The crime scene appeared to show all the earmarks of an attacker who was out of control.

As Emigh put it later, he had no evidence that Foley was a steroid abuser. And, of course, Emigh had supervised Foley for a number of years, so if anyone knew if such was the case, it ought to have been Emigh. But other aspects of Foley's life up to the early morning hours of April 13, 2006, at least raise the possibility of steroid abuse: Foley's incessant workouts, his barely concealed nervous aggression with the flicking of his knife, his intense, violent verbal reactions to the unfounded pedophilia allegations, his emotional volatility, his fantasies of Yelenic's death, taken together, are all signs of someone on testosterone juice. These symptoms, coupled with the evidence of the horrific attack—an indication of the uncontrolled outburst of rage—make secret steroid abuse a distinct possibility, albeit one never investigated. And if other PSP officers knew of or were complicit in this abuse—regrettably, such abuse is not unknown in some police departments around the country, as officers bulk up to counter similar abusers who are also criminals—this might have been one reason why the PSP higher command was anxious to keep a lid on the Yelenic murder. Because if there was a ring of PSP cops abusing steroids in Indiana County, the potential civil liability, not just for Yelenic's survivors but for many other potential litigants arrested or even assaulted by such a ring of substance-abusing officers, could be enormous: possibly millions of dollars if not tens of millions. And, of course, the abuse of steroids has been a federal crime for well over a decade, which might mean the end of a number of police careers . . .

Whatever the motivations of some in the PSP might possibly have been and whether they had attempted to sidetrack the investigation of Yelenic's murder or to stall Blairsville's Corporal Lydic, by May 11, 2006, almost a month after the murder, an effort was finally made to search Kevin's 2000 Ford Explorer for trace evidence, such as blood and fiber. Tape lifts were taken by Gonglik from the Explorer's ignition switch, windshield wiper switch, and the passenger side dashboard, with the thought that there might be minute traces of Yelenic's blood. Kevin voluntarily agreed to the examination, according to Gonglik. The lifts showed no signs of blood, and in fact there was no incriminating evidence to be found at all.

A week later Gonglik, again with Kevin's permission, attempted to search the house Kevin shared with Michele at Susan Drive in Indiana. Kevin wasn't present at the time, Gonglik recalled. Asked later why he hadn't obtained a search warrant—Bell would likely have had to approve one— Gonglik said he wasn't sure. "I don't know," he said. "I just do what I'm asked to do."

On this visit to the Susan Drive house, Gonglik first looked through a Nissan Armada apparently driven by Michele, and again found no blood. He wanted to go through the house, but a lawyer representing Michele essentially short-stopped him.

"I only had fifteen minutes," Gonglik said later. Michele's attorney insisted on limiting his search, Gonglik said. He thought, in a murder investigation, much more time for searching was necessary. "I would have liked to have had more time to search through the residence, and basically all I had time to do was open up closet doors and look underneath beds." Just why Michele had hired a lawyer to limit this consensual search at this early point in the investigation wasn't entirely clear, but without a court-ordered warrant, Gonglik had no authority to object to the limitation Michele's lawyer imposed.

It actually was highly unlikely that Gonglik would have found anything at that point, almost a month after the murder, although anything was possible; that's why thorough searches are always to be preferred, backed up by court-ordered warrants. But the hazy legality of this search—with Kevin apparently consenting, and a lawyer for Michele seeming to object (after all, she owned the property)— probably made anything discovered potentially inadmissible anyway. Just why there was no judicially approved search warrant, which would have made any such objections moot, wasn't entirely clear, unless Bell, for some reason, was hampering Corporal Lydic's investigation of the prime suspect.

Perhaps Bell was still dancing on the high wire between the politics of the PSP and Mary Ann Clark.

Whatever was going on, a month after the murder, it seemed apparent that the powers that be weren't particularly enthusiastic about going after Kevin Foley as the man most likely to have murdered John Yelenic.

While this was unfolding, Michele was taking steps to extricate herself from her own potential suspected culpability in her estranged husband's murder.

Legally, because John hadn't actually signed the divorce agreement so painstakingly negotiated by Alexander and Lovette—it was among the blood-spattered papers on the Yelenic living room floor—Michele was still John's wife. As his wife, and because of the will he had made in July of 1997, Michele stood to inherit everything. A little over $2 million, in fact, including the payouts from at least two life insurance policies, various investment accounts, and some remaining real estate.

Was this a motive, or what? Either as a wife or as the named beneficiary of the old will, Michele was now in a position to get all the Yelenic assets. It wasn't at all hard for the cynical to conjecture that Michele, facing the prospective loss of $2,500 a month in spousal support in the imminent divorce, had somehow cajoled Kevin to cut John's throat to make sure she kept a grip on *all* the dough, not just the measly $2,500 a month. The obvious fact that she stood to benefit so materially from John's death made her a possible a co-conspirator or even a potential suspect, at least on paper. After all, if Michele was Kevin's alibi, that meant Kevin was *Michele's* alibi, too. Could they have done the murder together? Or could Michele have done it alone while Kevin was driving home from Delmont, blissfully unaware of his paramour's deadly intent? On paper, both had motives, and neither had a truly solid alibi, other than each other. And any way you sliced it, so to speak, there was a lot of money at stake. That said, Michele was never charged with any crime.

Doubtless, whether such speculation had any factual basis or not, somewhere along the line, someone explained to Michele the implications of the unsigned final divorce papers, and what John's death meant as to her possible motive, and why that might make her a possible suspect in the murder. On May 4, Michele filed a notice with the Indiana court, disclaiming any interest in acting in any capacity in connection with her estranged husband's estate. Two weeks later, when Mary Ann Clark, acting as the "personal representative" of John for purposes of his estate, asked Judge Hanna to declare the divorce between John and Michele final and therefore valid, even if it had never been signed and notarized, Michele's lawyers joined with the motion. If granted by Hanna, this would have the effect of removing Michele from directly inheriting from John as a surviving spouse, although the will was murkier legal issue.

Eventually, however, Michele would disclaim rights under the old 1997 will, too, and Jamie would become John's sole heir, although Mary Ann Clark would be successful in getting the court to appoint a trustee to supervise Jamie's lucrative inheritance. Michele's legal filings in May of 2006 essentially removed her pecuniary interest in John's money: they essentially eliminated her potential motive, at least on paper, as a likely suspect in John's murder, although at some considerable cost to her control over John's estate.

Judge Hanna was confronted with a rather peculiar legal issue with Mary Ann Clark's petition asking her to declare the divorce between John and Michele final and therefore valid, even though John had not signed the final papers. In a hearing on May 18, 2006, just a month after John's murder, lawyers for Mary Ann, asked that the judge simply declare the divorce an established fact, despite John's missing signature. After hearing from both sides and thinking it over, Judge Hanna two months later, in mid-July, 2006, issued a rather comprehensive finding of fact, along with a court order. The order denied Mary Ann Clark's petition—actually an oral motion by lawyers representing her on the previous May 17—to declare the divorce final, even if posthumous.

"The facts of this case are emotionally compelling," Judge Hanna said in her ruling. "Husband's death was unjust and untimely. The court acknowledges the sorrow of those who were close to husband and their wish to give him in death what he sought in life. The court is aware the record shows that husband had a strong desire to be divorced . . . [W]hat the court cannot do is alter the fact that that this marriage ended tragically by death." Under such circumstances, Pennsylvania law made it impossible to declare that a divorce had actually occurred, Judge Hanna said. In the eyes of the law, John and Michele were still married, although Michele was now a technically a widow.

But the court could and would enforce the agreement signed by Michele: no more spousal support from John's estate. Michele would get no more from John Yelenic than what had been agreed to at the coffee shop meeting in January of 2006.

In essence, Judge Hanna cut the baby in half, Solomon-style. While the law didn't permit formal recognition of the divorce between John and Michele, the agreement signed by Michele the week before the murder was enforceable, in the judge's ruling. That meant Michele got the $54,000 final settlement, the child support for Jamie, but it also meant that the spousal support was ended. And the life insurance was for Jamie's benefit, not Michele's.

Three weeks after this hearing on the status of the divorce case—and while all sorts of rumors were flying about the

Indiana barracks about Foley and Yelenic—Emigh was named in a sexual harassment complaint involving the female trooper he supervised, Allison Jacobs. By this point Emigh had made his suspicions of Kevin well-known in the barracks and the PSP at large. Others, including some of Emigh's supervisors, had dismissed these suspicions and denigrated Emigh. Then Emigh was accused of inappropriate contact with a female trooper, stemming from an incident at a social gathering nearly two years earlier. He denied the allegation and soon became convinced that the complaint was cooked up by his enemies in the PSP, at least in part because of his persistently stated belief that Foley had murdered Yelenic. From June of 2006 on, Emigh would be at odds with the PSP, eventually suing the department and the state, alleging that the PSP had violated his civil rights under the First and Fourteenth Amendments to the United States constitution. The suit was dismissed by the trial court, but it is currently on appeal.

Emigh's statements as to what he knew and told his supervisors about Foley before and after Yelenic's murder would become critical evidence in Mary Ann Clark's eventual wrongful-death lawsuit, which held the PSP liable for John's murder. As a potential witness for Mary Ann Clark's lawsuit, at least some thought this might have been why Emigh was named as a sexual harasser by the PSP—a way to diminish his credibility as a potential witness.

Nevertheless, by late July of 2006, Corporal Lydic of the Blairsville Police Department was taken off the Yelenic murder case, and the investigation was placed in the hands of the Pennsylvania State Police, although investigators from the Indiana barracks were deliberately excluded. In the absence of any charges, Kevin Foley continued to work there, so allowing the Indiana barracks of the PSP to have any involvement in the investigation would have been untenable because of conflicts of interest if not possible tainting of the evidence. Kevin was popular in the barracks; therefore, could anything that the local PSP investigators generated be trusted? Even if it could, it would be a prime target for reasonable doubt at any trial: the potential for attacks of bias would be too great. It was far better to get some uninvolved investigators in to sort things out.

Just how this change of investigative jurisdictions unfolded, and what was involved in the transfer, was never completely clear afterward, although it appears that, independently, both Mary Ann Clark and Blairsville police chief Don Hess had significant influence in the decision. So, possibly, did State Senator Don White. The boundary line between policing and politicking is almost always very murky at the highest levels. Tom Riley was sure that Mary Ann Clark had bit the politicians in the leg and wouldn't let go.

"She was like a pit bull," Riley recalled. Mary Ann was too genteel to admit this, but later it was very clear that she wasn't about to allow the murder of her cousin to fade away without using every bit of her legendary persistence and her guile. In Mary Ann's mind, she owed at least that much to the cousin whose tales of harassment by the PSP she had doubted.

White recalled hosting a meeting between Mary Ann and her neighbor Bell. According to White, Mary Ann pleaded with Bell to give jurisdiction in the murder case to Pennsylvania attorney general Tom Corbett. Bell seemed reluctant to do this, according to both Mary Ann and White: on the surface, it would be an admission by Bell that his office was incapable of fairly conducting the investigation— hardly helpful to a politician facing reelection in two years. White recalled urging Bell to give the case up anyway. Bell seemed unconvinced, White recalled. Nevertheless, at some point in either the late summer or fall of 2006, Bell agreed to cede direct supervision of the investigation to Corbett, another Republican, who was preparing to run for governor. A pristine investigation of Foley's possible culpability in the murder of the politically active Mary Ann Clark's cousin could hardly hurt Bell under these circumstances, especially if Corbett agreed to share the credit—or blame—if any. An arrangement between Corbett and Bell was finally struck: they would jointly supervise the investigation into John Yelenic's murder. And so, by the end of July 2006, a new team was brought in to find the murderer. Corbett would soon convene a statewide grand jury to hear the evidence, and one of his top lawyers, Anthony Krastek, would take over the prosecution of the case.

The head of this new investigative team was a PSP corporal from Greensburg, Randall Gardner. And even if Gardner was telling the truth to Mary Ann Clark when they first met that summer of 2006—that this was his first homicide investigation—Gardner had his orders from his supervisor in Greensburg, PSP captain Harvey Cole: he had to conduct the Yelenic investigation without fear or favor. And that's exactly what Gardner did, although it took the better part of a year. Still, without the assistance of the Federal Bureau of Investigation, Gardner would have had no chance. The PSP "brotherhood" tried very hard to see to that, some thought. One dead alleged pedophile dentist measured against a living Pennsylvania state trooper—that, some thought, was no bargain.

16.

Gardner began by trying to reassemble all the physical evidence that had been collected so far: Gonglik's photographs of the bloody shoe prints; the bloody clothes taken from Yelenic's body; the autopsy records; the video from the Blairsville Sheetz convenience store at Market and Walnut; and the fingernail clippings from Yelenic's hands, which had been stashed for over three months in the Blairsville police department small refrigerator. It was very clear to Gardner, experienced as he was in murder cases, that this meager evidence was all the new team was likely to get, and it would have to tell the tale, barring someone's unexpected confession.

The first step in this new investigation took place on August 3, 2006, when Gardner dispatched Gonglik back to Blairsville to re-collect the evidence Lydic had stashed in the Blairsville refrigerator—most importantly, the fingernail clippings Wecht had obtained at the autopsy more than three months earlier. Once Gonglik retrieved this evidence, Gardner put the PSP itself to the test: he asked the state's crime lab to evaluate it, one item at a time.

The first test was of the shoe prints. Gonglik had taken quite a number of shoe print photos, some taken under normal lighting conditions, others under the effects of luminol. Gardner certainly saw Gonglik's point: if they could find a shoe that matched the bloody prints, they'd have the killer. Gonglik had already searched, at least cursorily, Kevin's car, Michele's car, and the house at Susan Drive, and had come up with nothing, certainly no bloody shoes or clothes. So the next thing to do was try to identify the tread of the shoe: from its impression in Yelenic's blood, what kind of shoe was it? That is, who made it? Nike? New Balance? Converse? Keds? PF Flyers? If the make of the shoe could be matched to a shoe known to be worn by one of the suspects, that would be a step forward. Gardner wanted the PSP lab in Greensburg to identify from the tread pattern, if it could—at least the manufacturer of the shoe that Gonglik's camera had documented in blood on the murder house flooring.

Gardner also submitted the fingernail clippings, with their associated potential genetic material—dried skin and blood found under the nails—to the same lab. If the PSP crime lab could identify the type of shoe and find a DNA profile from the fingernail clippings, it might go a very long way toward narrowing the field of suspects. Finding anyone who wore the right kind of shoes and who also had the right kind of DNA had to be a smoking gun, logic dictated. At the same time, the two clues could also eliminate suspects: if the DNA from the clipped fingernails didn't match Kevin's DNA, and if Kevin never owned a pair of running shoes matching the bloody tread pattern, that would almost certainly eliminate him. The same reasoning applied to Tom Uss: no shoes, no flesh, no service. Then, at least, Gardner would know the solution lay elsewhere.

But the crime lab in Greensburg was no help. It wasn't able to identify a tread pattern from Gonglik's photographs: "inconclusive," Gardner was told. And within a short time, Gardner was told by the lab that the tissue samples taken from under Yelenic's fingernails at Wecht's autopsy were insufficient to render a positive identification. There just wasn't enough DNA for a reliable test, the PSP lab expert told Gardner.

At that point Gardner asked for permission from his supervisor Harvey Cole to seek assistance from the Federal Bureau of Investigation. Gardner had the idea the FBI might be able to provide answers that the PSP either could not or would not, for whatever reason. This permission was very quickly granted. Sometime in late September or early October of 2006, he contacted Special Agent Michael Hochrein in the bureau's field office in Pittsburgh. Hochrein agreed to submit the Gonglik bloody shoeprint photos and the fingernail evidence to the FBI lab in Quantico, Virginia, for expert analysis.

Ordinarily, the FBI has no jurisdiction over state homicide cases. In effect, under such circumstances the bureau becomes a state police agency's "reliable informant," legally no better than a jailhouse snitch, although far more sophisticated, much more accurate, and therefore far more reliable. Essentially, the bureau's involvement in the Yelenic investigation in the person of Special Agent Hochrein had much in common with the second baseman in a baseball team's double play combination: Gardner to Hochrein to Quantico, Tinkers to Evers to Chance. By the time the bureau was finished with the Yelenic case a year later, several hundred thousand federal dollars would be spent, and the case against Kevin Foley would be scientifically established. Corbett's role in calling in federal chits to dragoon the FBI into the Yelenic mess would be crucial; so would, by extension, Mary Ann Clark's "pit bull" pressure on Corbett.

Corbett, of course, was by then the likely Republican candidate for the Pennsylvania governorship. The FBI was at the time under the influence of the George W. Bush administration's attorney general, Alberto Gonzales, and the bureau certainly also understood that there were two Republican

U.S. senators from Pennsylvania, one of whom, Arlen Specter, was the ranking member of the Senate Judiciary Committee, with power over the bureau's budget. So a little federal help to Corbett, however warranted, couldn't hurt, politically speaking, as far as the bureau, Corbett, and Mary Ann Clark's Pennsylvania Republicans were concerned.

There was likewise another political calculation: the PSP was an agency then under the nominal control of Pennsylvania governor Ed Rendell, a Democrat, the former mayor of Philadelphia. An indictment and prosecution of a PSP trooper like Foley couldn't help but make Rendell's stewardship of the PSP look lame. So the FBI mounted up. It remains true, wherever one is, that politics and policing are mostly inseparable concepts. Still, none of this is to say that the FBI improperly influenced the case against Kevin Foley, only that bureau's involvement from the beginning had political significance. If John Yelenic had been a shoe salesman rather than a well-connected dentist, the FBI would likely never have become involved: it just wasn't a federal case. It is true that the FBI has provided expert assistance for local law enforcement in many jurisdictions, but it's also true that it does so only when asked to do so by state or local authorities. The revamped Yelenic investigation had some powerful people behind it: Mary Ann Clark for starters, then Corbett, as well as possibly others higher up the political food chain.

By the end of December 2006, the bureau was well involved in the murder investigation, with Quantico experts examining different pieces of evidence. In the interim, Corbett, with Anthony Krastek in the lead, intended to convene a grand jury to examine the facts of the murder.

The statutes of the Commonwealth of Pennsylvania provided for a peculiar type of investigative body, the "statewide investigative grand jury," as it was called. This was in effect a regional assembly, drawn from jurors nominated by presiding judges from a number of coterminous counties—twenty-five counties, in fact, known as the "Western District." This district included Indiana, Armstrong, and Cambria counties. Two hundred potential jurors were to be selected from nominations by presiding judges in each of the counties; from this, one would think each presiding judge was entitled to pick only four possible jurors. Fifty of these two hundred were to be selected by a random draw, and of those, twenty-five appointed. The resulting body would be supervised by a judge of the state supreme court. In the Foley case, the supervisor would be senior judge Barry F. Feudale of Northumberland County, some miles east of Indiana County and north of Harrisburg. The grand jury was convened by an order from Chief Justice Ralph J. Cappy on December 20, 2006.

The idea was that with such a broad cross section from so many counties, the chance of the fix being put in by powerful people in any one county was greatly lessened. The investigative grand jury had the power of subpoena and, like most grand juries, could take hearsay testimony. Testimony was secret, and not disclosed to potential defendants unless it was used at trial, and then usually after a witness had testified. In a way, it was very similar to a federal grand jury. With the empanelment of a statewide investigative grand jury, Corbett and his senior deputy attorney general, Krastek, clearly signaled their intention to take the murder of John Yelenic seriously, no matter what the divisions within the PSP.

By this point in the fall of 2006, Kevin clearly understood that he was the prime focus of the attorney general's inquiry. He claimed not to be worried: he was just a family man, Kevin insisted, not the sort of man who would cut anyone's throat. Didn't he love children? As noted, even before Yelenic's murder, Kevin and Michele had adopted another child, the infant from Guatemala. This had, in fact, been partially the subject of discussion between Kevin, Michele, and Barbara Swasy at the Friday fish fry the week before John's murder, with Michele asking whether Barbara had spilled the beans about the adoption. Kevin and seventeen-year-old Nicole Kamler had gone to the Central American country in March of 2006 to conclude the adoption. Why Nicole accompanied Kevin to Guatemala rather than Michele for this isn't clear. However, for some reason, Michele apparently wanted to keep this event secret from John, at least based on Barbara's recollection of the conversation at the fish fry.

Now Kevin, despite the cloud of suspicion hanging over him and the loss of his badge and gun, was the main support of a family comprising four children: Nicole, Nathan, Jamie, and the new baby from Guatemala (although under the ruling of Judge Hanna in the posthumous divorce case, the $1,300 in child support from John's estate continued.) Kevin had become head of a family that had never been part of his life two or three years earlier. And mostly a family with an earlier father, Yelenic, dead, sliced to pieces on his own living room floor by a man with a very sharp knife. Which Kevin was known to flick habitually, nervously—or at least had done so until April 14, 2006. Since then he hadn't: the knife flicking had vanished as part of Kevin's persona, according to his brethren in the PSP barracks. Some also noticed that he now wore Nike running shoes, no longer ASICS . . . The gossip among the officers of the PSP continued: Had he or hadn't he?

Emigh, for one, was quite sure he had. Kevin continued to insist that he wasn't worried: he had done nothing to John Yelenic, he maintained. The force continued to be split between those who believed Kevin and those who did not. Emigh later claimed that computer e-mails flew back and forth among the troopers, including Foley himself and senior officers such as Emigh's archenemy, Fulmer, suggesting that the case would soon go away.

John and Michele Yelenic at the Chapel of Bells in Las Vegas, New Year's Eve, 1997. This wedding took place seven months after the death of John's mother, and six months after John made Michele his sole heir.

Photo by Chapel of the Bells, courtesy of Mary Ann Clark.

The Yelenic mailbox on the afternoon of April 13, 2006. The bloody streaks from the adjacent window caused the Uss boys to realize that something was amiss in the Yelenic house.

PA State Police photo.

The crime scene photo of the bloody broken side window at the Yelenic house, taken by Pennsylvania State Police. Investigators concluded from the evidence that Yelenic's murderer had shoved Yelenic's head through the glass just before cutting his throat.

PA State Police photo.

Bloody shoeprint in the Yelenic hallway. As John Yelenic was found barefoot, investigators suspected that this print matched the tread of the shoe worn by his murderer. Experts from the FBI concluded the tread matched that of a discontinued ASICS running shoe once purchased by Kevin Foley.   PA State Police photo.

More bloody shoeprints in the Yelenic house. Investigators found trace prints leading to the rear door, all of them seeming to match the ASICS tread, suggesting that there was only one killer. PA State Police photo.

This statue of the actor Jimmy Stewart, Indiana's most famous son, playing the role of Elwood Dowd in *Harvey*, occupies the front lawn of the courthouse in Indiana, Pa., where the town slogan is "It's a Wonderful Life." Carlton Smith photo.

The White Farm Road house in Indiana. John and Michele moved here in the late 1990s. After they split up, John moved back to Blairsville, and Michele and the children moved to Johnstown, apparently abandoning this house.

Carlton Smith photo.

A few months after leaving John, Michele and the children took up residence in this house in Johnstown, Pa. John drove here to leave a communication for Michele, which resulted in his arrest for violating a no-contact order. Carlton Smith photo.

Mary Ann Clark, John Yelenic's cousin. She was outraged by the murder of her cousin, and used her political skills to induce the Pennsylvania Attorney General's Office to take over the case.

Photo courtesy of Lifetouch Church Directories and Portraits.

Pennsylvania State Trooper Kevin Foley was arrested in September 2007 and charged with the brutal knife attack on John Yelenic seventeen months earlier.

PA State Police photo.

The vehicle owned by Kevin Foley, a Ford Explorer. Investigators actually tracked down this vehicle after Foley sold it, and used it in a simulation, hoping to match it to blurry images on a Sheetz video recording taken on the night of the murder.　　　　PA State Police photo.

One of several surveillance cameras at the Blairsville Sheetz gas stop/convenience store. John Yelenic once owned a portion of this property. Nine years later, one of these cameras recorded a vehicle that appeared to be the same as Kevin Foley's driving by a short time after the murder of John Yelenic.

Carlton Smith photo.

The Sheetz video recording from the early morning hours of April 13. FBI experts were unable to match the image conclusively to Kevin's Explorer.

Sheetz photo, exhibit at the trial of Kevin Foley,
still produced by the FBI.

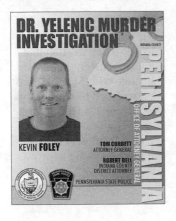

DR. YELENIC MURDER INVESTIGATION

INDIANA COUNTY

PENNSYLVANIA

OFFICE OF ATTORNEY GENERAL

KEVIN **FOLEY**

TOM CORBETT
ATTORNEY GENERAL

ROBERT BELL
INDIANA COUNTY
DISTRICT ATTORNEY

PENNSYLVANIA STATE POLICE

Following the arrest of Foley in September of 2007, Attorney General Tom Corbett issued this news release, saying the case would be prosecuted by his office in conjunction with Indiana District Attorney Robert Bell. After Foley was convicted, Corbett was elected governor.

Pennsylvania Attorney General's Office photo.

The Yelenic and Uss houses on South Spring Street, Blairsville, Pennsylvania. The two Uss boys who lived next door to Yelenic discovered his bloody body on the afternoon of April 13, 2006. Carlton Smith photo.

Dr. Thomas Riley, John Yelenic's mentor and eventual partner. Riley worried that John was rushing into his marriage with Michele, and then watched him fall into a deep depression as the marriage deteriorated severely. He wondered why it took the police so long to arrest Kevin Foley.

Carlton Smith photo.

The house on Susan Drive where Kevin Foley and Michele Yelenic resided with four children in the spring of 2006. After Foley's conviction, Michele Yelenic moved out of the house. As of the summer of 2010 it remained vacant and overgrown.

Carlton Smith photo.

John Yelenic in a happier moment.

Mary Ann Clark photo.

At the same time, Emigh was hip-deep in his own troubles with the PSP. The sexual harassment complaint lodged against him in June of 2006 was wending its way through the bureaucracy, and Emigh was losing ground, beset by hearings and inquisitions that he thought might have really stemmed from his suspicions of Foley. Meanwhile, Mary Ann Clark was pressing first White, then Corbett, to do something about John's murder—or else. This "pit bull" pressure on Corbett in turn put pressure on the PSP command, which resulted in the assignment of Randall Gardner to the case.

All the while, Mary Ann retained a probate lawyer to sort through John's assets: some remaining real estate after the initial 60/40 split with Michele, a variety of investment accounts, and—lo and behold, all of a sudden—a $1 million life insurance policy. It would take a little over a year, but by the time the probate lawyer totted it all up, John's estate was worth about $2 million when he died.

Little Jamie would inherit the lot.

Then Mary Ann heard from John's divorce lawyer, Effie Alexander in Pittsburgh. Alexander said John had told her that he was sure he was about to be murdered by Kevin, egged on by Michele. He wanted to give Alexander $10,000 to investigate his impending demise.

17.

This presentiment seems to have occurred sometime between John's unhappy encounter with little Jamie the day before Thanksgiving 2005 and perhaps March of 2006, only two weeks before his murder. Just why John had become convinced that Kevin or others in the PSP—in his mind he merged them all into the category of enemies—isn't entirely clear. What seems likely is that some event happened between Thanksgiving 2005 and March 2006 that alarmed Yelenic and led to his expression of fear to Alexander—but whatever it was, Yelenic never said. It seems possible that the harassment he had complained of earlier to his cousin Mary Ann Clark might have increased in this period as John and Michele were trying to finalize the financial terms of their divorce.

But six months after Yelenic's murder—after the Blairsville Police Department had failed to unravel the mystery, and Gardner and the Pennsylvania attorney general's office had taken over the case, and with the FBI on the job, along with the statewide investigative grand jury—progress was finally being made.

* * *

On the bloody shoe prints, for instance: when the PSP's crime lab told Gardner that the treads photographed by Gonglik were "inconclusive," Gardner wasn't so sure. He passed the Gonglik photographs onto Hochrein, who sent them on to the FBI's forensic laboratory in Quantico. There, drawing on a library of printed shoe treads, an FBI expert, Mike Smith, identified the pattern as one consistent with an ASICS running shoe, an ASICS Gel Creed or possibly an ASICS Gel Creed Plus running shoe, approximately size ten or eleven. Foley had been known to wear ASICS running shoes, and had even bought some for other troopers. PSP equipment records showed that Kevin wore a size 10½ shoe.

In the meantime, the tissue under John's fingernails was being examined by Jerrilyn Conway, a DNA expert employed by the FBI. While DNA evidence is often a smoking gun, in the matter of the Yelenic murder, it would turn out to be more like a faint wisp of smoke, barely seen, and no gun at all. It would take other, much more controversial analyses to tie the Yelenic fingernail tissue to Kevin Foley—presumably from his "hockey" scratch sustained the night before the murder was discovered.

The fact is, DNA analysis is subject to statistical interpretation, and all too many lawyers are ignorant of the principles of statistical calculation; words, not numbers, are lawyers' forte. And there are other possible problems with relying on DNA as conclusive evidence: First, it usually doesn't come with a time/date stamp. Knowing when and where a nonvictim sample of DNA is crucial to assessing its evidentiary value. Mere presence often means nothing. Second, so far in the United States, the control over the biological samples used to identify supposed DNA has been somewhat slipshod in many jurisdictions: samples have been known to be inadvertently mixed. Third, sometimes samples can be accidentally contaminated in the examining laboratory. In short, law enforcement laboratories are still chasing science in many places. And fourth: some police laboratories have been proven to have deliberately falsified test results, just to make sure the "guilty" do not go unpunished, as in the state of Texas. To date, several hundred people nationwide have been exonerated from their convictions, usually due to improper handling of DNA evidence.

Gardner probably knew what to expect from the PSP crime lab with regard to the shoe print photographs and the DNA from the fingernail clippings. He had to have an idea at that point, if someone already hadn't clued him in, that the murder of Yelenic was a hot potato, not least because one of his PSP brethren was odds-on the boy most likely. Which was why he had his superior Harvey Cole endorse the request to the FBI. In any bureaucracy, accountability runs both uphill and downhill. Cole did not want to hold the hot potato any more than Gardner.

In the meantime, Gardner met with Russell States, the director of security for the chain of Sheetz stores. Gardner already knew Kevin's story, at least informally: Kevin claimed he'd been at the ice rink in Delmont until around midnight, then had driven straight home to Michele and the kids. But any way you sliced it, Kevin had to take Route 22 east from Denton through Blairsville before catching Route 119 north to Indiana. That meant it was possible that the Sheetz store in New Alexandria, about ten minutes east of Delmont, had caught an image of Kevin's Ford SUV flying past on Route 22. If so, that might help establish a timeline for Kevin's movements on the fatal night.

Sheetz provided a DVD from the New Alexandria store. Gardner asked Robert Haar, a trooper in his unit, to review the DVDs from both the New Alexandria store and the one in Blairsville. Haar spent the next few weeks studying the disks copied from the Sheetz surveillance cameras at both

New Alexandria and Blairsville for the night of April 13, 2006. In the end, he thought he'd seen something—a vehicle that looked very much like Kevin's Ford Explorer passing the New Alexandria store at 12:18 a.m. on April 13. Approximately an hour and a half later, at 1:48 a.m., a similar vehicle was recorded by the Blairsville Sheetz surveillance cameras, this one heading in the direction of Indiana on Route 119. (Just why the New Alexandria Sheetz still had a copy of this video while the three Sheetz stores between Blairsville and Indiana did not remains a mystery.)

Was this Foley? The image on the tapes was too blurry to make a positive identification. Gardner asked Hochrein if the FBI could do anything to enhance the images. Hochrein forwarded the two DVDs to the FBI's laboratory at Quantico, and a technician there, Amanda Broyles, set to work trying to sharpen the images, and analyze them.

On October 11, 2006, Gardner served a search warrant on Kevin Foley, requiring him to provide samples of his blood and hair. Kevin accompanied two other troopers to a hospital in Greensburg, where the samples were taken. He was completely cooperative, even genial. Clearly, he had been expecting this: it was impossible to keep the thrust of Gardner's investigation secret within the PSP.

At the same time, the crime scene expert Gonglik returned to the house on Susan Drive in Indiana. In this more thorough search than the abbreviated, consensual one made in the spring, Gonglik collected two empty boxes for ASICS shoes, one for size 10½, the other for a size 11, as well as an older pair of size 10 ASICS shoes. Gonglik, accompanied by seven other PSP troopers, also collected seventeen snapshots of Kevin; in some of them he was wearing what appeared to be ASICS Gel Creed shoes. In addition, Gonglik seized a hockey equipment bag. It was just possible, Gonglik thought, that the bag might contain minute traces of John Yelenic's blood.

18.

By January 2007, most of the elements of a possible murder case against Kevin Foley were falling into place. Gardner and others who worked under him interviewed many of Kevin's fellow troopers. And while most considered Kevin a good officer, many also remarked on Kevin's obvious hatred of John Yelenic. The knife-flicking penchant was mentioned frequently. If any trooper knew of Kevin's supposed harassment of Yelenic, accompanied by other troopers, as later alleged by Mary Ann Clark and Tom Riley, they seem not to have mentioned it to Gardner's interrogators. Emigh—the investigators' supervisor—later said he knew of no such harassment. But then, Emigh said he'd never heard of Kevin's knife-flicking habit, either, despite widespread agreement among the troopers in the Indiana barracks that this was a definite aspect of Kevin's personality, at least up until April 13. So perhaps Emigh didn't always know what some of his subordinates were up to.

In any event, by early 2007, Gardner had the outline: motive, hatred; means, Foley's sharp-knife; opportunity, an apparently missing ninety minutes between 12:18 a.m. and 1:48 a.m. on April 13, the two times the two Sheetz cameras record a passing vehicle that looked very much like Kevin's, even though Kevin claimed to be home with Michele by 12:45 a.m. that morning.

By then, however, Kevin had sold his Explorer. Undaunted, Gardner tracked it down. He asked the new owner if the PSP might borrow it for a test. The new owner agreed, and one night in April 2007 the truck was driven past the Blairsville Sheetz in a reenactment, complete with water from fire trucks to simulate the rainstorm from the year before. The new video was sent to the FBI for comparison purposes with the original Sheetz DVDs.

By May, the statewide investigative grand jury was getting ramped up. Witnesses were called to testify, including Michele, along with various troopers who had known of Kevin's enmity toward John. Gardner was the primary witness, recounting what he had learned from the FBI, and from the divorce lawyer, Effie Alexander, including John's expression of fear that he would be murdered by Foley, and from Daniel Lovette regarding Michele's last-minute balking on the divorce settlement. Deana Kirkland testified about her two child molestation investigations of John. A Riley dental office receptionist, Georgette Johnson, testified that in the days before the murder, Michele had frequently called the office, demanding to speak to John, and that John had refused to speak with her unless she signed the divorce agreement that had been negotiated three months earlier at the coffee shop. Michele had been asking for money from John, Johnson testified—presumably the payment of the alimony from January, February, and March.

But up to this point the case against Kevin was made entirely of evidence inferred from circumstances. Circumstantial evidence is often very powerful evidence, but it is also evidence vulnerable to reasonable doubt: when a key circumstance can be shown to have multiple explanations, some of them exculpatory, a finding of not guilty or at least a hung jury is almost always within reach for a competent defense lawyer. What was needed to nail down the case was hard, incontrovertible physical evidence—like the DNA found under the fingernail of John's left hand.

FBI analyst Jerilynn Conway began working on this in July of 2007. She had three samples of material to work with: the scrapings from the fingernail clippings collected by Wecht's assistant at John's autopsy, a sample of John's own blood, and a sample of the blood taken from Kevin in the October 2006 search. Because the fingernail evidence was possibly a mixed sample—that is, containing DNA from John and others—the likelihood of obtaining a definitive match to a person other than John was fairly low. Usually, presumed mixed samples of DNA contain a large majority of material from the victim and a far smaller amount from the minor donor or donors. That was the ostensible reason the PSP crime lab had declined to do the test. As the PSP lab told Gardner, any test was highly likely to be "inconclusive," because any minor donors' DNA was likely to be almost impossible to tie to a specific person.

DNA analysis has come a very long way from its initial emergence as a forensic tool in the late 1980s. In those years, fairly large chunks of genetic material were needed to identify specific donors, or depositors. But at the 1990s progressed, methods to essentially expand the amount of DNA recovered were found. By taking some of the DNA, then using a chemical process to replicate its constituent molecules, a much larger amount of the genetic code—in a way similar to making many photocopies—could be obtained. Then, in further refinements, it was noticed that even small segments of DNA—short tandem repeats, or STR, as the science jargon now calls them—contained enough individual molecular variations to narrow the range of possible inclusion to very small odds. Thus, increasingly smaller amounts of DNA, coupled with the circumstantial evidence, could be used to prove a case beyond a reasonable doubt. That is, if the collection of the DNA had not been contaminated . . . if the laboratory treatments were done correctly . . . if the geneticists' assumptions of the rate of genetic frequency in large populations were accurate. And if the DNA lab was on the up-and-up.

As forensic science made use of these improved DNA identification techniques in the early 2000s, an arcane debate among experts erupted over the statistical standards for positive identification, particularly with regard to mixed samples, and the reliability of the identification of the smaller amounts of trace DNA not matching the majority sample. The FBI's lab, in fact, adopted a conservative standard. If the minority sample in a mixed DNA recovery registered below fifty relative fluorescent units, or RFU—a measurement on a piece of lab equipment that showed the quality of the DNA sample—it was considered insufficiently reliable for identification purposes.

Thus, the case for or against Kevin Foley as the murderer of John Yelenic came down to the FBI's DNA analysis. Was there a mixed sample of blood or tissue under John's right fingernail? If there was, would it match Kevin or someone else? And even if there was more than one DNA profile to be obtained, and even if there was enough obviously foreign DNA to satisfy the FBI's conservative RFU standards, did it have anything at all to do with the murder? For instance, had John scratched someone completely unrelated to the homicide?

On the other hand, there had been the abrasion on Kevin's face, noticed not only by Gaston on the night the murder was discovered but also by Kevin's fellow troopers, such as Deana Kirkland, only hours after the killing on the morning of April 13. Might John have scratched Kevin in a fight on the night of the murder? Could some of Kevin's DNA be under one of John's fingernails? If so, Kevin was probably going down for murder.

Meanwhile, a number of tales about the murder of John Yelenic had begun circulating within the criminal community, in Indiana as well as Pittsburgh, and generally among those in jail. As usual, these tales worked their way to the surface, from inmate to relative to snitch, and sooner or later came to the attention of Gardner and his team of investigators from Greensburg. Duty-bound to track these stories down, the investigators worked their way as far back as they could to the original sources. In one story, a former patient of Yelenic's claimed that he was present when the murder took place. In another, a well-known snitch claimed that three gang members from Pittsburgh had done the deed in a robbery gone wrong.

In addition, several Yelenic neighbors—all women— gave statements to the police, suggesting broadly if cattily that John and Melissa Uss had been having an affair, although one of them recanted later, allegedly out of concern about their status in the community if she testified to that effect. One woman claimed that she had seen the pair kissing. Another somewhat archly observed that the two had spent a lot of time together on John's front porch while Tom Uss was away. None of these women apparently knew that John and Melissa had been in high school together many years before, or that John had loaned the Usses $15,000 so Melissa could start a bakery, or that John had allowed Craig Uss to lift weights in his basement, or that John had lent Zachary Uss video games. Nor did they know that when the Yelenic divorce seemed imminent, John had asked Melissa to repay the bakery business loan, because the settlement required him to pay additional income taxes by April 15. That was why Melissa had given him the $14,000 check that had so aroused the initial suspicions of Bob Bell's investigators. Melissa had most of the money, just not the last $1,000. She later said she had told John she would pay him the rest as soon as she could, and John had said that was fine.

Gardner's investigators conducted all these interviews with snitches, neighborhood gossips, and felons alike, and dutifully filed reports of these conversations, which would eventually be turned over to Kevin's lawyers, providing grist for the defense theory that someone other than Kevin Foley had committed the horrible crime. This was, at least on paper, potential reasonable doubt.

Then, on September 11, 2007, the FBI's Conway forwarded her fingernail DNA analysis to Gardner. The examinations of the clippings from John's left hand showed that biological material found there had come from two different people, Conway said. Neither John nor Kevin could be excluded as a potential contributor of the DNA, based on comparisons of their DNA to the DNA found under the fingernails. Both of their DNA profiles could be included in the molecular analysis of the fingernail material. Still, the chance of a single Caucasian individual having the *overall* mixture of DNA found under the fingernail was 1 in 13,000, based on genetic frequency assumptions, or 1 in 46,000 among African-Americans. Kevin's DNA constituted only about 10 percent of the mixed sample, and while some segments matched Kevin's DNA, the rest of the sample was below the bureau's acceptable threshold of 50 RFU. That was why the number of possible matches was so large, at 1 in 13,000. (These were still exceedingly low numbers, a very far cry from the "million billion trillion" numbers often cited by Carl Sagan–ish DNA experts when testifying in court. Much higher numbers could be obtained if the FBI deducted Yelenic's profile from the analysis to only examine the minor donor, possibly Foley. But then, the amount of residual DNA was too undefined to be certain it belonged to

Kevin—consistent, yes; absolutely definitive, no, according to the FBI's standards.)

Based only on the residual DNA, after removing Yelenic's profile (after all, it was beyond question that the majority of material under the fingernails had to come from Yelenic himself, given that they were his fingernails to begin with), there could be thousands of people in Indiana County alone whose profile might fit the minor donor, as blurry as it was after the analysis. The finding that, statistically, there was 1 in 13,000 people who had a DNA profile that actually matched the combined genetic molecules found under Yelenic's fingernails seemed to undercut the FBI's assertion that there were *two* DNA donors. But the reality was, most of the fingernail DNA was entirely identical to Yelenic alone. And who was more likely to have DNA under his own fingernails, Yelenic, or some complete stranger, one of the supposed 1 in 13,000? How could Mr. X put his DNA under John's fingernails without John's DNA also being present? It was impossible.

The unexplained residue of the minor donor's DNA seemed to show conclusively that John had scratched some other person at some point—and since Yelenic had been a dentist who kept his hands immaculate for professional reasons, the residue had to have been acquired on the night of the murder. The minor donor residue was consistent with Kevin Foley having been present when the murder took place, even if it wasn't proof beyond a reasonable doubt.

One thing was sure, though: the FBI would never base a prosecution in federal court on such slim DNA findings alone. But the Yelenic murder was a state case. Federal standards did not necessarily apply. Krastek would soon try to find a way to focus on the minor donor, who, under the circumstances, he was sure was Kevin Foley.

Whether the DNA had deteriorated while in the Blairsville refrigerator for three months before being reclaimed by

Gonglik in early August of 2006—and if such deterioration had made it impossible to definitely include or exclude Kevin before it was sent by Gardner to Hochrein and from Hochrein to Quantico—was a moot question. It was what it was, however inexact, despite the hopes of Krastek.

Nevertheless, two weeks later the statewide grand jury investigating the Yelenic case brought a charge of first-degree murder against Kevin Foley, a "presentment," as the law in Pennsylvania termed it. The following day, Kevin was arrested at Pennsylvania State Police headquarters in Harrisburg, where he had been lured on a pretext, and taken to the Indiana County jail. The attorney general, Corbett, and his senior deputy, Krastek, had decided to roll the dice. They had nowhere else to go. It was either Foley or forget it.

"A Pennsylvania State Trooper was arrested today and charged with the 2006 murder of a prominent Indiana County dentist, John J. Yelenic," Corbett's office announced in a press release issued September 27. "It is extremely diffi-cult to have to arrest a member of the law enforcement com-munity, but as in any case, we follow the evidence wherever it leads," the release quoted Corbett. The case, Corbett said, would be jointly prosecuted by his office and Bell's office, thus giving the Indiana DA at least some political cover.

"State police worked side by side with the Attorney General's Office and the Indiana County District Attor-ney's Office in this investigation," the commissioner of the PSP, Jeffrey B. Miller, said. "It is a sad day for the Pennsyl-vania State Police when one of our members is arrested. But everyone, no matter what his or her position in society, must be held accountable for their actions."

IV.

The Trial
of Kevin Foley

19.

Kevin was held without bail in the same jail where he himself had booked so many suspects over the years: Indiana County Prison, as some county jails in Pennsylvania are archaically called. This had to be a shocking reversal of fortune for someone who had always seen himself as the good guy, the righter of wrongs to women and children—the one who locked people up instead of being locked up. Still, Kevin had to have known this was a distinct possibility, probably from the night of April 13, when he asked Jill Gaston who was "handling" the murder case of John Yelenic, and certainly from the time, several days later, when he was ordered to turn in his badge and gun and assigned to desk duty. Following his arrest, he was quickly in contact with a local lawyer, Thomas G. Johnson of Indiana, and a Greensburg attorney, Richard H. Galloway.

Galloway was a very prominent Pennsylvania trial attorney with more than forty years' experience in the commonwealth's courts. His retention by Foley was a signal that Kevin intended to fight the murder charge to the bitter end.

The first significant legal step after Kevin's arrest was the scheduling of a preliminary hearing to determine whether probable cause existed to believe that Kevin had committed the crime. This was first scheduled for early October but was postponed until the first week of November to give the defense time to prepare. A district judge, Guy Haberl, presided. Nine witnesses were called to testify, including Isherwood to describe the crime scene, Gonglik to identify the shoe print images, Wecht to detail the autopsy, Gaston to describe Foley's facial abrasions on the night of April 13, and several troopers to describe Foley's hatred of Yelenic and his penchant for flicking his knife. Gardner was called to summarize the investigation, including Foley's use of ASICS running shoes. Barbara Swasy told of her conversation with Kevin and Michele on the night of the fish fry, and her notification of Kevin and Michele of John's death on the afternoon of April 13.

At the end of the daylong hearing, Galloway said he had no evidence to offer to rebut the prosecution. But, he said, Judge Haberl should dismiss the complaint against Foley.

"I would ask that the charges against Kevin Foley be dismissed at this point in time for the failure of the Commonwealth to make out a prima facie case by competent evidence," Galloway said. "Let me point out some of the things that we don't have here. We don't have a knife, we don't have a fingerprint. We don't have an admission, we don't have any blood directly tied to Kevin Foley. We have a whole bunch of speculative testimony in the nature of the DNA."

The likelihood of anyone's DNA being included in a possible match was so broad, Galloway contended, that it was virtually worthless as evidence. Rather than the "billions and trillions" usually cited by the experts, the DNA found under the Yelenic fingernails was just a paltry 1 in 13,000. That meant any one of half a million people in Pennsylvania alone might have committed the crime, if one only used the DNA results.

"They took a year and better to investigate this case and called in the FBI and the crime lab and at least two and probably three law enforcement agencies and they haven't come forward with evidence that sufficiently ties Kevin Foley to this act to make it possible to hold it over for court, and accordingly, we would move to dismiss," Galloway argued.

On the contrary, Krastek responded, there was more than enough evidence to establish that a crime had taken place and that there was probable cause to believe that Kevin Foley was the person who committed it: the shoe prints matching the tread of shoes Kevin had been known to wear; his animosity toward John; his incessant, habitual knife flicking; his availability for the time period during which the killing had likely taken place, as shown by the two Sheetz videos—all were facts that pointed toward Foley. And the DNA—all the talk about "millions and billions," as Krastek put it, or even the much lower inclusion of 1 in 13,000—meant little, Krastek said.

"Those are just statistics, Your Honor," Krastek told Judge Haberl. "The fact of the matter is that we have all of this evidence that would suggest that Kevin Foley did this, and [then it was] 'Let's look under the fingernails of John Yelenic to see who he is telling us did this.' And it matches Kevin Foley. And if it didn't match Kevin Foley we are out of court. But it *did* match Kevin Foley. More likely than not a murder occurred, and a prima facie case [is] that Kevin Foley committed the murder."

Judge Haberl agreed with Krastek. "I do find that the commonwealth has met its burden, and this case is held for court and action in the Court of Common Pleas," he said, and with that, Kevin Foley was bound over for arraignment and trial. He would remain in jail for the foreseeable future. The case was set for trial in the court of William J. Martin, a judge of the commonwealth's Court of Common Pleas in Indiana County, akin to superior courts in most other states. Martin was a well-regarded judge, thought to be scrupulously fair and by no means anyone's tool, politics or no. In his mid-fifties, with a large, stolid, dignified presence, Martin was capable of staring down anyone, witnesses and lawyers alike, who veered outside the bounds of proper decorum. He'd grown up in Indiana and had served as Indiana County's district attorney prior to Bob Bell. He would keep the trial of Kevin Foley on track despite several attempted lurid digressions by the defense.

20.

By January of 2008, Galloway, his partner Dennis Rafferty, and Thomas Johnson had filed a motion asking that Judge Martin set a reasonable bail for Kevin, contending that Kevin's continued incarceration made it difficult for the defense to prepare for trial. At that point, Kevin had been in jail for more than three months. "It would substantially aid in the defense of the case if the defendant were able to participate in pre-trial discussion, strategy, planning, and investigation with defense counsel, and was not confined to a jail setting," the defense argued. Kevin was no threat to the community, and although he'd had ample opportunity to flee before his arrest, he hadn't done so. He had substantial ties to the community and "an impeccable record of employment" with the PSP. Under the law of the commonwealth, Kevin was entitled to release on his own recognizance: the evidence presented at the preliminary hearing was simply not compelling enough to warrant the no bail order.

Krastek and the commonwealth opposed the motion. The evidence presented at the preliminary hearing was sufficient to support a jury verdict of first-degree murder, Krastek contended, and because that was a crime for which a life sentence could be imposed, Pennsylvania case law permitted denial of bail.

Besides trying to get Kevin out of jail, the defense wanted something that was rarely if ever done in the commonwealth: the release of the transcripts of all testimony taken by the statewide investigative grand jury. Ordinarily, control of these transcripts belonged to the judge who supervised the grand jury—in this case Judge Feudale of Northumberland. However, Galloway and his team thought that Judge Martin had his own authority to order the transcripts released "in the interests of judicial economy," because it would save the defense considerable time in preparing for trial. Just because a judge supervising the investigative grand jury had "control" of the transcripts didn't mean that same judge could control them "in perpetuity," Galloway argued. He said Judge Martin could order the release of the transcripts because they had already been released to other parties—in the present case, to Krastek and his side. Once the transcripts had been delivered to Krastek, Galloway thought it was only fair that the defense get to see them too.

This was potentially vital for the defense. After all, Kevin's defense seemed to hinge on his major alibi witness: Michele. He'd said he reached Indiana and Susan Drive about 12:45 a.m. His story was that Michele could vouch for his whereabouts at the supposed time of the murder, forty-five minutes later, around 1:30 a.m., if the neighborhood ear-witnesses (excepting Isaiah Brader) had any validity. Michele, who had no spousal privilege protecting her from having to testify against Kevin, had been called as a witness before the grand jury. Surely she had been asked when Kevin had arrived home from the hockey game. If Galloway later put Michele on the witness stand to verify this alibi, and it turned out she had told the grand jury something entirely different, the case would blow up in Galloway's face. Sure, he knew what Michele had *said* she'd told the grand jury, but had she really? Would he bet Kevin's life on it? So Galloway needed to know conclusively what Michele had told the grand jury, which was why he wanted the transcripts.

Galloway argued that federal case law under *Brady v. Maryland*, which requires prosecutors to provide any exculpatory evidence to the defense, demanded that he get these transcripts, which had already been provided to Krastek.

No, Krastek said: the defense was in the wrong court. Under the law, only Judge Feudale could order the grand jury transcripts released to the defense. The defense would get the transcripts at the "appropriate time," meaning once a witness had testified during the trial. Because Krastek had no intention of calling Michele as a witness for the state—since she was Kevin's purported alibi, why would he?—that meant Galloway wouldn't be able to see what Michele had told the grand jury until after she testified for the defense—if she ever would now, with Krastek holding Michele's grand jury testimony behind his back as a potential cross-examination bombshell. Could Galloway take the risk of putting Michele on the witness stand in those uncertain circumstances? Probably not. The denial of the grand jury transcripts was a critical blow to the defense.

Judge Martin agreed with the prosecution. The transcripts were beyond his jurisdiction, Martin said.

Judge Martin also denied the defense motion asking for bail for Kevin.

In the meantime, Krastek had been doing some thinking about the problematic DNA, which had turned out to be a mere whiff of smoke, rather than the gun itself. He had been told that there were at least two DNA experts who might be able to make more sense of the minority donor's sample and possibly tie it more definitively to Kevin. Both of these scientists were in private practice as forensic consultants and not employed by the FBI. Therefore, their testimony might expand on the findings of Jerrilyn Conway. One was Dr. Robin Cotton, who had gained fame years before for her testimony in the trial of O. J. Simpson, at a time when DNA was just beginning to be widely used in criminal prosecutions. Cotton was an associate professor at Boston University's College of Medicine and director of the university's master's degree program in forensic science. The other expert was Dr. Mark Perlin, who had devised a controversial technique of computerized analysis of DNA fragments at his own privately held company, Cybergenetics of Pittsburgh, using a process that he declined to divulge as proprietary, but essentially employed a computer program based on statistical probabilities to narrow the field of possible DNA matches rather drastically. He had been retained by New York authorities to help identify the human remains from the World Trade Center terrorist attack of 2001: eighteen thousand biologically different samples from the three thousand victims, a DNA identification problem that obviously demanded outside-the-box thinking.

That spring, the FBI's DNA results were sent to both Cotton and Perlin for their own independent analysis. Essentially, both subtracted John's DNA profile from Conway's findings and then closely examined the remaining results, presumably the profile of the unknown minor DNA donor. Neither actually tested the combined DNA itself; instead, both employed mathematical methods of teasing out additional genetic indicators that theoretically brought the findings far closer to the one in "millions and billions" that the prosecutors wanted. These techniques were on the cutting edge of DNA science, and controversial. Neither expert's technique had as yet been accepted as scientifically valid by a court under the so-called Frye test, which held that scientific evidence had to be widely accepted as proven valid before it could be used in court, which was why Conway and the FBI did not use them. But then, Krastek's side had little to lose—unless the controversial methodologies wound up proving that Kevin *hadn't* done the crime. Given the rest of the circumstantial evidence, Krastek didn't think that was very likely.

So Krastek wanted a continuance in the trial date from the spring until at least the summer, to give the two scientists time to finish their work. Galloway, who wanted to know these results as much as Krastek, readily agreed to the continuance. Either the new methods would wind up identifying Kevin as one in the "millions and billions" range—in which case Galloway would attack them as bad science—or they would show by the "millions and billions" that the biological material had *not* come from Kevin—in which case he would embrace them with evangelical fervor and use them to ask that the murder charge be thrown out of court. An adept lawyer has to be flexible.

Then, in early April of 2008, the defense fired another arrow, hoping to derail or at least delay the prosecution: it wanted a change of venue. The trial could not be held in Indiana County, the defense contended, because of pervasive and prejudicial publicity against Kevin, for which the prosecution was primarily responsible. Galloway knew the political ambitions of Corbett and Bell as well as anyone else in Pennsylvania, and was already preparing the ground for a later claim that his client Kevin Foley was a sacrifice on the altar of Attorney General Corbett's gubernatorial ambition.

"The homicide engendered great publicity in the county of Indiana from the date it occurred to the present," the defense lawyers averred in their motion. "Said publicity was slanted, sensational, and inflammatory." A good part of the bad press, the defense said, stemmed from Kevin's "relationship with the victim's estranged wife." This almost seemed to suggest that in taking up with Michele Yelenic, Kevin was being unfairly persecuted by a moralistic prosecution, seconded by a salacious and hypocritical news media—the cuckolder as yet another victim.

After all the publicity that had erupted at the time of the murder, the defense argued, a further spate had taken place on September 27, 2007, with the announcement of Kevin's arrest. "The commonwealth convened and held a televised press conference in the Borough of Indiana . . . to announce the arrest of the defendant and to distribute to the print and electronic news media, who had been invited and gathered thereat, a press release, including . . . a grand jury presentment concerning the defendant, containing purported evidence, speculation, and inflammatory and prejudicial material . . ."

The press conference announcing Kevin's arrest had been attended by Corbett, Krastek, Bell, and "a host of other prosecution officials and officers. "Said press conference was carried on all Pittsburgh, Johnstown, and Altoona TV outlets. In addition, the same was covered by, and carried in the Pittsburgh and Greensburg *Tribune Review*, the Pittsburgh *Post Gazette*, the Indiana *Evening Gazette*, and the Blairsville *Dispatch*, which trumpeted 'Crime Solved' in its next edition."

Not only had the law enforcement community piled on with this sort of thing, the case had also generated substantial negative publicity toward Kevin as a result of Mary Ann's unusual lawsuit seeking to have John's divorce of Michele declared posthumously valid. "Said action resulted in extensive publicity in Indiana County and throughout western Pennsylvania, and generated substantial discussion and strong opinion in Indiana County."

Besides this, "police and prosecution officials" had "repeatedly released information to the news media concerning the case," including statements allegedly made by John and his lawyer, Effie Alexander, "all of which have additionally saturated the county of Indiana with slanted, prejudicial and inflammatory information."

The barrage of publicity, contended the defense, made it impossible to obtain an unbiased jury in Indiana County. The only fair solution, they said, was to move the trial somewhere else. To prove this, the defense had retained an expert to document the prejudice discernible in the news media coverage.

But this motion gained no traction with Judge Martin. In early June, the judge rejected it, in an order covering only a little more than a single page. The mere existence of publicity, Martin ruled, did not justify a change of venue. Before a court could establish prejudice against a defendant, there had to be at least an attempt to seat an unbiased jury. "There is not sufficient evidence before the court at this stage to support a change in venue," Martin concluded. But Martin said that he might be willing to reconsider if, when it came time to actually try to select a jury, it was obvious that prejudice against Kevin really existed.

By June of 2008, Drs. Cotton and Perlin had provided preliminary results from their mathematical analyses of the FBI's DNA tests. Perlin's secret process resulted in a finding that the minority donor included one in 677 billion possible genotypes, perhaps 10,000 times as many human beings than could possibly have existed—in total—since Neanderthal Man, 50,000 or so years ago. Cotton's report was much more conservative: she found that the minor donor's DNA was the same as 1 in 59 million—about one in four Americans—men, women, children, from Alaska to Apalachicola, Florida—which was still a lot of people. The vast disparity between the two outside-the-box opinions had to frighten Krastek: Who would believe either of them, as widely separated as they were? Galloway could use Perlin's findings to attack Cotton's credibility and Cotton's to attack Perlin's. And with such a wide variation in the experts' numbers, a jury was very likely to dismiss *all* DNA evidence as simply eggheaded poppycock. And waiting in the wings would be Galloway's cross-examination of the FBI's Conway, who would testify that the bureau routinely rejected findings that were under 50 RFU. The wisp of DNA smoke, which even Krastek had admitted was the main reason why the murder charge against Kevin had been brought, despite the circumstantial evidence, looked likely to blow away. The experts explained that there really wasn't much difference in the findings. It was only that each expert used different assumptions and methods, with Conway's being the most conservative and Perlin's the most radical, using an enhanced computer program to calculate rarities. But Krastek knew he would have his hands full trying to explain these apparent discrepancies to a jury of ordinary people who often had trouble balancing their checkbooks.

At that point, Galloway wanted his own continuance. He wanted a defense DNA expert to examine the findings of Cotton and Perlin.

21.

The trouble with the DNA numbers continued for Krastek throughout the summer of 2008 and into early 2009. In September, Dr. Perlin reiterated his finding that the minor donor of the DNA under John's fingernails matched only 1 in 677 billion human beings. Then, in a new report, Perlin said it was actually even rarer than that: one in 19 *trillion*. Good grief! There were fewer stars in the Milky Way!

By February of 2009, though, Dr. Cotton had revised her own assessment: she'd miscalculated by a factor of more than 2, she admitted: the match wasn't 1 in 59 million, it was really 1 in 23 million. The next day, Dr. Perlin revised his estimate too: the inclusion was 1 in 189 billion.

So here it was, the usual "million billion" cotillion—so many dancing numbers as to lose all meaning. Krastek might convince a judge that these were "just statistics," but a jury inured to disbelieving experts from incessant television advertising was highly likely to throw all the DNA testimony out as unreliable, even crazy.

In light of this statistical confusion, Kevin's defense team asked for and received several more trial continuances throughout the fall of 2008, to allow their own experts to attempt to make sense of the wildly vacillating numbers of the FBI's Conway and the independent experts, Drs. Cotton and Perlin. Galloway had the idea that his side could get the Cotton/Perlin ideas about the DNA thrown out as unscientific and unreliable, now that they had pinpointed Kevin as a possible donor. That was the role he envisioned for his own expert witness—someone who could say that Cotton's and Perlin's analyses were inflated baloney, not generally accepted within the scientific community.

As early 2009 arrived and the date for trial loomed, the defense also focused on trying to get rid of some of the other damning parts of the prosecution's case against Kevin. This, after all, was the role of any defense lawyer: to find legal ways to jettison so many bits and pieces of the prosecution case that it no longer held together. In some sense, an effective defense attorney has to climb into the mind of his or her client, take his or her brain as his own for a time, and then use every opportunity to debunk the case as if he or she *were* the client, only with finely honed skills of logic and oratory that are usually beyond the capacity of the accused. That's the way the American adversarial system of justice is meant to work. That's what you get—or should get—when you hire a competent criminal defense attorney.

First up for Galloway and his team were defense motions *in limine*—that is, efforts to cut down at the outset the evidence the prosecution wanted to present against Kevin—on arguments that were unacceptable hearsay or otherwise inadmissible. Many of these issues were on the admissibility borderline: some could come in, others had to be kept out. It depended on the arguments of each side and how the judge saw decisions in similar cases. But this is where most lawyers earn their paychecks, because these motions *in limine* have the potential of framing an entire trial and spelling the difference between winning and losing.

All these pretrial efforts to limit the evidence were the work of Galloway and his side. This was hardly unusual. In most criminal proceedings it's almost always the defense that wants to trim down the prosecution's case to the bare minimum: the less the prosecutor has as evidence, the better it is for the defense.

In January of 2009, with the trial finally set to begin in early March, Galloway filed an initial motion to limit the evidence to be proffered by the prosecution. A week or so later, he filed an amended motion after Judge Martin demanded more specific objections. Both of these *in limine* motions zeroed in on vulnerabilities the defense thought it saw in the prosecution's case.

After a hearing on February 19, Judge Martin agreed with the defense that the prosecution could not be allowed to ask Effie Alexander about John's supposed statements to her that he feared that he was going to be killed by Kevin, or that he had asked her to set aside $10,000 of his estate to investigate his death before it had even happened. This was surely hearsay, the judge agreed, and not permitted under Pennsylvania rules of evidence and case law. Krastek and his side agreed to not ask Alexander about these supposed statements from John: the hearsay from Alexander was clearly prejudicial to Kevin.

As to a related issue—whether Kevin had ever said "someone" should kill John—Judge Martin ruled this also out of order. Without specificity as to who the "someone" might be, this was prejudicial and untied to any provable facts beyond Kevin's possible state of mind, which could not be evidence. But as to any specific statements by Kevin himself that he wanted to kill John or "solicit others" to do the same, those were in. They were statements by a "party opponent," Kevin, and therefore against his penal interest, which, even if hearsay, made them fair game under the law allowing exceptions to the hearsay rule: statements allegedly made by the accused were *always* admissible against the accused. It would be the defense's prerogative to attack the credibility of the witnesses who might claim such statements had been made, but only after they were heard by a jury. Galloway appeared to agree that these supposed statements by Kevin were admissible as evidence while not admitting their truthfulness.

While the defense wanted all the shoe print identification evidence out, Martin wouldn't do it, at least right away. He said he'd rule on that one after experts—from ASICS, no less—provided more definitive testimony, one way or another. As for the gory photographs from the Yelenic living room and hallway, as well as Wecht's autopsy, all of them were admissible, Martin decided. Still, he agreed to give the jury an instruction not to let the horrible images inflame their passions.

Galloway also wanted the judge to restrict testimony from Kevin's fellow state troopers as to whether his personality had changed after John's murder. That did not mean those witnesses couldn't testify to specific observations and to their own feelings about those changes, if any, Martin decided. Any testimony about Kevin's habitual flicking of his knife—that was also in.

Martin knew as well as anyone that the most critical testimony against Kevin involved the DNA analyses—first Conway's, then Cotton's, then Perlin's. The defense had anchored itself on the FBI's generic findings of 1 in 13,000 Caucasians—certainly a small enough inclusion to encompass reasonable doubt, given the millions of Caucasians in Pennsylvania. Cotton's findings and, worse, Perlin's were far too specific for the defense to agree to their admission as viable evidence: with the numbers both Cotton and Perlin calculated, whether in the millions, billions, or trillions, the hint of gun smoke would suddenly seem thick enough to choke an elephant, however wispy they might be in reality. The defense had to get rid of Cotton and Perlin as mercenary purveyors of "junk science" if they had any chance of getting Kevin off the hook.

Realizing that this might be the whole ball game, Judge Martin took particular care with this DNA ruling. The issue was whether Dr. Cotton's and Dr. Perlin's techniques of mathematical analyses of the FBI's findings were acceptable evidence despite their cutting-edge methodologies. In another hearing both sides argued their points vociferously.

Then, on March 3, the day before jury selection was scheduled to start, Martin made his findings.

The defense had demanded that Cotton's and Perlin's findings be withheld from the jury under the Frye standard, which held that "novel" science had to be excluded unless it had gained wide acceptance within "the scientific community." After the hearing, and after perusing forty-five different scientific articles on Perlin's method—which, like Cotton's, involved subtracting John's DNA, then analyzing RFU results that fell below the FBI's standard of 50—Judge Martin found that Cotton's method met the Frye standard. Her findings could be presented to the jury.

As for Perlin's rather more extreme approach, the judge found that it was in use in the United Kingdom and that it had been used by the Allegheny County crime lab and the University of Pittsburgh; all three had validated Perlin's approach.

"Based upon a review of the evidence the court finds that Dr. Perlin's methodology is admissible pursuant to the Frye rule . . ." Judge Martin held.

Just before this, the defense delivered its proposed witness list to the prosecution, ninety-seven prospective witnesses altogether. Krastek was particularly intrigued by three names: Michele, Nicole, and Nathan Kamler. All three were Kevin's alibi witnesses for the night of April 13, 2006. If the three Kamlers stood up for Kevin—if they said he was home when the murder occurred—that might be reasonable doubt. That is, assuming they weren't lying. But then, Krastek had grand jury testimony to possibly impeach them with.

The trial opened on March 4 with jury selection. Foley sat quietly at the defense table neatly attired, the very picture of a young professional police officer. To look at him—a young father, well-known in the community for his volunteer work as a youth sports coach—one would hardly consider him capable of any murder, let alone one so barbarous. Tom Riley thought Kevin seemed very confident he would be found not guilty. There was absolutely no nervousness betrayed in his behavior, no fiddling with his hands or swift, darting looks around the courtroom. Through the entire trial he would seem almost preternaturally calm.

On the following Monday, March 9, after preliminary instructions from the judge, Krastek gave a summary of the case the state expected to prove against Kevin Foley.

Most murder cases, Krastek said, weren't at all like those shown on television, with lots of scientific evidence that proved who did it, usually within an hour. But this one was an exception to that rule: this time, science *would* prove who did it, he said.

To that end, the prosecution had arranged for four flat-screen television monitors, two for the jury, one for the judge and witnesses, and one for the public. Krastek intended to use the monitors to link all the parts of the case in a visual, even interactive way: photos, videos, maps, documents—all would appear on the four screens simultaneously at the click of a mouse as the presentation moved forward during the trial. The means of presentation Krastek would employ actually reinforced the subliminal message: this case was high-tech, science in pursuit of the guilty.

"In a way, as jurors, you are also detectives here, trying to determine what happened," Krastek said. "And through photographic evidence, through documentary evidence, through science, you will be able to . . . re-create what happened here, and not just what happened, but who did it."

Krastek now set the scene of the night of April 13, 2006: John Yelenic lying on his living room sofa with the television on, thinking of his divorce from Michele, which was to become final the following day when he signed the papers in front of a notary.

"He had married Michele Yelenic, his wife, back in 1997. They had adopted a child, Jamie, from Russia. But the marriage soured. And they separated and then things got in fact nasty. This was in no way an amicable divorce. There were questions of custody. There were allegations raised that Dr. Yelenic even perhaps molested his young son. Allegations which at every step were found to be unfounded, and allegations that were raised by Michele Yelenic with the help of Kevin Foley, who was living with Michele Yelenic."

This was a necessary move by Krastek, to be the first to raise the molestation allegations, and he did it rather deftly by tying it to the defendant, Kevin. Keeping quiet about them would have given the defense a chance to shock the jury and diminish sympathy for the victim, John.

Krastek continued with the scene of April 13. "Dr. Yelenic is there, and those papers with little tabs on them to be signed, just watching television or sleeping. And someone comes in that back door, one or one-thirty in the morning, and confronts him, or awakens him . . . [I]t's not certain what happened exactly but at one point you will see from the evidence, the assailant and Dr. Yelenic were in that living room and they were facing each other. And the assailant, you will learn, had some kind of knife or knife-like instrument, and began slashing Dr. Yelenic."

Krastek went on to describe the numerous wounds suffered by John in the attack.

"You will also see from this evidence that after he was slashed, at some point in time, Dr. Yelenic tried to run to the front door. Slash marks, you will see on his back, the assailant still trying to kill him. You will see evidence that Dr. Yelenic got to the front door, but it was locked. The bolt was there and he couldn't open that front door. You will see that his head gets pushed through a side window to that door. In doing so, the glass pops out, but two shards of glass remain, two triangular pieces of glass remain, and his neck was caught there.

"You will hear from neighbors, who put that time around one-fifteen or one-thirty, and hear bloodcurdling screams, hear a male voice yelling, enough to wake them up and set dogs barking . . ."

Krastek briefly summarized the findings from Dr. Wecht's autopsy. "You will see the cause of death was loss of blood. You will see where he died and how he died. You will also see the beginning of the evidence which will let you know who killed him . . ."

There were bloody shoe prints; because John was barefoot, these had to have come from the killer, Krastek said. And the prints matched the sort of shoes worn by Kevin Foley. The jury would hear from Kevin's colleagues in the state police that he hated Yelenic "and wanted him dead, wanted him to die in a car crash."

At that point Galloway interrupted and asked for a sidebar conference with the judge, out of the earshot of the jury. He thought Krastek had just violated the judge's edict on not referencing Kevin's wish that "someone" would kill Yelenic.

"I move for a mistrial," Galloway said. When a defense lawyer moves for a mistrial early in a prosecutor's opening statement, it's usually a sign that the defense is weak and is already trying to establish grounds for an appeal.

"Statements that he wants this guy dead are clearly relevant and are not within the court's [previous] ruling, as I understand it," Krastek said.

"I agree," Judge Martin said, "and I will overrule the objection, and motion for mistrial is denied."

Krastek resumed describing Kevin's antipathy for John.

"You will hear not only did he have the ill will and the motive, the reason to kill Doctor Yelenic, but you will also hear how he had he had the opportunity." The jury would see videos of a "vehicle very much like Kevin Foley's burgundy Ford Explorer" passing the two Sheetz stores before and after the approximate time of the murder.

"Heck, he had enough time to drive back to Indiana, where he lived with Michele Yelenic, and still get back to Blairsville . . . [H]e had plenty of time to be there in Blairsville, and was heading in that direction and was driving by, in fact you will learn, around the time that the murder occurred."

The jury would hear that in a struggle, John had scratched his attacker, which left some of the assailant's DNA under his fingernails.

"It matches Kevin Foley," Krastek said. "That DNA profile matches Kevin Foley, the man that said he wanted Doctor Yelenic dead, the man who was driving by that day, and the man with the size ten ASICS shoes."

That prompted a request for a sidebar conference from Galloway.

"In no report that I have seen," Galloway told Judge Martin, "does it say that the DNA 'matches' Kevin Foley. It gives certain rates, one in thirteen thousand, one in one trillion, et cetera. But no one says that it 'matches' Kevin Foley, and there is a huge difference between saying there are some statistics that are going to be offered . . . and saying that it 'matches' him, and that is a misstatement to the jury, and I move for a mistrial."

Krastek countered that the profile did indeed "match" Kevin Foley. He did not add, however, that it just did not match perfectly. That which was there "matched," but not all of it was there, because there just wasn't enough of it.

The prosecution knew that the experts weren't going to use the word "match," Galloway persisted. "They don't use that term at all. That leaves the jury with a conclusion that is unfounded." Krastek's remark "totally misstates the evidence," he said.

No it didn't, Krastek insisted.

Yes it did, Galloway said.

"All right," said Judge Martin. "Well, the word 'match' is not a scientific term." He said he would deny Galloway's second motion for a mistrial—this in the first half hour of the proceeding—but instruct the jury that they could judge for themselves whether the word "match" applied after hearing from the DNA experts "and give it the weight that they think it deserves."

"Okay," Galloway said, apparently unmollified, "the court has ruled."

Krastek resumed trying to summarize the case, touching on the injury to Kevin's face and the timing of the attack, roughly coincident with, first, the loud screams in the night and then the video taken at the Blairsville Sheetz.

"It will speak volumes," he ended, "and by the conclusion of this case you will see that Kevin Foley had the motive, the opportunity and the ability to commit this crime to the exclusion of anybody else . . . that the man who talked over and over again about how much he wanted Doctor Yelenic dead is the one who caused his death."

Now it was Galloway's turn. In the months leading up to the trial, Galloway had ended his partnership with Dennis Rafferty and formed a new one with his daughter and son-in-law, Jeffrey Monzo. Galloway had Monzo deliver the defense's opening statement to the jury.

"Ladies and gentlemen of the jury," Monzo began, "you will learn that this case is about the commonwealth leaping, jumping, to a conclusion that Kevin Foley killed John Yelenic, and the commonwealth's desperate attempt to build a case toward that conclusion. Ladies and gentlemen, the evidence will show they leaped to the wrong conclusion. The evidence will show that Kevin Foley did *not* kill John Yelenic."

This was pretty strong stuff, claiming that the evidence would prove the exact opposite of what the prosecution contended it did. It wasn't just that the commonwealth couldn't prove that Kevin did the crime "beyond a reasonable doubt" because the evidence was insufficient—surely a safer assertion for any defense—but that the evidence would prove he couldn't possibly have done it.

There were two reasons why the commonwealth was so desperate, Monzo went on. One reason was because Kevin had been living with Michele and therefore it was "real easy" to say "the boyfriend of the victim's ex-wife" was responsible for the crime. The second reason was George Emigh.

"He has been forced to retire from the Pennsylvania State Police but you will learn how desperate he was to point the finger at Kevin Foley, because of differences that he had with Kevin. You will learn that on April 13, 2006 . . . George Emigh was the first person to point the finger, and when he did, he specifically stated, Kevin Foley was dating his [*sic*] ex-wife, and those were his words." Hopefully Monzo's unfortunate syntax did not leave the jury confused as to whose ex-wife Foley was dating, John's or Emigh's.

Monzo sketched in Kevin's background: his age, then forty-three, "a very proud father of his adopted three-year-old"; a man who served his country in the U.S. Army; and someone who has "dedicated his life since 1994 to serving the citizens of this state as a member of the Pennsylvania State Police." Kevin was a youth soccer coach, a Little League baseball coach, and a youth hockey coach, all in all a stalwart, worthy fellow.

On April 13, Monzo continued, Kevin "drove directly home to his home in Indiana County . . . and got home about 12:45. The next day he was at work . . . at eight o'clock in the morning." They would see evidence presented on the four television monitors that didn't necessarily mean what the commonwealth contended it meant.

"And let me just talk about these television screens," Monzo continued. "These television screens are an example of the commonwealth continuing to try and build a case against Kevin Foley . . . [T]hese are the commonwealth's television screens. They are here to inflame you against Kevin Foley." They would be used to show "gruesome photographs" and "the purpose of all that is to inflame you against Kevin."

Kevin was innocent, Monzo reiterated. "How will you learn that?"

For one thing, Monzo said, the scene at 233 South Spring Street "was in fact very bloody . . . [Y]ou're going to be able to conclude from that evidence that whoever killed John Yelenic had contact with that blood. Guess what? You will learn that no blood was ever traced to Kevin Foley . . . there was no blood on any pair of shoes owned by Kevin Foley. No blood in the SUV you heard about.

"No weapon . . . you will hear that no weapon and no knife was ever traced to Kevin Foley, and not without trying." Just the mere fact that Kevin had possession of a knife was hardly unusual among state troopers, Monzo said.

More than that, he went on, the jury would hear "that in the commonwealth's desperate attempt to build a case against Kevin Foley they ignored and did not pursue several other suspects." And they would hear from one witness who would put the time of the crime much later than the commonwealth contended—as long as two hours later—when the witness heard two men arguing loudly, and the shout, "I will never loan you money again!"

"John Yelenic never loaned Kevin Foley any money, ever, but you will learn about some other suspects that John Yelenic did loan money to. Other suspect Number One you will learn about, Thomas Uss. You will learn that the Uss family lived right next door . . . You are going to learn a lot about why Thomas Uss had the motive to kill John Yelenic and why it fits that he did."

Jurors would hear neighbors testify that when Tom Uss was away, his wife Melissa "hung out with John Yelenic." They would hear that John had loaned the Uss family $15,000, that John had asked to be repaid, "and it wasn't at the time of his death." Here Monzo was skating on thin ice, insinuating an improper relationship between John and Melissa, and almost falling in with the assertion that the money had not been paid back at the time of John's death, when he knew full well that a check for $14,000 had been found in the murdered man's living room. Still Monzo plunged on, trying to erect the some-other-dude-did-it defense, wryly known as SODDI among criminal defense attorneys.

Tom Uss was seen mowing John Yelenic's backyard grass as well as his own a few days after the murder. That was unusual, Monzo told the jury: "Thomas Uss never cut his grass, hardly ever." If there was evidence in the grass, Monzo suggested, Tom Uss could have used the grass cutting as an excuse to pick it up and get rid of it.

"Suspect Number Two," Monzo went on. "Tracy Jacobs." Jacobs, Monzo said, had borrowed $20,000 or so from John. When police first questioned him, Monzo said, he had denied borrowing money from John, but then later admitted it.

"Suspect Number Three, a man by the name of Brian Ray, who knew John Yelenic, was a patient of John Yelenic back in the earlier part of this decade, who admitted, while in Westmoreland County Prison, because you will learn that Brian Ray is a thief, is a drug user [who, in the spring of 2006 was committing burglaries in the Indiana County area] . . . months after the killing, admitted to his involvement. But not only did he admit his involvement, but he knew specific details about where in fact the killing had occurred, and that the killer had exited the back door." At the time, Monzo said, Ray's mother had noticed that he had recently been in a fight.

Besides Uss, Jacobs, and Ray, the police also "ignored information that they received from Blairsville [Police] by a gentleman named Scott," who had told a woman acquaintance that he knew of three men who had bragged of killing Yelenic, and that when they had made this boast, they were wearing clothes covered with blood. The PSP had ignored that lead, Monzo said.

"So instead of pursuing those suspects they continued to try to build a case, and [they said], 'Well, Kevin Foley had ill will toward John Yelenic.' The evidence will show that you should not confuse a dislike with a motive.

"You will learn that Kevin Foley had hardly ever seen John Yelenic and that the last time he saw John Yelenic was in November of 2005, five months before the killing."

Whatever Krastek said about the contentiousness of the Yelenic divorce, Monzo said, all that had been resolved by April 13.

Despite all the broken glass at the Yelenic house, there was no evidence that Kevin had been cut by any of it. As for the shoe prints, the evidence would prove that the shoes could not be "connected to Kevin Foley." As for the videos, not even the FBI could definitely say that the vehicle recorded by the Sheetz cameras was Kevin's Explorer.

And the DNA—when the commonwealth's Krastek said it "matched" Kevin, that was not exactly true. It was only that the DNA experts could not conclusively eliminate Kevin as the minor donor. And even the experts disagreed as the probabilities that the DNA came from Kevin, with numbers all over the universe.

"On cross-examination you will see that this piece of evidence demonstrates how desperate the commonwealth is. Six different numbers for the same data will show you just how inherently unreliable this evidence is . . . [T]he evidence will point you to the right conclusion. Kevin Foley is not guilty of killing John Yelenic. Kevin Foley is innocent."

And with that, Monzo sat down, and Krastek called the case's first witness, Craig Uss.

22.

Craig was now twenty years old, and a student at IUP, Indiana University of Pennsylvania. Krastek wanted Craig to set the scene for the discovery of John's body on the afternoon of April 13. But first he wanted to delve into the relationship between John and Craig, to defuse any insinuations the defense might make that there was anything untoward in their friendship while Craig had been a teenager. Krastek had read the reports of Bell's investigators, too, and was well aware that Galloway and Monzo would use this uninformed innuendo to add more weight to the argument that Tom Uss could have perpetrated the murder.

"And can you just explain briefly what your relationship was with him?" Krastek asked.

"When John moved there," Craig said, quite matter-of-factly, "he had a stepson Nathan. We became friends and every weekend, or every other weekend, Nathan would come, and I would come over and play with Nathan, and that is how our relationship grew. Over time I would just go over to hang out with John just to watch TV with him and hang out and he helped me with my homework, and I used his home gym in the basement to work out every day. And that is basically my relationship with John."

John usually left his back door open so Craig could use the weights in the basement when he wasn't home. He saw John frequently, usually every other day or so.

Under questioning by Krastek, Craig described the discovery of John's body on the afternoon of April 13.

"I unlocked it and I went in and took a couple of steps in and just to see if he was okay and if he was not. And I saw that he wasn't so I went over, back to my house, called my grandpa to come over and when he came over we called the police and the ambulance and all of that to come."

He tried to avoid stepping in all the blood he saw in the entry foyer, Craig said. "When I first opened up the door, I saw a lot of blood and I tried to avoid the blood and I tried to go where the blood wasn't and I just went about to, right where the cloth is right on the picture." He indicated a point on a photograph of the scene that Krastek had displayed on the monitors.

In his cross-examination, Galloway had Craig acknowledge that he'd told investigators later on April 13 that his dog had begun barking between 2:00 and 3:00 a.m., because of some disturbance outside. This was an effort to bolster Isaiah Brader's forthcoming testimony for the defense about the disturbance he had heard, an hour or so after the time that the prosecution said the murder had occurred.

Then Galloway asked Craig about his shoes.

"What size do you wear now?"

"I wear a ten and a half."

Galloway was trying to suggest that it might have been Craig's shoes that made the bloody shoe prints photographed by Gonglik. But Galloway did not ask what type of shoe Craig was wearing, whether it was an ASICS or even a running shoe, probably because he knew the answer wouldn't help his case.

On his redirect examination, Krastek returned to the relationship between Craig and John.

"And just to address some of the innuendo out there, what was your relationship with Dr. Yelenic?"

"He was a very close friend."

"Okay. And as far as you know, what was your parents', what was their relationship with Dr. Yelenic?"

"They were the same, very close friends."

Krastek next called former Blairsville patrol officer Donald Isherwood, who described his actions after reaching the scene. Galloway's main cross-examination was intended to direct the jury's attention to the fact that Isherwood hadn't taken the names of different people who had been on the porch when he arrived, the implication being that some of them might have been inside the house and therefore left bloody shoe prints. This was part of the defense's rush-to-judgment theme: a thorough investigation would have recorded all these names, Galloway's questions implied.

Krastek now called Paula Ernst, a "visual information specialist" for the FBI. Ernst had been with the bureau for eleven years. Before that, she had been a specialist in accident reconstruction. She held a degree in mechanical engineering. It was her job to document crime scenes, supervise digital mapping, and preparation of documents for trial exhibits. She had worked on the shootings at Columbine High School and the 9/11 airliner attack at the Pentagon. Among her specialties was the creation of three-dimensional representations of crime scenes, which permitted the viewer to see the scene from virtually any angle and greatly assisted a crime's reconstruction. She and another FBI specialist, Susan Brown, had prepared such a three-dimensional view of the Yelenic house with the help of FBI special Agent Hochrein, and then overseen its incorporation into the extensive multimedia exhibit Krastek was displaying on the monitors.

After Ernst explained the process of preparing the three-dimensional exhibit, Krastek had his trial assistant, operating a computer that controlled the display, click on various places within the view, including the locations of the shoe prints. In a way, this told a far more intelligible story than simply showing the jurors flat still photographs of bloody shoe prints. One could move around the representation of the house, see it from any perspective, and actually view the print trail in its entirety, including their direction toward the rear door. The rest of the exhibit included various documents from the divorce and the videos from the Sheetz stores, represented by icons on an aerial view that could be activated by a mouse click. An animated aerial view of the neighborhood showed the direction of the vehicle past the Blairsville Sheetz. The overall effect was to provide an almost movie-like presentation of the entire crime in real time. Altogether, about forty-four separate still photographs or documents were also embedded in the presentation, each of which could be accessed by a mouse click on its own screen icon.

On his cross-examination, Galloway zeroed in on the icon, which, when clicked, represented the track of the moving vehicle as observed by the Blairsville Sheetz video camera. Ernst acknowledged that the information of the SUV's path had been provided to her, along with its apparent rate of speed and the timing. Galloway suggested that the FBI's own analysis of the Blairsville Sheetz video could not positively identify it as Kevin's Explorer and, therefore, including it in the multimedia exhibit was improperly prejudicial.

"I would just relate what was provided to me to show where it is located on the diagram," Ernst said.

"Not necessarily that it's a matching car or has relevance to this proceeding and et cetera?" Galloway asked.

"No, that is irrelevant to my diagram."

"So Mr. Krastek said or somebody—was it Mr. Krastek?"

"It was either him or Corporal Gardner."

"And said they needed something that showed a car moving at the same rate as that video?"

"Correct."

Galloway thus buttressed the defense theme of rush to judgment camouflaged by high-tech legerdemain. In other words, GIGO: garbage in, garbage out, in the techies' own phrase.

Krastek then asked that the multimedia presentation be placed into evidence. He intended to use it in his later examination of witnesses like Gonglik and Gardner.

Galloway objected. He said he wasn't sure, but there might be portions of the presentation that were inadmissible. The problem was, with the presentation all mixed together, it might be difficult, even impossible, to segregate the admissible from the inadmissible, the Sheetz video and related animation being a case in point. If the judge ruled the Sheetz video out as unreliable and prejudicial, it would be too late if the whole thing had already come in.

One possibility was to run through all the portions of the presentation then and there and have the judge rule on each component before proceeding with further witnesses. That wasn't anything Krastek wanted to contemplate: it would throw off his whole plan for presenting his case.

As far as he was concerned, he'd established the "authenticity" of the presentation, and if Galloway had any doubts, he should ask Ernst.

Galloway asked Ernst if she had any idea of how much it cost the FBI to produce the mixed-media presentation. Ernst said she did not. Galloway asked her if she could estimate how many hours were spent by the bureau in preparing it.

Ernst said she'd received the underlying data from Hochrein and the others in October of 2007, just after Kevin had been arrested. From that point forward, her section had worked on it an average of "a good twenty hours a week" into February of 2008.

"So twenty hours a week from October, November, December, January, February, five months?"

That was correct, Ernst said.

Galloway asked Ernst how much she and her assistant earned per hour. Her pay was about $50 an hour, while her assistant was about $35 an hour, Ernst said. Her assistant had come on board in July of 2008, and after that, the presentation had been worked on another twenty hours a week or so until two weeks before the trial—altogether, another eight months.

"So if we wanted to calculate what it cost, we could simply multiply those numbers for that period of time and get at least a rough approximation of the cost of producing it?"

"It would be a rough approximation, yes."

"And that couldn't include the cost, for example, [of] Agent Hochrein going out to do the measuring of the site?"

"No. His time would be independent of ours."

"And do you know how long it took him to do that?"

"No, I don't."

Galloway didn't stop to calculate the rough estimate of the cost, but he had certainly planted the idea in the jurors' minds: thirteen months—say, fifty-six weeks—at twenty hours a week, times an average salary of, say, $40 an hour . . . The cost of the presentation came to around $44,000. And this did not include Hochrein's time spent measuring the house. Here again the defense was bolstering its argument that the prosecution was intent on using electronic razzle-dazzle to stampede the jury, and would pay whatever it cost.

Galloway said he was satisfied with the "authenticity" of the presentation but reserved the right to object to certain portions of it "from time to time." Apparently, Galloway was relying on the judge to later instruct the jury on which portions of the presentation were evidence and which should be ignored. Krastek agreed with this procedure, and the presentation was admitted, at least provisionally.

Krastek now called Trooper Gonglik to establish his crime scene photographs.

Gonglik's testimony was as tedious as it was gory, establishing as it did the location of the body, the blood splashes, and the bloody shoe prints. Krastek used Gonglik to essentially "host" the virtual tour of the house prepared by Ernst, having him describe the various rooms and the evidence, buttressed by his still photographs, which would pop up on the monitors as required. Galloway renewed his objection to some of the photographs as being unnecessarily graphic, which he contended was prejudicial to any defendant, a standard tactic by most defense lawyers when confronting gory pictures. Another problem with presenting the photographs as part of the mixed-media presentation, he said, was that the record did not reflect which "button" or "hot spot" on the display Krastek was referring to when he triggered each picture. That might be important to an appeals court, he said.

All of this led up to Gonglik's taking possession of the fingernail clippings from Wecht at the autopsy and then getting them back more than three months later.

There wasn't much Galloway could do with this testimony; the photographs spoke for themselves. But in his cross-examination, he was able to make the point that Gonglik's crime investigation unit's procedures for safeguarding evidence were rather more sophisticated than those employed by the Blairsville Police Department, and that Gonglik had no way of knowing what had happened to the items, including the fingernails, once Blairsville's Brant had taken possession of them on April 17, four days after the murder was discovered. Gonglik did not see the items again until about August 1, 2006. All that time they had been in the custody of the Blairsville police. Because Galloway believed that John's two hands had not been bagged at the scene or subsequently preserved in a secure location at Blairsville, he suggested by his questions that it was possible that the material found under the nails might have become contaminated by someone else's DNA after the murder. After all, the minor portion of DNA that had been found partially matched an awful lot of people, at least 1 in every 13,000, according to the FBI. To that end, Gonglik's testimony was something of a wash—he just didn't know.

The following day, Dr. Wecht was the first witness called. Judge Martin warned the jurors that photographs to be presented by the prosecution would be unpleasant to look at. The jurors would have to put aside any feelings that the photographs might engender and try not to judge the facts of the case emotionally. He ordered the monitor facing the public section of the courtroom turned off, to spare the trial spectators the unpleasantness.

Krastek spent the better part of an hour leading Wecht through his autopsy, cataloguing the numerous knife wounds to Yelenic's body, which Wecht said had been made in frequent slashing motions, along with the wounds to the victim's neck from the broken glass. There was little Galloway could do with this testimony, either; again the photographs spoke for themselves. The best he could manage was to suggest, through his questions of Wecht, that the nature of the wounds might be consistent with more than one assailant. Wecht was on the witness stand for more than two hours, and at times, one or more of the gruesome pictures from the autopsy were up on the screens for many minutes. That prompted an outside-the-presence-of-the-jury objection by Galloway, who contended that the long displays of the bloody wounds was prejudicial. Judge Martin denied the objection, finding that Wecht was on the stand the entire time the pictures were displayed. Galloway marked this down as perhaps another appellate issue.

After Wecht, Krastek called Deputy Coroner Conrad and Blairsville police officer Jill Gaston to tell of their notification of Michele and Kevin of John's death on the night of

April 13. On cross-examination by Monzo, Conrad said that John's hands had been bagged, contrary to Galloway's suggestion the day before. Conrad also said he did not see any injuries to Kevin's face that night.

Gaston, however, was clear about the injuries.

"During this time did you have a chance to look at Kevin Foley's face?" Krastek asked.

"Yes."

"And what, if anything unusual, did you see on his face?"

"He had a mark above his left eye, above the eyebrow."

"And would you describe that mark?"

"It was about one to two inches, I am going to say closer to one inch, gash, cut above the left eye."

"Okay. And did it have a shape to it?"

"Kind of like a half-moon."

"Okay. And just that one?"

"There was a very tiny scratch under the left eye."

"And being a police officer since '99, could you tell us how fresh that mark was above his—"

Galloway objected. In a sidebar, he complained that there was no way to tell what "fresh" might mean to Gaston. Krastek's term was too inexact to be meaningful. Did Krastek mean an hour old or a week old? Although the point was fairly critical, Gaston's answer could mean anything. Besides, Gaston was hardly an expert in how fast wounds healed.

Krastek said he was just asking for a lay opinion, what an average person might observe. Judge Martin said he would allow the question if Krastek could establish that Gaston had experience in seeing wounds heal. Yes, she did, Gaston said. Krastek asked her to describe the mark again.

"It was red, swollen. It appeared to be fresh. It had no scab."

Krastek asked what she meant by "fresh."

"That it happened recently."

What did she mean by "recently"?

"That day," Gaston said.

Under cross-examination by Galloway, Gaston acknowledged that she knew, from talk among police officers at the Spring Street house before the notification, that Kevin was a likely suspect in the murder. But when Galloway tried to suggest she knew this from Kevin's nemesis, George Emigh, Gaston denied it. She hadn't talked to Emigh at all that day, she said. She had never been told that Emigh had named Kevin as the most likely suspect.

On redirect, Krastek asked if Kevin had said anything as he noticed her looking at his face.

"He made a remark about hockey," Gaston said.

On recross, Galloway badgered Gaston about her testimony. Wasn't it true that at the preliminary hearing, she'd said the injury was above Kevin's right eye, not his left? Hadn't she said both left and right eyes at different times? Hadn't she described the injury as an oval, not a half moon? Didn't her written report, filed the day after the notification, and including a diagram of the injury drawn shortly thereafter by Gaston, seem to contradict her testimony at the preliminary hearing? Hadn't she taken an oath to tell the truth? Did she think the court reporter had taken her words down wrong?

She hadn't had her notes with her when she testified at the preliminary hearing, Gaston said. Galloway's treatment of Gaston on the stand was harsh, probably harsher than necessary. Gaston came across as simply a police officer trying to do her best.

Galloway may have believed that he had impeached Gaston's testimony about Kevin's facial injury—after all, Conrad had just testified that he'd seen no injury—but Krastek wasn't worried. He had several state troopers lined up to testify that they, too, had seen an injury on Kevin's face the day after the murder.

*   *   *

Following Conrad and Gaston, Krastek called a number of witnesses who lived on South Spring Street near the Yelenic house to testify to what they had heard in the early morning of April 13. All recalled the screaming, breaking glass, and the barking dogs around 1:30 a.m.

"I just remember waking up with some ungodly scream and then an argument, is what I woke up to," said Harold German Jr., who at the time lived down the street from the Yelenic house.

"I heard what I thought was a screaming and that is when I did get up out of bed and proceeded to look out of a couple of our windows, and I didn't see anything," said James Ferguson, another neighbor.

"It was loud screams," said Maria Alexander, another neighbor. "We have always known it to be quiet and safe, very silent, so a noise like that outside would definitely awaken somebody, especially that loud of a scream. And then the second time, I heard another scream, about, I am going to say, maybe five minutes after, after I was starting to doze off again, and it set me up to the point where I turned to my husband and I said that frightened me, that scream frightened me." The screamer was definitely male, Mrs. Alexander said. "Definitely male. I knew all the time it was a male scream. I couldn't get, I wouldn't call it an old yell, but male and curdling, a curdling scream."

Vincent Ugoletti said he had awakened to hear two loud male voices arguing, also at about 1:30 in the morning. He wasn't sure what it was all about.

But after the ruckus, all went back to sleep.

Galloway and Monzo tried to punch holes in this testimony, first by trying to question the time frame: they wanted to push the time of the disturbance ahead to about 3:00 a.m. rather than 1:30 in order to support Brader's upcoming testimony about the squabble he'd heard at about 3:00. That in turn would backstop Brader's recollection that he'd heard one man say to another, "I'll never loan you money again," all in support of the some-other-dude-did-it defense. But several of the neighbors said they'd looked at their clocks at the time of the screaming and it was about 1:30, not 3:00.

For his final witness for the day, Krastek called Robert Worcester, a Pennsylvania state trooper who worked with Kevin. Worcester would be the first in a long string of state troopers, thirteen in all, some of them Kevin's closest friends. This was the result of Gardner's unit's interviews with Kevin's colleagues, and they didn't paint a pretty portrait of Kevin.

23.

Worcester had been a Pennsylvania state trooper for eighteen years. He'd been assigned to the Indiana barracks for almost fourteen years, the last two in criminal investigations. Before that, he'd been in the patrol division. He'd been friends with Kevin, Worcester said, sharing activities like basketball, softball, hockey, and golf. As a hockey player, Worcester said, Kevin was enthusiastic "but not too good—sorry." Kevin was just a bit too unsteady on his skates, Worcester said, apologizing to Kevin for his frank opinion.

Krastek wasn't really interested in Worcester's evaluation of Kevin's athletic ability. Worcester had been at the hockey game the night of April 12 at the arena in Delmont. Krastek wanted Worcester to say whether Kevin had been injured in that game and whether he had a facial cut when he left the arena.

No, Worcester said. Had he seen Kevin change out of his hockey uniform into street clothes after the game? He had, Worcester said. (Kevin had said he had not.) Kevin had left the ice rink around midnight.

The next morning Worcester had seen Kevin at the Indiana barracks.

"He had a scratch," Worcester said.

* * *

The next day of the trial, Krastek called a dozen PSP troopers as witnesses, some of whom, like Worcester, had known Kevin for years. The first was Deana Kirkland.

In an in-chambers conference before Kirkland's testimony began, Krastek said he wanted her to testify about the molestation allegations that had resulted in the two investigations of John Yelenic. Krastek wanted to show, first, that these investigations had been instigated by Foley, and second, that they were unfounded. This all went to establish Kevin's motive for killing John, Krastek said. He said he would make sure to avoid any reference to the two lie detector tests John had passed, even though these were the main reasons why Kirkland had stopped the investigations.

"Basically, for that reason, is why the charges were never filed," Krastek said. "Additionally, they attempted to polygraph Michele Yelenic, and she refused to do that." He only wanted Deana Kirkland to testify that she had stopped her investigations of the molestation allegations, and that she had good reasons for doing that. But if the defense pressed Kirkland on this issue, he would ask her about the lie detector tests. Although the results of the polygraphs were inadmissible, the fact that John had taken them might be, if it explained Kirkland's subsequent actions. He thought the prosecution should be entitled to do that, if the defense suggested that Kirkland had made the wrong decision.

Well, Galloway said, he certainly didn't want the jury to hear about any polygraph tests taken by John Yelenic—or *not* taken by Michele. In Galloway's assessment, that would only make Kevin look like a lunatic for continuing to believe in Michele's assertions. The whole idea that John was truthful and Michele was "dodgy," as Galloway put it to Judge Martin, gave him the willies. If testimony was produced to suggest *that*, he would move for a mistrial—again. Lie detector tests were simply unreliable, Galloway continued, and the jurors might infer from their very mention that John was honest and Michele was a liar, and that could hardly help his defense of Kevin.

Judge Martin agreed that any testimony about the polygraphs was out of bounds, but Kirkland could certainly testify that John was cooperative with her investigation. And as for Michele and her cooperation —

"I won't get into that, Your Honor," Krastek interrupted, although it was not clear what he wouldn't get into.

"I thought—" Judge Martin began, apparently about to suggest a means for Krastek to address the subject of Michele's credibility. But Krastek interrupted again.

He had no intention of asking Michele about her refusal to take the lie detector test, Krastek said, but he might ask Kirkland if Michele had been as cooperative as John had been. "I was distinguishing the two," Krastek said. "Michelle Yelenic is listed as an alibi witness and may be testifying, and I think that [asking her about her refusal to take a lie detector test as to the molestation allegations] would be definitely inappropriate." But as to Kirkland's opinion of Michele's cooperation, and thus her veracity, that would be fair game. On the other hand, a suggestion by reference to the declined lie detector test that Michele was dishonest in advance of her testimony, through questions to Kirkland, would be improper, as Krastek had acknowledged, if Michele was to be an alibi witness for Kevin.

This was a warning shot across the defense's bow: Krastek was telling Galloway he was ready to use Deana Kirkland to reveal Michele to be at least "uncooperative" in determining the truth or falsity of allegations against John, if not a fabricator. The molestation allegations she had made against Yelenic were, after all, "unfounded," in Kirkland's assessment. Any attack by the defense against the victim, John, as a child molester whom the jury should care less about would blow up in the defense's face.

Now Galloway seemed to make an about-face. Whereas Krastek had from the outset expected him to raise the molestation allegations at some point in the defense, Galloway now informed the judge he had no intention of doing so.

"Let me stop you for a minute," he told Krastek. "I am going to object to all of the testimony about the investigation of Doctor Yelenic. I think that is a side issue. We are going to try a case within a case if we get into it, and I object to that as not being relevant to the charges, and if it has any relevance, its prejudice outweighs its probative value."

What was this? It struck Krastek that Galloway now realized that Kirkland's testimony against Kevin would gain immeasurable weight once the jury heard that Kirkland had repudiated—with two investigations—Kevin's constantly reiterated suspicion that John was a child molester. Suddenly, blaming the victim could be toxic for the defense: testimony about Kevin's complaint to Kirkland might make him look obsessive, someone who couldn't accept no for an answer, which was why Galloway wanted to avoid the issue like the plague.

Absolutely not, Krastek argued. It was Foley's complaints about John, and "how they were foiled at every turn, that led to his frustration, led to his expressions of ill will, which led, we think, to this homicide, Your Honor." Kirkland's testimony about the unfounded allegations was crucial to the prosecution, Krastek said.

Judge Martin overruled Galloway's objection to the molestation allegation testimony. It would come in, along with Kirkland's findings that they were unfounded.

Kirkland took the witness stand on the morning of Wednesday, March 11. She was the first of the day's Pennsylvania State Police witnesses.

There were a number of points Krastek wanted to get from Kirkland's testimony: the two molestation investigations instigated by Kevin, of course, along with her observation that Kevin wore ASICS shoes up until the time of the murder; his habitual knife flicking; and his oft-stated wish that John would die. Kirkland would substantiate every one, although it was clear that she was a reluctant witness against her friend Kevin.

Under Krastek's questioning, Kirkland related how she had first become involved in the alleged molestation case: Kevin had told her that Michele had told him that Jamie had made claims that John had molested him. A few weeks later, after Kirkland had informed Kevin that she wouldn't investigate unless someone responsible for Jamie's care initiated a complaint, Michele contacted her and told her of Jamie's claims. That had begun her first investigation of the claims, in April of 2005. She had met with John, who was cooperative if arrogant. A parallel investigation had begun with CYS. A court order had been entered forbidding John to have contact with Jamie while the investigations proceeded. In September of 2005, both Kirkland and CYS determined that the claims had no merit: Kirkland concluded that Jamie had been "coached" on what to say: the words he had used seemed rehearsed.

But that wasn't the end of it, Kirkland said. As the end of the ban on John's one-on-one contact with Jamie neared, Kevin again complained. In the Thanksgiving Day handoff of custody in 2005, after Jamie's fit at the Indiana police station, Kirkland had started a new investigation, this one quashed a few days later by the intervention of Judge Hanna after the judge met with Jamie alone in her chambers.

Having disposed of the bogus molestation allegations, Krastek moved on to Kirkland's recollections of Kevin's attitude toward John. Kirkland told the story of Kevin's stated wish that John would die in a car wreck, and how she had admonished him—this, only two weeks before the murder.

That left the habitual knife flicking. "Did you know him

to carry a knife?" Krastek asked. She did, Kirkland testified, a folding knife with a blade about four inches long. She had one just like it.

"He would flick it. Not only would I see that it was clipped on his pocket but I would see him open and close it, and that kind of thing."

Krastek asked Kirkland if she's seen Kevin on the morning after the murder.

She had, Kirkland said. "And did you see his face?" Krastek asked. Yes, Kirkland said. "And what did you see on his face?"

"I saw what I, what appeared to me as an abrasion, I believe it was above his right eye but I am not certain, approximately maybe one inch in length."

On his cross-examination, Galloway tried to soften the image of Kevin using his friend Kirkland to investigate John; Galloway did so by inducing Kirkland to acknowledge that Kevin had been reluctant to get involved with Michele's allegations about her estranged husband. That was true, Kirkland said—at least initially. The second time the topic came up, Kevin wanted her to initiate an investigation. Kevin seemed "stressed" by the claims, according to Kirkland. Not angry or raging, just worried.

Now Galloway tried to throw a curveball.

Who was in charge of the Indiana barracks crime investigation unit at the time the allegations were under investigation?

"That was Sergeant George Emigh," Kirkland said.

"Would it be fair to say that George Emigh didn't like Kevin Foley?"

Kirkland said she had "gathered that" from hearing talk at the barracks, although she had no personal knowledge of it.

"Was George Emigh disciplined, ultimately?" Galloway asked.

Krastek was on his feet, objecting. From the moment of Monzo's opening statement, he'd known that the defense was going to attempt to make an issue of Emigh's friction with Kevin in order to buttress their claim that he had only been charged with murder because of Emigh's enmity for him. At the same time, the defense hoped to portray Emigh as a bad officer, someone who had converted a personal animus into a vendetta that had resulted in Kevin being charged with murder.

Emigh's early retirement from the PSP had nothing to do with Kevin Foley, Krastek told Judge Martin. It was irrelevant to the murder case.

"He was disciplined, not over Kevin Foley, but he was disciplined and drummed out of the state police," Galloway retorted, "and he has filed a lawsuit complaining of that, and . . . that he was not given an honorable discharge, and suspended for thirty-five days, later reduced to fourteen days. But he was not allowed to purchase his gun, take his hat and all of those things. And he was disciplined." Galloway seemed excited. He wanted to get as much of the bad blood between Kevin and Emigh in as possible as part of the defense case. (On retirement, PSP troopers were permitted to purchase their state-issued weapons and to retain their troopers' hats as symbols of their service. Not being permitted to do so was the PSP's way of saying that an officer had left the force under untoward circumstances.)

"How is it relevant to this?" Judge Martin asked.

"George Emigh's character is going to be an issue in this case," Galloway said.

"Not yet, it isn't," Krastek said defiantly.

"We are still in the prosecution of the case," Galloway acknowledged, "but I am going to assert to you that it will be an issue in this case, George Emigh's character, and the fact that he is the one that directed the investigation toward Kevin Foley, and that is clear."

Well, this was a somewhat slippery statement by Galloway: the use of the word "directed" could mean either that Emigh had supervised ("directed") the investigation of Kevin as the suspect, which wasn't the situation at all, or that he had merely pointed ("directed") the other police toward Kevin. Galloway seemed to be ignoring or perhaps was unaware that Mary Ann Clark and Melissa Uss had also "directed" the police toward Kevin perhaps half an hour after Emigh's call to District Attorney Bell, and that in any case, given the well-known enmity between Kevin and John, the police would have been idiots not to consider Kevin a suspect from the beginning. Krastek could have made much about the fact that the Pennsylvania State Police did not interview Kevin on the morning of April 13 as evidence that Emigh's supposed malign influence had no effect whatsoever on the investigation. But that would have meant a confusing detour into the politics of the PSP, so it wasn't worth it. But having erected a straw man, Galloway was in no hurry to blow it down.

Well, Judge Martin said, the defense might want to raise Emigh as an issue, but now wasn't the right time for it: it more properly belonged to the defense of the case once the prosecution was finished, if the defense still chose to do so. He sustained Krastek's objection.

On his redirect examination, Krastek tried to delve into whether Kirkland thought Jamie had been "coached" to make the molestation allegations. He asked her whether, ordinarily, the fact that a custody dispute was going on had any effect on her assessment of molestation charges.

"I would say it becomes more of a relevant issue," she said. "The suspicion tends to become raised as to whether or not the allegation is legitimate."

Now it was Galloway's turn to object. At the bench, he wanted to know where Krastek was going with the line of questioning. Krastek said he intended to bring out the fact that, to Kirkland, Michele had been less cooperative than John. No, no, no, Galloway said. Michele Yelenic was irrelevant to the case, which was about whether Kevin had murdered John. Getting into issues involving Michele would bring on the trial-within-a-trial that Galloway wanted to avoid. Besides, there was no upside for the defense in having to defend Michele as well as Kevin.

Galloway told the judge that Krastek was heading toward the polygraph examination that Michele had refused to take. No he wasn't, Krastek said. He only wanted Kirkland to testify that Michele was less cooperative than John, despite the fact that she had initiated the molestation claims.

Galloway said "lack of cooperation" was practically the same as saying she'd refused the lie detector test, and "cooperation" from John was like saying that he had passed.

No it wasn't, Krastek said. To Krastek, it was like walking up to a door but not going in.

Judge Martin cut through the debate by asking Krastek if, other than refusing the polygraph, Michele was "cooperative" with Kirkland. Krastek said she was "generally cooperative."

Based on that, Judge Martin sustained Galloway's objection. The jury would not hear Kirkland say that Michele had not been as "cooperative" as John in her two abuse investigations. A judge's job is to permit a fair trial, one without inflammatory, prejudicial testimony, and so far Martin was doing this very well.

Krastek now called a parade of state troopers to the stand to testify about Kevin's appearance and behavior in the years since he had taken up with Michele.

Trooper Martin Knezovich said he was a friend of Kevin's, often playing sports with him in off-duty hours. He had been at the hockey game in Delmont on the night of April 12. As far as he could recall, no one had been hurt in the game. Foley had left almost immediately after the game. Knezovich had stayed in the parking lot talking with another trooper until about 1:30 a.m. The following morning he'd noticed "kind of a deep-type scrape over his eyebrow, down by the bridge of his nose." When he'd asked Kevin about it, Kevin told him that his hockey stick had sprung back from the seat belt and hit him as he was putting his gear in the back of his Explorer after the game.

Kevin habitually wore ASICS shoes, Knezovich said.

Krastek asked Knezovich if he knew what Kevin thought of John Yelenic. "I just know from things at the barracks that Kevin didn't think very highly of the man."

Trooper John Aloi also said he was a friend of Kevin's. He'd also seen Kevin on the morning of April 13. "I noticed that he had a mark on his right eye and it appeared to be a scratch, approximately from the eyebrow across the eyelid toward the nose." He thought the wound looked like a fingernail scratch. He'd joked about it with Foley, Aloi said. "I threw out a gesture like, 'Can't you take no for an answer?'" Kevin told Aloi about the boomeranging hockey stick.

Trooper Joy Goodyear also said she saw a wound on Kevin's face around the time of the murder that looked to her like it might have been a fresh fingernail scratch. Trooper David Franks said he'd seen a "fingernail-type cut" on Kevin's face. Trooper Douglas Snyder said he noticed a "small red mark, injury-type of scratch" on Kevin's forehead around April 13.

For each of these witnesses, Galloway or Monzo emphasized the bouncing hockey stick as a possible cause of Kevin's appearance on the morning of April 13. They seemed to be conceding that Kevin had a facial injury, all right—but that it had not been caused by anyone's fingernail.

Trooper Daniel Zenisek, a patrol officer assigned to the Indiana barracks, was called to the stand. He considered himself more of an acquaintance of Kevin than a friend, unlike some of the other troopers who had testified. He said that Kevin had always worn ASICS running shoes until the time of the murder, after which he switched to Nikes. Zenisek said Kevin frequently played with his knife. He did not know Michele or John Yelenic but knew of John because Kevin frequently talked about him.

"And was that talking to you or to just other people that you overheard?" Krastek asked.

"Talking to me, talking to anyone who was around, we heard about it . . . [H]e talked about him a lot."

"Okay, when he talked about him, how did he refer to him?"

"He was a cocksucker."

"Did he ever have a more direct conversation with you about John Yelenic?"

"Yes."

"Tell the jury about that."

"He made a statement to me one time that he would like to kill the cocksucker some night and wanted help."

"Okay. And what was your response to that?"

"I really didn't have any response and I didn't think he was serious."

"And how did he sound to you when he said that?"

"It is hard to describe because I mean, he was upset, but he said things so much in a joking manner that you didn't know. He just said it, you know?" This had happened either in April 2005, a year before the murder, when the molestation allegations had first been raised, or during the fall of 2005, when Judge Hanna was revisiting the child custody issue; Zenisek couldn't remember.

Still, this was pretty damning testimony under the circumstances: in fact, John *had* been killed at night. The point wasn't lost on the jury.

Galloway had known this was coming, of course, because he'd been given copies of all the witnesses' statements to Gardner and his team. He wanted to blunt the effect of the testimony by getting Zenisek to agree that Kevin was clearly joking, that it was just a flip remark, not an indication of serious intent.

"You laughed, or Kevin laughed, and kept on walking; didn't he?"

"When I say laugh, if you knew him, he just says things; it is just the personality," Zenisek said. Apparently Kevin was always saying outrageous things to get a laugh from his fellow troopers.

"When Kevin said something to you about killing Yelenic, he was obviously joking and definitely joking, correct?"

"Correct, yeah."

"Okay. Thank you. Now, in the state police barracks at Indiana it is not unusual for persons, troopers up there, to say things like, 'Somebody ought to kill that son of a bitch,' or words to that effect?"

"No, it is not unusual."

"And people, state policemen, talk about people who give them a hard time or people who are just, they are upset with, that are suspects or whatever, and make offhanded statements about somebody ought to kill that SOB, or that kind of thing?"

"Correct."

In other words, it was just a flip remark by Kevin and shouldn't be taken out of context, Galloway implied. Zenisek agreed.

Krastek now called another Indiana trooper, James Fry. Fry had known Kevin since 1997, considered him a friend, and frequently observed him playing with his knife.

"Was there ever an incident that involved you and that knife?" Krastek asked.

"Yes. One time, I couldn't even tell you the date of it, but as he was playing with the knife he sliced my pants in the groin area accidentally."

"Just the pants?"

"Yes, just the pants, which I was thankful for that."

"I take it that you weren't happy; is that right?"

"No, I wasn't, and he apologized immediately and it was, as I recall he even called our supply and obtained me a new pair of pants."

"What was he doing with the knife that he got that close to your groin and cut your pants? What was he doing with it?"

"As I recall when he was walking by me he had the knife out and just made the motion, like he had his knife out."

"And was he, do you recall what hand he was holding it in?"

"Oh, I would say the right hand."

"And do you know if he was holding it blade up as I have it here, or blade down?" Krastek had produced an open flick-knife with the sharp edge of the blade up.

"It would have been blade up," Fry agreed.

"And he was going back and forth like this?" Krastek asked, swishing the blade back and forth, creating an image for the jury.

"Right."

Trooper Douglas Berezansky said he'd sold a hockey equipment bag to Kevin, along with his equipment, except for two sticks and his skates, for about $180. Krastek showed Berezansky the hockey bag Gonglik had seized during his search of the Susan Drive house in October of 2007.

"Have you ever seen this hockey bag before?" Krastek asked.

"No, I have not," Berezansky said. The implication was that Kevin had ditched the bag he had bought from Berezansky and replaced it with another one after the murder.

24.

The rest of the day was taken up by testimony from three other troopers who had worked on the investigation, including Corporal Gardner.

John Dell was the sergeant in charge of the Pennsylvania State Police criminal investigation unit in Greensburg; he was also Gardner's supervisor, much as Emigh had been Kevin's supervisor in Indiana. He had served the search warrant on Kevin in October of 2007 that resulted in the blood sample forwarded to the FBI. Krastek wanted to establish the chain of custody for the blood so the DNA experts' upcoming testimony could be admissible. Kevin had been served with the "body warrant," as Dell referred to it, and taken to a hospital in Greensburg, where the blood was drawn and hair samples were taken; these were then provided to Gardner. Kevin had been cooperative throughout, the defense elicited on cross-examination, the implication being that he had nothing to hide.

Then Gardner took the stand to recount all the steps he and his team had taken in the investigation and to relate how the FBI's Hochrein and others became involved. That set the stage for the battle over the DNA on the next day of the trial, March 12, 2009.

* * *

Both sides knew this was probably the ball game. Krastrek had to get his three experts to explain the apparently wild differences in their findings while also making those explanations seem coherent and reasonable to a jury hardly conversant with the arcane sciences of molecular biology and statistics. Then Galloway had to make the same findings seem crazily contradictory and therefore improbable. He need the jury to conclude that the whole area of DNA was just too fraught with imponderables to be reliable, and that therefore Kevin's possible guilt was subject to reasonable doubt.

First Krastek needed to get the DNA from the fingernail clippings to the FBI by continuing to establish the chain of custody. Any break in the "chain" could allow the defense to argue that the critical DNA evidence had been compromised somewhere along the line. He called the former Blairsville police officer John Brant, who told how he had picked up the blood, clothes, pictures, and fingernails from Gonglik on April 17, delivered the clothes and blood to the PSP lab the same day, and brought the pictures and the package containing the bloody nails back to Blairsville, where it was placed in the unsecured small refrigerator. The defense tried to use Brant to illustrate that the DNA under the nails might well have been contaminated during their stay in the Blairsville mini-refrigerator, but Brant wasn't much help: he really knew nothing.

It is somewhat curious, however, that Janelle Lydic, the Blairsville police officer who was in charge of the investigation from April to August, and the official custodian of the evidence and the mini-refrigerator, was not called as a witness. If the defense felt the need to establish contamination of the fingernail material at some point along the line, Lydic was probably vital for the purpose. But neither the prosecution or the defense called her, which seemed to suggest that the defense's intimations about possible DNA contamination had little substance.

After Brant, the prosecution called the FBI's Hochrein, who described his Tinkers-to-Evers-to-Chance role in assisting Randall Gardner and the reactivated PSP in their investigation in late 2006, including his forwarding of the vital fingernail material to the FBI laboratory. This set up the testimony of the FBI's DNA expert, Jerrilyn Conway, who had estimated that the likelihood of a DNA match for the fingernail material was the rather wide-ranging 1 in 13,000 people, none of them either John or Kevin, since their own DNA did not perfectly match the material found under John's fingernails. In a way, though, the 13,000 number was sort of a red herring.

Conway had been with the bureau for nine years. She had a master's degree in molecular biology. She had begun examining the small amount of DNA taken from the fingernails of John's right hand in July of 2007 and finished her analysis in September of 2007, just two weeks before Kevin was arrested.

After describing the process of amplifying the DNA by replicating its molecular constituents, Conway moved on to the subject of mixed DNA samples. The genetic characteristics of the amplified DNA distinguished each component part of the mixture. It was like having a jar of 1,000 marbles, Conway said. If 900 of the marbles were red, and the remaining 100 were blue, she could say with certainty that the red marbles represented the majority of the marbles and the blue the minority. The same went for DNA samples: if all of the sample had the same DNA characteristics, it would be an unmixed sample; but if a small portion of the sample had different characteristics from the majority, that would indicate a mixed sample. That was what she had found under John's fingernails. She compared this DNA to reference samples from John and Kevin and concluded that neither could be excluded as a donor of some of the DNA.

"There was a major contributor type which matched Mr. Yelenic," Conway said. "There was also a minor contributor type that matched Mr. Foley. I then did a statistical calculation to say what is the probability of collecting an individual at random from a population that could be a contributor of that mixture independent of who was included in the mixture, and it is any possible combination of the DNA types. So when I did that calculation, in the African-American population, it was 1 in 46,000 individuals. In the Caucasian population, it was 1 in 13,000 individuals. And in the southeastern Hispanic population, it was 1 in 16,000 individuals. And then in the southwestern Hispanic population, it was 1 in 28,000 individuals." But because she had John's DNA profile and the DNA profile under the material under the fingernails did not exactly match John, she knew there had to be another DNA contributor. The small amount of DNA from the minor contributor, while insufficient to give a positive identification, nevertheless included Kevin among the possible donors. It did not exclude him, as would have been the case if none of the DNA had been his.

Krastek knew where his experts' vulnerabilities lay, and it was clearly in the fact that Conway's numbers were not the same as those of Cotton and Perlin—the "million billion" problem. He wanted to take some of the mystery out of this situation, so he asked Conway if she was familiar with Cotton's and Perlin's work.

She was, Conway replied. She was aware that Cotton and Perlin had reviewed her work. She also knew Cotton personally, Conway said.

"And her numbers are different than yours; are they?" Krastek asked.

"They are."

"Can you explain that difference to the jury?"

"Well, when I do my calculation I make no assumptions as to how many contributors might be present, or whether or not the victim's profile is present. My understanding of her calculation is that she *does* make those assumptions, so when you start making assumptions about a profile, you can narrow down the possible contributors that could be contributing to that minor profile."

"And why don't you use her method of calculation?"

"Well, making assumptions is by [FBI] policy, really. Our protocol sort of keeps us from making those sorts of assumptions. That is really why we don't do it."

So here it was, the explanation for the "million billion" problem. Cotton's procedure entailed throwing out John's DNA and focusing only on the minor contributors' to see if more could be learned from it. The FBI's procedure didn't allow that, even though Conway knew for sure that the large majority of the DNA had to come from John, because they were his own fingernails. Cotton's "assumption" wasn't much of a leap, just one the FBI wouldn't take with its one-size-fits all philosophy of DNA analysis.

"Well, are you wrong and she is right, or vice versa?" Krastek asked.

"I wouldn't say either one of us is wrong. I would say that it would really be up to you all, the jury, to determine whether those assumptions are appropriate to make or if you would be more comfortable not making those assumptions." Conway clearly trusted the jury to understand her explanation, even if they didn't agree with the FBI's conservative approach.

"Nevertheless the method, you are aware of the method that Doctor Cotton uses?"

"I am."

"And is that reasonable or unreasonable?"

"I think it is reasonable."

"Regardless of, again, her method or your method, does either one change that Kevin Foley's DNA profile matches the minor contributor?"

"No, it does not."

On his cross-examination, Galloway asked Conway if she was aware that Cotton and Perlin had come up with vastly different, much larger numbers than she had. Yes, Conway said, she knew that. Galloway produced the various Cotton and Perlin reports—the ones that seemed to shift the numbers rather wildly in each rendition—and asked Conway if she'd read them. She had, Conway said. These were numbers millions and billions of times rarer than her findings, weren't they? he asked. Yes, Conway said.

By reciting the varying numbers from Cotton and Perlin and inducing Conway to acknowledge them, Galloway was implying that all the numbers were pie-in-the-sky evidence, conjured up only to help the prosecution win. Conway did not agree: it was only that Cotton and Perlin had concentrated on the minor donor, which the FBI did not permit, when there was insufficient data.

Galloway zeroed in on this: *Why* was the data insufficient? The typing process, Conway explained, involved a piece of laboratory equipment that measured "spikes" on a graph showing the strength of various components of the DNA. If the spikes were less than 50 RFU—relative fluorescent units—the FBI did not consider them to be sufficiently reliable DNA indicators. In the case of the minor donor's DNA under John's nails, there were a number of spikes that registered below 50 RFU.

"And if it's below 50 relative fluorescent units, the FBI is unwilling to use those, because your protocol does not consider them sufficiently reliable to be used for this purpose?"

"That is right. Peaks that are below the 50 threshold are not necessarily reproducible. They are almost certainly not allelic information that we could use." In fact, the FBI standard required the spikes to be above 200 RFU for "matching purposes," Conway said. Clearly much of the minor donor's DNA was not above 200 RFU, otherwise a complete profile would have been found. But, said Conway, in most cases a below-50 RFU *could* be used to exclude someone as a donor. The implication was that none of the below-50 RFU spikes had eliminated Kevin as a contributor. Otherwise, he would probably never have been charged.

"And are you aware that Mark Perlin used those below-50 peaks?" Galloway asked, meaning that Perlin had used them to calculate his inclusion results despite the FBI's more conservative policy.

She didn't know how Perlin had made his assessment, Conway said.

Well, was she aware the Cotton had also used the spikes that were below 50 RFU?

Conway said she couldn't speak to Cotton's methods, either.

After all this rather dense testimony, Judge Martin ordered a break.

After Conway, Krastek called Cotton, then Perlin. Each acknowledged using the below-50 RFU spikes to make inclusion calculations, with Perlin contending that his proprietary statistical software was capable of refining the numbers even more than Cotton's methodology. That was how he'd first obtained the 19 trillion assessment, but after further refinements he had reduced his estimate to the billions. Soon Galloway was enmeshed in an arcane argument with Perlin over whether his process was widely accepted in the scientific community, implying that it was rash when compared to the more conservative FBI standard.

With the jury's eyes in danger of glazing over after all this, Krastek wanted to get his case back to human size. He called Barbara Swasy, the wife of John's cousin, who had known both Kevin and Michele from Jamie's school, to recount Kevin's remarks at the Friday-night fish fry. It was also Barbara who, on the afternoon of April 13, had told Michele and Kevin that John had been murdered, even as George Emigh was telling Bob Bell that Foley had to be a prime suspect.

"After I found out about John being murdered I talked to Michele on the phone," Barbara testified.

"What did you tell Michele?"

"That John was gone."

"Okay. And did you talk to Kevin at all that day?"

"Yes."

"And what was that circumstance?"

"Well, after I was done talking to Michele. I told her John was gone. She said, 'What do you mean, gone?' and I said he is dead, murdered, and I said, 'Let me talk to Kevin.'"

"Okay. And why did you want to talk to Kevin?"

"Kevin was a criminal investigator for the state police, and I thought he would know something."

"And did you talk to him then?"

"Yes, I did."

"And what did you ask?"

"I asked Kevin if he could find anything out."

"And what did he say in response to that?"

"He said, 'No, I'm off today, and that is not within my jurisdiction. You'll have to call the Blairsville police to find anything out.'"

Later, both Mary Ann Clark and Tom Riley pointed to this remark by Kevin as evidence of his guilt. How did Kevin know that the crime had occurred in Blairsville? Of course, he could have assumed it, since John lived and worked in Blairsville, and it was the most likely place for the crime to have taken place. Still, John could have been murdered elsewhere. But Kevin's reluctance to call his own agency to find out what was going on—out of natural curiosity about what had happened to the man he'd long hated—should have compelled him to make such a call, if he wasn't involved in the crime himself. Almost anyone else who was innocent of the murder would have done so.

And how did Kevin know the case was "not in his jurisdiction"? That had just been decided minutes before by Hess and Bell. So it seems likely someone had already called Kevin to fill him in on the latest from inside the investigation even before Barbara called. But who? That was also a mystery.

Next, Barbara told the story of the fish fry, and Kevin's remark that he wished John would die, and her admonishment of him.

"He said, 'I wish that guy was dead.' "

"Was he joking? Was he angry, frustrated? How would you describe it?"

"No. That is exactly the way he said it: 'I wish that guy was dead.' " Barbara had a somber tone in her voice as she mimicked Kevin.

"And was Michele there, right in that same conversation?"

"Yes."

"And what was your—how did you respond to that?"

"I said, 'No, no, you don't wish that.' "

25.

The prosecution was nearing the end of its case. Krastek had only seven more witnesses to go, and most of them were housekeeping matters, needed to tie up various loose ends, such as the identification of the tread in the bloody shoe prints by an expert from ASICS, and the circumstances of the two Sheetz videos, from the Sheetz security coordinator, and investigator Haar's subsequent review for Gardner's team. Gardner himself was recalled to testify about the midnight reenactment with the Bronco and the fire trucks and to tell how the videos, now three of them, were passed on to Hochrein and then the FBI video expert, Amanda Broyles. Broyles was then called to say that the vehicle in the Sheetz videos closely resembled the vehicle in the reenactment, which, of course, had been Kevin's before he sold it.

"That is all I have for today, Your Honor," Krastek said. Judge Martin then adjourned the trial at a little after 3:00 p.m. on Friday afternoon.

The prosecution had one more witness to call: Effie Alexander, John's divorce lawyer. She would take the stand on Monday morning. Krastek's decision to call no more witnesses until Monday was either the result of circumstance or strategic. Clearly, Alexander was Krastek's cleanup witness, the one any prosecutor wanted to put on the stand to sum up the emotion of the case. If he'd put Alexander on the witness stand Friday afternoon to tell of her experiences with the victim, John Yelenic, the jury would have had the whole weekend to contemplate the emotional impact of her testimony and maybe even think it over. On the other hand, if she testified on Monday morning, he might undercut the start of the defense case. In telling Judge Martin he had no more witnesses Friday afternoon, Krastek had seemingly opted for the undercutting: Alexander's testimony would loom over Galloway's first defense witnesses.

When the trial resumed on Monday, March 16, 2009, Krastek called Alexander to the witness stand. But as he did so, Galloway wanted another secret sidebar conference with Judge Martin. He wanted to know exactly what Krastek expected to hear from Alexander before the jury also heard it.

Krastek summarized what he expected to get from Alexander's testimony: a general description of the toxic divorce with Michele, the child custody fight, the allegations of molestation, the ultimate agreement with Michele and Lovette at the Blairsville coffee shop, Michele's balking just before she signed the final agreement, and the fact that the formal agreement, with Michele's signature, was found blood-spattered and scattered all over the Yelenic living room floor on the afternoon of April 13.

"There will be no—I have advised her further—that there will be no mention of the ten thousand dollars that he once offered for a private detective . . . to find out who did this," Krastek said, referring to John's premonition of his murder. Judge Martin had already ruled that out of bounds.

When Alexander took the stand, Krastek guided her through her representation of John in the divorce case, with its associated custody issues. While all this was certainly at the bottom of the whole story, its relevance to Kevin's guilt or innocence in the murder wasn't clear. But the defense made no objection to this background, and within a few minutes Krastek turned to the subject of Kevin.

When was the first time she had seen Kevin Foley? Krastek asked.

Alexander thought it was probably in fall of 2005, during the protection-from-abuse hearing before Judge Hanna.

"While we were in court for the PFA, we had a recess, and as we were leaving the room to go to the recess, Trooper Foley winked at [John] . . . he and Michele were staring all of us down and really trying to intimidate us . . . throughout the proceedings, both Michele and Trooper Foley were behaving very intimidating, and trying to stare John down, and trying to stare me down. And as we were leaving the courtroom, Trooper Foley winked at John and John kind of gave him a, like that." Alexander was referring to John's *Seinfeld* gesture of pointed finger and thumb. Kevin seemed to react to this negatively. Alexander said she asked John, "What was that all about?"

"John said, 'I just gave him a *Seinfeld*, because he winked at me.'"

When they returned to the courtroom, Michele's lawyer tried to get John, who was on the witness stand, to admit that he'd made a threatening gesture at Kevin. Alexander said Judge Hanna dismissed that notion, and was about to explain why, but Monzo objected to whatever Hanna had told Michele's lawyer as hearsay.

Krastek asked Alexander if she'd given John advice on how to deal with Michele and Kevin generally.

"Sure," Alexander said. "John was a very kind person and probably didn't have a lot of, I would say spine. He was very open to suggestions regarding money issues, and I think that he was far too generous with Michele, and he never held his ground . . . But we did reach a point in the case in early 2006, where we settled the case in a four-way meeting . . . We were going to try to resolve everything . . . [I]t was early January 2006. We met at Valley Dairy outside of Blairsville. There was Mr. Lovette, Michele, myself and John. And I felt we reached a complete settlement on all of the economic issues and we shook hands. I started to write, hand-write the settlement right there. And Mr. Lovette couldn't see why I was doing that, but I felt it was important to have something signed at the time."

Instead, Lovette convinced her to go back to her office and have the agreement typed up and sent to him, Alexander said. Then Michele had refused to sign it.

"And what advice then specifically did you give John Yelenic after that?"

"Well, I felt we had a binding agreement and I felt that we could take it to court and have what we shook on enforced, and I told him to stand his ground. She wanted more money . . . she wanted the terms for the support changed. Michele had new demands and—"

Monzo objected to Alexander testifying about what Michele wanted, but was overruled by Judge Martin.

"She was going to lose her share of the support order. The order that he was paying was a combined spousal and child support order, and in Pennsylvania you pay that while the case is pending, regardless of your circumstances . . . but when the case is final and everything has been decided . . . you negotiate the alimony or not, and in this case there was no room for negotiations, because Michele lived with the trooper, and that is one of the reasons to deny alimony, is cohabitation with an unrelated adult male. So there was not going to be any alimony."

Alexander said she encouraged John to "stand his ground and not to give in to any demands, and not to take her phone calls, and not respond, and that we had a deal and we would make it stick."

"Okay. And do you know the estimated amount of his finances, how much he was worth?"

"Maybe two hundred to three hundred thousand dollars, but there was life insurance that was in excess of a million dollars." (Alexander underestimated John's net worth before the insurance by about a million dollars, according to the inventory filed by the estate lawyer after John's death.)

"And who was the beneficiary of that life insurance?"

"The beneficiaries [*sic*] of the life insurance was Michele Yelenic."

The life insurance issue had come up at the settlement meeting in January 2006, Alexander said.

"The terms of the [divorce] agreement actually called for John to be able to name whoever he wanted as beneficiary of his life insurance policy, once everything was settled, and Michele Yelenic was to receive a portion of the life insurance as beneficiary, sufficient to cover his child support obligations until the child reaches eighteen. And that was the last point that we negotiated that day at Valley Dairy . . . [S]he wanted the life insurance."

"And as of April 13, 2006, had John Yelenic changed the beneficiary of his life insurance?"

"He had not. He was going to do it after the agreement was signed."

There wasn't much the defense could do with Alexander's testimony except try to blunt the implication that Michele stood to benefit directly from John's estate. Monzo induced Alexander to acknowledge that because the divorce agreement had been upheld by Judge Hanna, and because Michele had signed it, she had agreed to forgo the bulk of the lucrative life insurance payout even before John was murdered. All the money would go to Jamie, limited each month to the $1,300 Michele was to receive under the child support provisions of the divorce agreement. The rest was to stay in a trust until Jamie's eighteenth birthday. In other words, Michele couldn't get at most of the money until Jamie turned eighteen, and even then he'd have control of it.

After Krastek asked Alexander if, to her knowledge, John had paid for Michele's house on Susan Drive—Alexander erroneously said he had, and that the couple had lived there together for a time (she had confused the Susan Drive house with the one on White Farm Road)—the prosecution rested its case.

Galloway then asked Judge Martin to dismiss the charges against Kevin.

"At this time, if it please the court, the defense would move for a judgment of acquittal on the charges, all of the criminal homicide charges, on the ground that the commonwealth's evidence does not rise to the level that a reasonable jury could find proof beyond a reasonable doubt as to first degree murder, third degree murder, involuntary or voluntary manslaughter."

"I believe it does, Your Honor," Krastek said.

"All right. Motion is denied," Judge Martin said.

Once the jury was out of the room for the morning recess, Galloway wanted the judge to approve testimony from a defense witness who did not want his name used in open court. The man claimed to know Brian Ray, who had supposedly confessed to having killed Yelenic in a robbery gone wrong. The witness, Galloway said, "has expressed to us an absolute terror of being branded as a snitch. He said in the world that he lives in that if the word gets out that he has done this, he is as good as a dead man. And he is willing to testify but he would like to provide his name and that sort of background [and] identification to the court but not have it stated out loud in court so that it can be picked up by the press and put in the paper and the TV and all that stuff. He is, I am telling you, terrified of it getting back to Pittsburgh that he was, to use his term, a snitch here on Brian Ray. And as I said, he is not unwilling to testify. He is simply reluctant to use his name in court where it would be reported and get back to where he lives."

"So you want him to testify without giving his name to the jury?" Judge Martin seemed skeptical.

"Maybe some arrangement, alternate arrangement could be made, where his name is provided to the jury in writing. That is one thing I thought of, and the jury would be instructed that they are not to reveal that name or some such name. It is the only time I have ever had it, and I am telling you that the guy is just absolutely petrified, not of testifying, but of it getting out that he testified in the place where he lives. And again, we won't be using him until tomorrow, so we have a little bit of time, but I want to alert the court to that."

Krastek said he couldn't agree to the witness not giving his name.

He didn't want to put anyone's life in danger, Krastek said, "but this really is not a game . . . this is a homicide trial, and this guy is a snitch witness. That is what he is, and I need to cross-examine him about that . . . [T]here is no specific threat here. It isn't like there is some cabal out there that is watching this case. This is just generally . . . Being a snitch, I don't think, gives grounds for extraordinary testimony, and indeed the— I object to it, Your Honor." John's death wasn't a "mob killing," Krastek added. Besides, if the court permitted Galloway to get away with this, it would provide the judge's own credibility to the witness, even if he was just a jailhouse snitch who had told a tall tale to state police in order to curry favor.

Judge Martin said he wanted to think it over before deciding whether to comply with Galloway's request.

26.

Now the defense called witnesses in its attempt to establish their "two reasons" for the charging of Kevin Foley: the "rush to judgment" by the state police, supposedly instigated for personal reasons by George Emigh, and the alleged failure to adequately investigate other suspects, including Tom Uss. Their first witness was former district attorney Bob Bell.

Bell had lost his seat in the election of 2008. Some said this was because of the way the Foley-Yelenic matter had been handled at its outset. He was now in private practice in Indiana, with an office on the corner of Philadelphia Street, next to the courthouse where he had held sway for so many years.

After Bell briefly filled in his background as the former elected district attorney at the time of the murder, Galloway asked him how he had first heard of the death of John Yelenic.

He was just pulling into his driveway on the afternoon of April 13, Bell said, when he received a telephone call from Indiana coroner Mike Baker, who told him of the murder. Baker suggested that he go to the scene, which was nearby, Bell said. At some point after he arrived at South Spring

Street, Bell continued, he was contacted by the 911 dispatcher, who asked him to call Emigh at the Indiana barracks.

"Initially Sergeant Emigh asked me if the state police would need to respond to the scene. At the time, I believe, Chief Hess had shown up and he advised me that it was his intention for the Blairsville Borough Police to maintain jurisdiction of the investigation, and that he, at this point in time, didn't need any assistance. So I advised Trooper Emigh of that. Trooper Emigh asked me who the victim was, and I advised him that it was a dentist from Blairsville by the name of John Yelenic. At that point in time, Trooper Emigh said that he needed my cell phone number." Apparently Bell was talking to Emigh on some sort of radio link that could be monitored by others; that was why Emigh wanted Bell's cell phone number, which he thought would be more secure.

"It wasn't a couple of minutes until the phone rang and it was Sergeant Emigh," Bell continued, "and he asked me if I knew who John Yelenic was, and I said, aside from him being a dentist in town, I did not. He then advised me that he was the individual that was involved with, well . . . that Kevin Foley was living with his soon-to-be ex-wife."

Bell in his testimony made no mention of his encounter with Mary Ann Clark and Melissa Uss on the sidewalk in front of John's house, in which they had told him that it would be wrong to allow the Indiana barracks to investigate because of Foley's relationship with Michele, and in which he had supposedly denied there was someone named Kevin Foley assigned to the Indiana PSP barracks. If the recollections of Mary Ann and Melissa are correct, it would seem that Bell was dissembling—either to Emigh about not knowing who Yelenic was, or to Mary Ann and Melissa about not knowing who Foley was. But Bell must have realized soon after he arrived at the Yelenic house that the case was going to be a major headache. Whatever, Bell never mentioned the encounter with Mary Ann and Melissa when he testified.

Throughout the evening, Bell continued, he'd had three conservations with Emigh, and "pretty much all of them" concerned Foley.

"Do you know if there was any animosity between Sergeant Emigh and Trooper Foley?" Galloway asked. He wanted to drive home the notion that Emigh's dislike of Foley was the main reason Kevin had become a suspect.

"Yes, sir."

"And was there?"

"Oh, yes, there was."

"Did Sergeant Emigh, for want of a better term, have a dislike for Trooper Foley?"

"I would say that would be correct, yes."

"Was Sergeant Emigh the first person who brought up the name of Kevin Foley to you as the chief law enforcement officer, official of Indiana County?"

"He was." Here again, Bell made no mention of Mary Ann Clark and Melissa Uss.

Galloway asked Bell about Wecht's autopsy. No one told him, Bell said, that a knife had been involved in Yelenic's murder. As far as he knew, the wounds that had killed John Yelenic had all come from the broken window.

Krastek first needed to blunt the implication that it was unusual for Emigh to have called Bell in the wake of a murder. After all, that was Emigh's job, as the supervisor of the Indiana barracks' crime unit. There was hardly anything nefarious about this; it was just routine.

"And if a homicide occurs in Indiana County," Krastek asked on his cross-examination, "well, if it occurs in Blairsville, as this one did, certainly the Blairsville Police Department would have jurisdiction. But it would not be uncommon, would it, for the Indiana barracks of the state police to also be involved?"

"It would not be uncommon. That is correct."

"So, is there anything uncommon whatsoever with you having a conversation with George Emigh about a homicide that occurs in Indiana County?"

"Absolutely not."

In fact, when Emigh called him, Emigh hadn't known the identity of the dead man, wasn't that correct? Krastek asked. It was, Bell said. It was Bell who had given that information to Emigh, not the other way around. Then it was only when Bell told Emigh the name of John Yelenic that Emigh said he wanted to talk to Bell on his cell phone? True, said Bell.

Emigh had been completely professional in providing the information about Foley? Yes, said Bell. It was Hess, Bell said, who insisted that Blairsville should conduct the investigation. He had even tried to talk Hess out of this in the ensuing days and weeks, Bell said, but Hess had been insistent that Blairsville would handle the case. Bell did not know then that Mary Ann Clark had initially insisted to Hess that the Pennsylvania State Police be kept out of the loop.

Here was some confusion: Mary Ann distrusted the PSP, and while Hess was trying to satisfy her concerns and take over the case, Bell didn't have all the facts—or more exactly, wasn't aware of all the politics involved—which made it difficult if not impossible to do the right thing. All three were working at cross-purposes but with the best of intentions. These were the main causes of the delay in getting the PSP to finally do its job in the murder of John Yelenic.

"Was he trying to get you to do something bad?" Krastek asked, returning to the implication that Emigh might have been up to something on the evening the murder was discovered.

"I don't believe so," Bell said. "He was providing me the name of somebody he believed may be involved in the case, that just happened to be a member of the Pennsylvania State Police."

"And did he say, with any particular animosity, or say, 'You got to get this guy, Bob; we want to pin this one on Kevin Foley'?"

"The only thing he said, he was adamant about believing that we should get a search warrant for Kevin Foley's [house] that night, and I advised him that at this point in time we did not have a probable cause for a search warrant to be issued. Other than that, no."

Krastek pressed Bell about Yelenic's wounds. Wasn't it true that he'd read Wecht's autopsy report? Yes. Wasn't it true that Wecht had described wounds that could have been inflicted only by a very sharp object, almost certainly a knife? Yes. But on redirect, Galloway was able to get Bell to admit that nowhere in Wecht's autopsy did the doctor use the word "knife." It was a shallow victory, however.

Using the defense's own witness, Bell, the prosecution seemed to have knocked down the claim that the arrest and prosecution of Kevin Foley was nothing more than the consequence of George Emigh's personal dislike of Kevin Foley—this, even without testimony from Mary Ann Clark and Melissa Uss about their sidewalk encounter with Bell.

The defense next called Daniel Lovette, Michele's divorce lawyer. Monzo's aim with Lovette was to suggest that the divorce between John and Michele, at least up to a point, had been fairly amicable, with John agreeing to split the couple's real estate assets 60/40 in Michele's favor. He needed to undercut, or at least mitigate, the idea that anger from a bitter divorce had been a motive for the murder—that Michele had somehow incited Kevin to get rid of John once and for all, or that she had a pecuniary motive for doing so.

"And you recall that being an amicable split of that property; do you not?"

"Yes."

"Okay. And that continued throughout the course of the separation . . . did it not?"

"The property didn't seem to be a problem after we reached a 60/40 split."

"And would you describe them, Mr. Lovette, as being fairly amicable?"

"Yeah. I mean, I have had a lot worse. Let's put it to you that way. These people weren't yellers. They weren't obnoxious. Doctor Yelenic was pretty professional."

"And were they respectful of each other?"

"They had their times, and I kind of remember, both Effie and I had to cool it down, when they started to get a little excited, because we were trying to keep the negotiations on an even road."

"And you were able to accomplish that?"

"Yeah. Michele was not difficult to deal with. I kind of have a rule, that you better listen to what I tell you, or we probably won't be together very long . . . I am an old dog and I don't have to put up with it."

Michele's reluctance to sign the divorce agreement, Lovette said, stemmed from John's decision to terminate the spousal support once the agreement was negotiated in early January, even though Michele hadn't yet signed it. That decision by John, in Michele's view, was costing her $2,500 a month. She wanted John to pay up for January, then February, March, and April, before she would sign . That was why she had been calling him frequently in the week before the murder, and why Alexander had been pressing him to stand his ground: to Alexander, they already had a deal, Michele was reneging, and in Alexander's mind there was no reason why Michele's procrastination should cost John money he hadn't agreed in January to pay.

On his cross-examination, Krastek tried to put the onus for the delay in signing the agreement on Michele.

Lovette agreed that Effie Alexander had sent him the formal, typed agreement in February of 2006, and Michele had refused to sign it until April. That only changed when Alexander scheduled a hearing to have Michele held in contempt of court, wasn't that true? Krastek asked Lovette.

"I would say it went this way," Lovette said. "I sent the agreement to Michele, probably got a call from her saying, 'Hey, Dan, he hasn't paid me, and I am not going to sign this until he *does* pay me, and until the thing is settled.' And I said okay, and I would believe that I would have called Effie and said, 'What's going on, and why has he quit paying, and let's get him paying again, and then let's get this thing signed.' That would be my recollection."

But by then Alexander was urging John to show some "spine" and stand fast. In fact, she had included a termination date of December 2005 for the spousal support in the typed agreement she sent to Lovette. That was another reason Alexander had advised John not to pay.

In the end, Lovette indicated, he'd told Michele to sign the typed agreement provided by Alexander without the four months' additional spousal support. One senses that Lovette had become at least slightly aggravated by Michele at this point. Just about the time of the fish fry, Michele went to Lovette's office in Johnstown and signed. Michele's apparent unhappiness in forgoing $10,000 more in spousal support might have contributed to Kevin's "I wish that guy were dead" remark at the fish fry.

Now came the star witness for the some-other-dude-did-it defense, Isaiah Brader, the Yelenic neighbor who had told the police that the disturbance he'd heard the night of the murder had occurred at 3:00 or 3:30 a.m., not two hours earlier. The defense wanted Brader to tell his story because it set up the "I'll never loan you money again" remark that Brader claimed he'd overheard, and that, in turn, led to the

$14,000 John had loaned the Usses, which in turn supported the defense theory that Tom Uss should be suspect number one.

Brader in March of 2009 was twenty-four years old and unmarried. He now lived in New York, after finishing his training at WyoTech. He had just moved to Blairsville in the spring of 2006 to take classes in metal fabrication. He lived across the street from John Yelenic, although he did not know him. On April 13, in the evening, while on a meal break from WyoTech, he saw the commotion in front of the Yelenic house, with the police, the paramedics, the crowd, and the news media, and on the way back to school he stopped a Blairsville police officer and told him what he had heard and seen the night before. The Blairsville officer wrote this down, and by around 10:00 p.m. on April 14, Brader was sought out by the investigators to tell his story of his early-morning hours of April 13. This is what Galloway now wanted him to tell the jury.

"Then you went to bed about what time?" Galloway asked.

"Probably around 3:30."

"And did there come a point in time when something awakened you, after you had gone to sleep?"

"Yeah. I heard loud arguing."

"And now, in the course of the arguing, how many people's voices did you hear?"

"I believe two. There was one dominant voice and that is what I could make out the most."

"One dominant voice that you could hear, better than the other?"

"That is correct."

"How long did the arguing go on?"

"Not more than five minutes."

"In the course of the argument, were you able to hear any of the things that were said?"

"The only thing I could make out the whole time was

someone, the dominant voice, saying that they would never loan them money again."

"And that statement that the person said, 'I'll never loan you money again,' words to that effect, was that part of the argument?"

"Yes, I believe so."

"And was it, you said it was said by the dominant voice?"

"That is correct."

"After the arguing stopped, were you in bed?"

He was, Brader said.

"Did you hear any other noises?"

"I heard glass shattering, and I got up and looked out the window. The only thing I could see was a garbage truck down the road, driving toward me. I went back to bed and heard it drive past, so I thought maybe it was just somebody throwing some glass into the back of the garbage truck." He now thought this might have actually happened between 4:00 and 5:00 a.m.

Well, of course there was a big difference between 3:30 a.m. and 5:00 a.m., let alone between 1:30 and 5:00 a.m. Brader's times thus seemed fairly elastic, and cried out for more definition. He'd left the trade school around 2:00 a.m., stopped at the Sheetz to pick up a video—on chassis manufacture, of all things, or so he said—was home by a little after 2:30, watched the video, and was in bed by 3:30. The next thing he knew, he'd been awakened by the disturbance: the arguing about a loan, the sound of breaking glass, then the movement of the garbage truck. But Brader's estimate of the times involved, even for the length of the disturbance, seemed hard to accept. He said the argument might have occurred over the span of five minutes. Five minutes is a very long time for most arguments, and would ordinarily contain a lot of phrases that Brader might have overheard, even over loans. Thirty seconds was probably more like it.

Krastek had an idea about what Brader had heard, and it certainly wasn't the deadly confrontation between John Yelenic and his murderer. How else to explain the fact that everyone else on the street heard screams at 1:30, and Brader's testimony that he'd heard an argument at 3:30—or was it between 4:00 and 5:00? Krastek didn't think Brader was making things up—he probably *had* heard some commotion between 4:00 and 5:00—but it just wasn't what had happened to Yelenic. To Krastek, it was highly unlikely that of nearly a dozen ear-witnesses to the screams and breaking glass, only Brader could have had the time right. It just didn't add up. After all, Brader had been in class at Wyo-Tech at 1:30—nowhere near the scene, at least as described by the other neighbors. Krastek thought Brader was honest but just being used by the defense to throw up insubstantial shadows.

"And you said that the yelling woke you up, and at that time, at the same time as the yelling, you also heard the garbage truck; is that correct?" Krastek asked, on his cross-examination.

"Well, I heard the arguing first, and then I heard the garbage truck, as the arguing was dwindling down. But the glass shattered before the garbage truck went by, so that is why I thought, you know, when I got up and looked out the window and saw the garbage truck, well, maybe it was just that."

"Okay. Well, did you tell the Blairsville Police Department within one day of hearing this, that you heard the garbage truck at approximately the same time as the yelling?"

"Yeah, because I thought that would be important, because then they would be able to figure out a time when it happened," Brader said. "Because I had been sleeping, so I didn't know an exact time."

This was a particularly acute observation by Brader, and it might have saved a lot of difficulty later if someone had effectively followed up on it at the time of the murder. Brader had seen and heard a garbage truck about the time of the disturbance he had heard. It shouldn't have been too hard to discover who had been driving the garbage truck and the approximate time it had driven down South Spring Street, whether at 3:30 or between 4:00 and 5:00 a.m. But this was never done by the Blairsville Police. Whether the garbage haulers had anything to do with a loan or throwing glass into the back of their trash truck that stormy morning was soon an unrecoverable fact. By the time anyone else thought of it, it was too late: there were no more records of which garbage haulers went where on the morning in question.

Still, Krastek was pretty sure of the explanation for Brader's observations: what Brader had heard, unlike all the other neighbors, was an argument between two trash haulers, sometime around 4:00 or 5:00 a.m., sparring about a loan from one to the other while throwing glass bottles into the truck. What Brader had heard, Krastek implied, had absolutely nothing to do with the murder of John Yelenic, who was already dead by the time Isaiah Brader had come home from school.

Undeterred, the defense still tried to maneuver Tom Uss into the jury's crosshairs as the man most likely. They now called Melissa Uss. Galloway questioned her. Both Melissa and Tom worked at WyoTech by the time of the trial. Back in April of 2006, Tom had been employed at a steel manufacturing plant in Johnstown. He had just retired from twenty years' service in the navy.

Galloway asked how long Melissa had known John. They had first met when she was in the ninth grade, she said; John was two or three years ahead of her. They'd been in band and had several classes together, and had both worked on the high school yearbook.

And years later, when they were living next door to each other in Blairsville, had she ever asked John for a loan? Galloway asked.

Yes, she had, Melissa said. It was in the summer of 2005.

"I was going to go to a bank, but I had saved money to get a loan to open a bakery, and I had asked him if, because I found out it would be, we would need a little bit more down for the bakery, if he would consider loaning it to me until we opened . . . and I would pay him back." John loaned her $15,000, Melissa said. The loan was unsecured, even by a note, Melissa said.

"And in April of 2006," Galloway asked, "did he come to you and say that he needed the money back?"

"Yes, he did."

"And did he ask for the money?"

"Yes. He did ask me for the money."

"And when was that?"

"He came to me about a week before, it was on Friday evening, and he wanted to know if he could have the money back on that day, and we wrote him a check." That was the check for $14,000 signed by the Usses that had been found in the Yelenic house on the day the murder was discovered.

Friday, April 7, was the same day that Michele had signed the divorce settlement—the night of the fish fry and Kevin's remark wishing that John was dead.

Faced with Galloway's questions, and probably knowing of his insinuations to follow, Melissa was the exemplar of cooperation and politeness, answering all of Galloway's queries directly, simply, and with a respectful "sir." If Galloway hoped to make Melissa "the other woman" in a fatal triangle, he was getting nowhere fast.

He turned to the $14,000 the Usses had repaid John. John had explained that his imminent divorce agreement required him to pay more in income taxes by April 15. Could he have the money he had loaned back? Melissa had written him a check for $14,000 that same night; she didn't have enough for the last $1,000. John had taken the check with him. Later, after John had been found murdered, she had stopped payment on the check. After that, she'd written a $15,000 check payable to John's estate.

Galloway turned to the subject of Melissa's husband, Tom. He asked Melissa what time in the morning Tom usually got up to get to his job in Johnstown.

"He had to be there very early, so I think he got up around 3:30 or 4:00 in the morning," Melissa said. From this question and response, it was clear where Galloway was headed with this: he wanted to put Tom Uss on South Spring Street about 4:00 a.m., on his way to work, so he could also be present for Brader's overheard argument, "I'll never loan you money again." And who had John loaned money to? The Usses. Galloway's implication was obvious: it was Tom Uss, not Kevin Foley, who had murdered John Yelenic.

Melissa handled this line as if she had no idea of what Galloway was implying with his question, which tended to boost her credibility considerably. Her seeming naïveté in responding to Galloway's insinuations only made Galloway seem manipulative, maybe even cruel. Or perhaps desperate. Her guileless acknowledgment that Tom might have been up around 4:00 a.m. had the effect of knocking the pins out from under Galloway's elaborate house of cards.

Galloway asked Melissa if the Uss family, or Craig, had a key to the Yelenic house. Melissa said they did not. Galloway produced a police report by Indiana County detectives from their interview of Melissa on April 13 that seemed to indicate otherwise. Melissa steadfastly insisted she had never said any such thing. Why the Indiana County Sheriff's office investigators might have made such a mistake in their initial report was hard to fathom, unless they were trying to bend the investigation's focus toward the Uss family at the time. Given that the lock on the rear door of John's house was broken and could not be opened with a key, even before the murder—a fact already established in earlier testimony—once again Melissa seemed to have gotten the better of Galloway with her fundamental honesty. Relying on police reports for facts that seemed so obviously in error was no help to the defense.

On his cross-examination, Krastek asked one very pertinent question: What shoe size did Tom Uss wear? Thirteen, Melissa said. Clearly the bloody shoe prints in the Yelenic house could not have been made by Tom Uss.

Now the defense called five more witnesses, two of whom had been living on South Spring Street on April 13. Pamela Ferguson, who lived next to the Uss family, two doors down from the Yelenic house, noticed Tom Uss cutting the grass in his backyard and the Yelenic backyard a few days after the murder. She thought this was unusual, along with the fact that Tom put the clippings into plastic bags. He'd never done that before, as far as she knew, she said. This was while the yellow crime scene tape was still up around the Yelenic house, she added.

After Pamela Ferguson, the defense called Darla Ferguson, who lived next door to Pamela Ferguson—in other words, three houses away from the Yelenic house. Weirdly, both Pamela and Darla were married to men named James Ferguson, and even more coincidental, each had a son named Jeremy, although the two James Fergusons were not in any way related. Go figure: What were the odds of two unrelated men with the same first and last names, and with sons with the same names, living next door to each other on one small street in a small town? But those were the actual facts.

"The postman did very well with it," Darla Ferguson told Galloway.

He asked Darla Ferguson if she'd ever seen John keeping company with Melissa Uss when Tom Uss wasn't around.

Krastek objected.

"That is highly speculative," he said, "and, by the way, the witness, the woman in question [Melissa Uss], was just here on the stand this morning, and wasn't asked that." The defense was trying to slip in some innuendo about John and Melissa Uss through a third party, when he could have asked Melissa herself while she was testifying, Krastek contended.

Judge Martin sustained Krastek's objection. Galloway tried again in a different way. The defense's objective was to create doubt in the jury's mind: Was it possible that John had been murdered by someone other than Kevin, perhaps a jealous husband? Tom Uss, perhaps? It took only one juror insisting on acquittal to create a mistrial, as Galloway knew well.

"The interactions that you saw between Melissa Uss and John Yelenic . . . did they take place while Mr. Uss was there, or while he was away?" Galloway asked.

Krastek was on his feet once more, objecting. "Again, this is the worst kind of innuendo. Unless she [Darla Ferguson] has reason to know anything more intimate, I object to this being asked."

"I'm taking this [from] the police report supplied to me by the commonwealth," Galloway retorted. The Pennsylvania State Police team under Gardner had interviewed all the neighbors. If there was innuendo, it had first been recorded by the same PSP that had eventually arrested their own colleague, Kevin Foley. He had every right to inquire into the possible relationship between the dead man and the woman he'd loaned $14,000 to, Galloway said.

"There are all kinds of stuff in there," Krastek said, referring to Gardner's PSP reports. "He had the woman [Melissa] on the stand, and didn't have the decency to ask her." Krastek was getting upset. This in turn upset Galloway.

"I object to a speech being made," Galloway told the judge. All this unfolded in front of the jury.

"Stop. Stop. Stop!" Judge Martin demanded. He summoned the lawyers to yet another secret sidebar, outside the hearing of the jury.

"I object and move for a mistrial," Galloway said. "Mr. Krastek engaged in highly animated actions and, I think, kind of fake emotional actions, in front of the jury, and I ask for a mistrial."

Judge Martin denied this mistrial motion, at least the third by Galloway since the proceeding had begun. But Galloway wasn't done.

"Secondly," he pressed on, "the statement that was given to me by the police says this, that she would see Melissa Uss and John Yelenic together all of the time, and she formed the opinion that the two of them are more than just friends. And was quick to say that she never saw the evidence of that impropriety directly. Although the interactions between Melissa Uss and Yelenic were when Tom Uss was not living at the Spring Street address. Tom Uss had obligations in the Navy. She then does say when Tom Uss returned to the Spring Street address, she saw the victim and Tom Uss and Mrs. Uss hanging out together. Melissa said that it seemed to end abruptly as if a problem was in the relationship."

Melissa said this? No, clearly Galloway had misspoken: he meant Darla Ferguson, who after all was the witness he was questioning. But perhaps this also showed that Galloway did not have a solid grasp on his facts, never a good thing to reveal in front of a judge.

Krastek missed this misstatement by his opponent: he was still focused on trying to keep Darla's ideas about Melissa's relationship with John away from the jury. It was only Darla's opinion, he said; there was nothing to back it up. Galloway said Darla's notion should still be admissible; how else was the jury to get the full picture?

"That doesn't make it admissible in court," Judge Martin said. "I understand, you have the right to present evidence that someone else may have committed this crime, but it has to be more than just speculation. It has to be admissible evidence and her opinion, I mean, it is no better than *my* opinion."

Well, it was different from Judge Martin's opinion, Galloway said. After all, Darla had seen John and Melissa together "a number of times," while Judge Martin had not.

Monzo chimed in: "She observed them and it is not opinion. She observed them doing, she can testify to what she observed, talking and together, all of the time."

"And what does it prove?" Martin asked. "So let the jury guess and speculate?"

"The jury is allowed to draw inferences from evidence all of the time," Galloway said. Circumstantial evidence could cut two ways.

Judge Martin still didn't think it was relevant to the issue of whether Kevin had murdered John Yelenic. Just because two neighbors were seen sitting together on a porch, in full view of the public, didn't mean anything, he said. "The fact that two neighbors talk and sit on the porch together, I mean, unless you have something more that they acted inappropriately together, or something like that . . ." The judge didn't finish the thought, but his meaning was clear; in order to put forward the notion that Yelenic's murder had something to do with his possible love life, the defense had to offer much more substantial evidence.

Galloway now said he could produce witnesses who would say they had seen John and Melissa "touching each other, kissing, him with his hand between the lady's legs, and et cetera, and this is part of that continuing of evidence of what occurred between the two, Miss Uss and John Yelenic."

Before Krastek or Judge Martin could react to this assertion, Galloway galloped on. He was upset at Krastek for delivering speeches in the form of objections, he said.

Okay, Judge Martin said, enough. From now on, if either

side wanted to make an objection, they could explain in a sidebar, not in front of the jury. But he still wasn't about to admit Darla Ferguson's opinion as to the relationship between John and Melissa. She could testify to what she observed, but not more.

Okay, Galloway agreed, he'd ask her about what she'd told the state police. "And I will ask her if she saw them kissing, holding hands or anything like that, and I will review that, and she will say no."

Well, this was hard to parse: Did Galloway mean that Darla would deny what the state police, in their post–August 2006, investigation, had reported? Was this an attack on John or the state police? It didn't seem to make any sense.

Krastek tried again.

"I object to this, Your Honor, as being . . . it is completely innuendo. They are trying to get two and two and make it seventeen. And I think this is really improper and unfair, and I think it proper to raise an objection. This woman was on the stand, Mrs. Uss, and they didn't ask her about that [then], so they are trying to do it [now] by innuendo, that [which] they could have asked her directly. And it is completely improper."

Judge Martin wanted to know if the defense had any witness who could substantiate the implication that John and Melissa had been having an affair.

Yes, Galloway said. Monzo agreed. They would produce a witness who could back up Darla Ferguson's observations.

All right, Judge Martin said—only as long as the witnesses confined their testimony to what they observed, not what they thought about it.

"Agreed," said Galloway.

Galloway now asked Darla if it was true that she had told the police that she had seen John and Melissa together "all of the time," as the police report indicated. Darla tried to explain what she meant.

"Her husband was away in the service. I am sure she was very lonely and having a hard time and needed a friend and he was going through a divorce and I am sure having a hard time and needed a friend and they supported each other," Darla said.

"Now, to be fair, you never saw them kissing, holding hands or anything of an intimate nature?"

"No, no, I did not," Darla said.

Galloway said he had no further questions, and Krastek chose not to cross-examine. Afterward, there was another sidebar conversation between the judge and the lawyers, this one not reported, but which probably had to do with other defense witnesses Galloway expected would offer testimony as to John's relationship with Melissa. Which was probably why the court reporter, Kimberly Serafin, never put it down in writing. Judge Martin likely found it to be, as Krastek would have put it, "speculative" and unfair to the reputations of innocent people, not to mention a dead man.

After Darla Ferguson, the defense called David Okopal, another state trooper, also assigned to the Indiana criminal investigations unit of Emigh and Foley. Galloway asked him whether Kevin had a reputation for being honest, and Okopal said yes. What was the relationship between Emigh and Foley?

"Tumultuous, rocky," Okopal said.

The defense now called John Ogden, a former police officer from El Segundo, California, who had served as the Indiana police chief for a little over a year after retiring from the Southern California department. He had known Kevin through youth hockey. Galloway wanted the former chief to testify about Kevin's reputation.

"In my opinion, Kevin has always been looked at as a very good citizen, peaceful. His demeanor in activities at the ice rink was excellent compared to many other parents, unfortunately. He was always very calm, cool," Ogden said.

"Everybody that I have come in contact with has always thought of him as a law-abiding, peaceful, gentle person," Janet Ogden, John Ogden's wife, testified.

By then, the defense had run out of witnesses. Judge Martin adjourned the trial to the next day, Tuesday, March 17, 2009, when the defense planned to call its big gun, a DNA expert of their own.

27.

Well, it was all too easy for Kevin's defense lawyers to suggest that John had had an affair with Melissa Uss as the possible motive for the murder, but that was simply more shadow casting, really, searching for something potentially plausible that, on further review, seemed much larger than it really was. This was a tried-and-true tactic with the SODDI defense: always find an explanation that encompassed other possible perpetrators, "some other dude." The fact that the defense hadn't pressed Melissa Uss on this issue, or even called Tom Uss as a witness, were silences that spoke volumes: clearly, if there had been any substance to the "innuendo," the defense would have exploited it by grilling the best witnesses.

As Krastek had argued to Judge Martin, there was actually no hard evidence of any affair between John and Melissa, only suggestions generated mostly by the defense counsel's choice of words in questioning their own witness, Darla. What might go quite a bit further for Kevin was significant evidence that the DNA findings of Drs. Cotton and Perlin were wildly inaccurate—back to the "million billion" conundrum. To that end, on March 17, 2009, as his first witness, Galloway called Dr. Laurence Mueller, a professor at the University of California, Irvine's department of ecology and evolutionary biology, where he specialized in the mathematics of population genetics.

Galloway took Mueller through the DNA testing process, essentially echoing Jerilynn Conway's testimony. But Mueller added something interesting: sometimes, during the replication process of the DNA, the chemicals used to amplify the DNA copied more of one parent's genetic pattern than the other. The underrepresented half was called "allelic dropout," and one effect of this, when it happened, was to give a misleading picture of the overall DNA pattern. Some portions of the amplified pattern could then fall below 50 RFU because of the "dropout." If there had been no "allelic dropout" in the test of the fingernail DNA, it was possible that the test might well have excluded Kevin as the minor donor, Galloway's questions implied. But because the residue of the minor donor was so small, the bureau had assumed a standard range of allelic dropout.

Mueller agreed. Essentially, the FBI had made assumptions about allelic dropout, then used those assumptions to say that Kevin could not be excluded. After that, Cotton and Perlin used even more assumptions to include him in their "millions and billions" analysis.

"From your review of the FBI's protocol, do, again, they find those simply not reliable enough to make an inclusion?" Galloway asked, referring to the FBI's standard of not using any results below 50 RFU.

"Right. And following up on that, or to include in their statistical calculations."

But Cotton and Perlin *did* use results below 50 RFU, didn't they? Galloway asked. Yes, Mueller said.

"Let me skip to Perlin's method," Galloway said. "Is the Perlin method simply a computer that he makes and sells?"

"Computer program, yes."

"A computer program. Do any legitimate scientists have

the ability to look behind his computer and see if his software is appropriate or is inappropriate?" In Galloway's question, Perlin was transformed into the Wizard of Oz: pay no attention to the man behind the curtain.

"It is proprietary, so only he and his coworkers know what is in it," Mueller agreed. It was impossible to verify Perlin's "billions and trillions" results, Mueller said, because Perlin wouldn't let anyone else know how his computer program worked. That was how he made his money.

"By the way," Galloway asked, "are you aware of any labs, anywhere, that are using the TrueAllele system that Mr. Perlin uses for mixed sample DNA forensic cases?"

"I have never encountered its use before until this case," Mueller said.

If the FBI had not assumed there was little or no allelic dropout on the amplified DNA sample, Galloway asked, wouldn't it then be true that a greater number of people would not be excluded, not just Kevin?

Yes, Mueller said. The FBI's assumption that there was little or no allelic dropout in the amplified DNA could be wrong.

"And that means even by the FBI—and even making the assumptions that the FBI had to make here, about allelic dropout—if you went out into the general population of Indiana County, or western Pennsylvania, or wherever, you have a one in thirteen thousand chances of finding somebody else who is in the same class, has the same markers?"

"Correct." The numbers could be even lower than 1 in 13,000, Mueller suggested, because those were calculated on the presumption of little or no allelic dropout."

"And that is because we are talking about a sliver of the DNA?"

True, said Mueller. In fact, he said, there was no way to say for sure that there weren't more than two donors of the fingernail DNA. This was an oblique reference to Monzo's opening statement that police had been told that John had been killed by several men in a robbery gone bad. Galloway was trying to make it appear that the FBI had cherry-picked the DNA information—had seen a glass half-full rather than half-empty—and that Cotton and Perlin had then thrown out most of the contents of the glass, leading to an even more skewed result.

It was also possible, with such a small amount of DNA for the minor donor, that the FBI's lab had made an error resulting in false positive results for the small number of spikes that did not exclude Kevin, Mueller said.

"And again, the size of the sample, can the size of the sample tend to make the results even less reliable?" Galloway asked.

"Yes. As I said, if the starting amount of the DNA is very low, you most often encounter these problems of allelic dropout, which, as I said, not only complicates the interpretation, but weakens the value of the evidence, or *should* weaken the value, of the evidence."

After a recess to give the jury a chance to stretch their legs and recharge their brains following this rather dense testimony, it was Krastek's turn to cross-examine. Mueller's testimony had thrown some sand into the prosecution's gearbox with the implication that the DNA results had been cherry-picked, that only the most damning results were used to decide whether to arrest Kevin. Krastek needed to clean this up, somehow. He decided to take a whack at the messenger, Mueller.

"You . . . testify quite frequently; do you not, sir?" Krastek asked.

"I have, yes."

"Okay. How many times do you think you have testified concerning DNA in criminal cases?"

"Since 1989, an exact count . . . it is hundreds now, [but] I don't have an exact count."

"And some little research, by 2002, I think you guessed, about a hundred and fifty times, you testified as a defense expert?"

"That is a reasonable ballpark."

"And have you ever testified for the prosecution in any case?"

"Yes,"

"How many times have you testified for the prosecution?"

"Once."

Krastek was employing a time-honored tactic of a prosecutor when confronted by an expert scientific witness for the defense: trying to portray Mueller as a hired gun who only testified for money and almost always only for the accused.

"And you are paid for what you testify for; is that correct, sir?"

"I am paid for my time, yes."

"And how much are you paid in this case? What are your rates?"

"Two hundred dollars an hour, plus expenses."

"You probably made over a million dollars testifying as a defense expert in DNA cases?"

"Since 1989, over twenty years, probably a reasonable estimate."

Having established, at least in his own mind, that Mueller's testimony was bought and paid for, Krastek moved on, satisfied that he had made the jury believe that Mueller would say whatever the defense wanted in return for a paycheck. Of course, the defense could make the same insinuations about Cotton and Perlin: they got paid, too, but by the taxpayers of Pennsylvania.

Mueller himself had never done any actual DNA tests, wasn't that correct? Hadn't he only evaluated the statistical likelihood of inclusion? Krastek asked. That was so, Mueller said.

The fingernails were still around, weren't they? As far as he knew, Mueller said. So the DNA test could be done again, true? Yes, if it was true that a sample remained, Mueller said.

"Okay," Krastek asked. "Do you know of any other attempt by the defendant, Kevin Foley, to have those tests redone? Anybody else redo those tests, to your knowledge?"

He hadn't heard of any, Mueller admitted.

When Cotton and Perlin made the choice to subtract John's DNA pattern from the mixed fingernail sample, those were reasonable assumptions, weren't they? After all, they were John's own fingernails, weren't they?

Yes, Mueller agreed, although with fingernails, as opposed to semen or saliva, there might be a more tenuous conclusion as to the identity of donors of mixed samples. The problem was in the assumption that said there was only one other minor donor: there could have been two or even more minor donors. The more donors, the broader the genetic swath it might represent, which was why the FBI estimate was so large, at 1 in 13,000. The DNA remnant could not be used in any definitive identification, he said: it simply could not provide enough information to be forensically useful. Although Conway had said the recovered DNA matched John and Kevin to greater or lesser degrees, there was no way to say for sure that the DNA didn't also include a vast number of other people. It all depended on what one assumed, whether about allelic dropout or RFU assessments, Mueller said: it was a matter of what one chose to include or exclude as possibilities. The FBI had assumed one thing, while he would not have assumed anything at all.

"And, sir, you are here, and you have come from California. And can you exclude Kevin Foley as a contributor here?" Krastek asked.

"No." But neither could Mueller exclude tens of thousands

of other men living in west-central Pennsylvania, at least not on the DNA alone.

Krastek now conducted Mueller into a morass of academic controversy over statistical genetics, in which Krastek suggested that Perlin's approach was considered by some to be state of the art. Mueller wouldn't go there, and the questions and answers between prosecutor and witness soon deteriorated into arcane inside baseball involving genetic experts, statistical methods, and erudite articles in scientific journals, a sort of verbal fencing match involving weapons no sturdier than foils, when a broadsword would have settled the issue definitely, although neither side had one.

By this point, the jury was surely wondering when the next recess would be decreed by Judge Martin. And by then, the fundamental question had already been answered: the small amount of DNA found underneath John's bloody fingernails that did not match John's own DNA *could* include Kevin Foley—among many, many others, thousands, millions, billions, trillions: the experts could argue until the Last Judgment, but no one could say for sure. It didn't *prove* it was Foley, but it did not exclude him—not unless one did not trust the FBI. The bureau might not have told all there was to tell, but it certainly wasn't lying. Still, if Mueller was telling the truth, the bureau could have excluded Foley if only it hadn't made the assumptions that it had about the allelic dropout. But no one could say for sure: the science was still in dispute.

The DNA battle was essentially a draw. But to Galloway, a draw was tantamount to reasonable doubt.

28.

Following Mueller, the defense called eleven more witnesses, most of them to testify to the good character of Kevin Foley. Russell States, the Sheetz security supervisor, was called by the defense to clarify if video cameras were in position to face the Route 119 roadway in Homer City. Despite the worries of his jailhouse witness over being publicly named, Galloway called him anyway.

Several of these character witnesses were also Pennsylvania State Police troopers in the unit that had been supervised by Emigh. As far as they knew, these troopers said, Kevin Foley was honest, never one to tell a lie. That was a useful foundation for Galloway, who intended to call Kevin to testify on his own behalf: it couldn't hurt to have a reputation as someone known to tell the truth.

From Russell States, Galloway wanted an acknowledgment that investigators had failed to recover any northbound Route 119 video records from the night of April 13. While it wasn't proof positive that Kevin hadn't committed the murder, the police failure to take them into custody at least supported the defense theme that someone wanted no evidence suggesting Kevin had *not* committed the crime. Galloway could now argue that if the police had done their job properly, there might have been Sheetz surveillance videos show-ing Kevin's Explorer rolling north on Route 119 *before* 1:00 a.m., well in advance of the screaming heard by the neigh-bors.

If the police had taken the trouble to obtain those videos, Galloway would suggest, Kevin would never have been ar-rested: he would have had a clear alibi. The failure to collect these video records reinforced the notion that the PSP had cherry-picked the evidence simply in order to make a case against Kevin.

As for the jailhouse informant who wanted to remain anonymous, this was the man who had named Brian Ray as the man who had confessed to the crime while both were in jail a few weeks after the murder. In a lengthy conference outside the presence of the jury, Galloway again pressed the judge to permit this man to testify without publicly provid-ing his name because of his fear of retaliation. In doing so, Galloway conjured up a number of stereotypes about gang-sters in the Pittsburgh 'hood. In the end, Judge Martin re-jected this: if Galloway wanted the jury to hear from this witness, he had to give his name, just like everyone else; it was part and parcel to his credibility as a witness.

Acceding to this requirement by Martin, on the after-noon of March 17, Galloway called William Bagley as a witness for the defense.

"Mr. Bagley, did you have occasion to be at the Westmore-land County jail when there was another prisoner there who made certain statements to you relating to the death of John Yelenic?" Galloway asked.

"Yes, sir."

"Can you tell the jury what that person told you?"

"He told me that he was responsible for the doctor's death."

What had he been told?

"He told me that he was a former patient of the doctor's. He told me that he was very friendly with the doctor, because he was a patient of his for years. He told me that the doctor used to buy him gifts and whatnot, and also told me that he had a bad drug problem at the time. And he was using drugs and going through things like that. And he basically told me that him and his friend were out doing burglaries and looking for a robbery, looking for some easy cash, and they plotted on the doctor and they went to go rob him and get some money, and things went haywire, and here we are now."

The inmate had told him that he and another man intended to rob Yelenic and had gone to the house armed with a pellet gun and a knife, Bagley said. But then things had turned nasty, and in the melee John had been cut to death.

"And when the doctor came downstairs, that is when they proceeded to frighten him, and he said that he tried to run, the doctor tried to run away, and the things got out of control and there was a scuffle in the home, and then he said he blacked out. And he said, the next thing that he remembered was running out the door"—the back door, Bagley said.

On his cross-examination, Krastek tried to induce Bagley to admit that he had read about the murder in the newspaper—that that was where he had gotten the details.

"Okay. This isn't the only homicide that you solved while you were in prison; is that right?" Krastek asked.

"Only homicide that I solved. I never saw a homicide before."

"Okay. Well, did you give information about another homicide to the police, while you were in the same prison or same jail?"

"I don't recall."

But, of course, Krastek had the records: Bagley had provided information on a second murder case too. While in jail, Bagley had claimed to have information on yet another murder, this one of a woman, a crime completely unrelated to the one involving John Yelenic. Krastek was trying to demonstrate that Bagley was someone who fabricated tales in order to get better treatment while in jail.

Krastek now pressed Bagley on his earlier revelation, which had involved a Pittsburgh woman whose throat had been cut. But the more Krastek pressed Bagley for details, the more Bagley said he couldn't recall. Clearly, somewhere along the line, some lawyer had prepped Bagley on the most appropriate answer to uncomfortable questions asked in court. Bagley could have been a Fortune 500 CEO, at least insofar as his memory was concerned.

Krastek asked Bagley about his criminal record; while extensive, it wasn't for major crimes. But to every question Bagley said he couldn't recall. Krastek had driven his point home: the testimony of William Bagley was hardly worth the time spent to hear it.

After a few more character witnesses for Kevin, a new row erupted between Krastek and Galloway over yet another Yelenic neighbor, one Bette Morris. In mid-August of 2006, after Corporal Gardner's crew had supplanted the Blairs-ville Police Department on the case, a trooper had taken a statement from Ms. Morris. The statement asserted that she had seen John and Melissa Uss kissing and hugging and otherwise involved in seemingly intimate acts while Tom Uss was away. But with the trial now in progress, Ms. Morris had denied that she had ever said such things. Galloway wanted to question Morris and use the trooper's report to "refresh her recollection." This would add weight to the defense's idea that John had been killed by a jealous husband, not Kevin Foley, Galloway told Martin.

"They [the PSP] generated a long and detailed report saying that she [Morris] pays attention to most things that she sees in the neighborhood," he told Judge Martin. Galloway meant that Morris had told the police that she had watched her neighbors closely. But, Galloway told Martin, "she now says she never told the police officer any of this." Ms. Morris had apparently recanted what she had allegedly told the trooper in August 2006.

Galloway told Martin he wanted to put Morris on the witness stand to make her admit that she *had* told the trooper what the report said she'd said. In Galloway's mind, Morris's supposed statements supported Darla Ferguson's observations. Taken together, they opened the door to the possibility that the killer of John Yelenic was someone other than Kevin Foley.

"I want to treat her as a hostile witness," Galloway told Judge Martin. "A reoccurring theme in this proceeding is . . . the people in the neighborhood, and that would include Darla Ferguson . . . are all concerned about their status . . . if they testify contrary to the Mary Ann Clark theme." Galloway was now suggesting that John's neighbors were all so intimidated by Mary Ann that they now could not recall ever seeing John and Melissa behaving inappropriately. This fit, at least somewhat, with the defense theory that Kevin was some sort of political scapegoat thrust into the spotlight of suspicion by Emigh, Mary Ann Clark, Tom Riley, and others, and that pressure on PSP higher-ups had resulted in Randall Gardner's allegedly skewed investigation.

"And this lady has now said that she never said . . . any of these things," Galloway went on, still referring to Bette Morris. "She had seen them on two occasions embracing, and one of them on the front porch of Melissa's house, where Yelenic was seen with his hand between her legs, rubbing her leg." Galloway was again referring to the PSP report. Still, Ms. Morris must have had very acute vision, if not binoculars, as well as an obsessive fascination with the goings-on of her neighbors—if not a vivid imagination—to have been able to tell the Pennsylvania state trooper the sorts of details she later denied giving. "And at one time, upon Yelenic returning from work, they met between the homes, and were hugging and kissing," Galloway went on, paraphrasing the PSP report. According to the report, Ms. Morris had also told the trooper that John had been involved with another woman at the same time. But now that Morris had denied she'd ever said anything like that, Galloway said, he wanted to put her under oath and question her as a hostile witness, which would permit him to ask leading questions: Wasn't it true she had told the Pennsylvania State Police that she had seen John and Melissa engaged in intimate relations?

It wasn't relevant to the case, Krastek said. "Even if that is true, I mean, God forbid, if one of us should be murdered, and then have romantic suggestions [that] we have had, with someone not our spouse, [it] comes into a courtroom. I just don't see, unless there is more, and I don't think there is more in this case, how that is relevant."

It *was* relevant, Galloway insisted, because it was Melissa who had accepted the $15,000 loan from John.

"A jury could infer that somebody who was having a romantic affair with Doctor. Yelenic, the husband might be inclined to do something, and that is a fair inference," Galloway argued. John was both a lover and a lender, according to Galloway's theory, and Tom Uss hated the former and resented the latter, Galloway contended. It was ample motive.

"I don't think it's a fair inference, and I think it is *way* out there," Krastek said.

"How are you going to establish that he [Tom Uss] knew?" Judge Martin asked Galloway.

"I'm just going to establish that it happened a lot, and—" Martin interrupted him.

"Don't you have to connect those dots to him?" the judge asked. He meant that Galloway would somehow have to prove conclusively that Tom Uss knew or believed that such an affair was going on before introducing such inferential evidence from third parties such as Darla Ferguson or Bette

Morris—both of whose testimonies had been contradictory at times.

"I don't think, Judge, that I have to show . . . There are certain inferences that jurors can draw, simply because common experience tells us that Mr. Uss is not going to come in here and say, 'I knew she was having an affair, he was having an affair with my wife, and therefore, I killed him.' And that is probably not going to happen in this case, and so all I will do is, put out the facts—that somebody thought that he was romantically involved, and they saw him doing something as intimate as rubbing [Melissa Uss] between her legs, and at times hugging and kissing . . . and let the jury infer what they infer from that. It is not a rape shield case." In other words, Melissa had no privacy rights, under the circumstances. Her reputation was not a pertinent issue to Kevin's guilt or innocence.

"I understand that," Judge Martin said, "but motive is not evidence. The reason that this guy—that is, your theory is that Mr. Uss is the one that murdered Dr. Yelenic?"

"Yes. That is the theory of this case," Galloway said.

He didn't think, without more evidence, that such a motive from a third-party witness would be admissible, Judge Martin said. There had to be something much more substantial than the defense's mere supposition.

"Why wouldn't it be?" Galloway demanded. "Why would it be less admissible than what Mr. Krastek has put in, about Michele Yelenic, [that she] was mad about the marital settlement, and therefore, Kevin would have some reason to kill? How is that relevant, and that is throughout this proceeding; what Michelle was happy about, Michelle was unhappy about, the PFA, and all of that stuff?"

If the prosecution could impute a motive to Kevin, Galloway was saying, why couldn't the defense impute a motive to Tom Uss? Why was the prosecutor's evidence of motive relevant while the defense's was not?

"Holy cow!" Judge Martin said, apparently giving in to his own frustration. The prosecution was able to support its theory of motive with other evidence, he said, not least of which was Kevin's multiple assertions that he wished John dead—all uttered while the divorce and custody cases were at issue.

Krastek agreed that made it relevant: he had shown that the unhappy divorce and the custody issue had led to Kevin expressing the desire that John would "just die." The defense had provided no facts at all to support the notion that Tom Uss had killed John or even, really, that John and Melissa had been having an affair. Without substantive facts, there could be nothing to support such a motive.

Galloway did not agree. Inferences were inferences, he said; one should be as equal as another.

"Again, you have to draw an inference that [Kevin] had a motive to kill, because he was mad about the Michele Yelenic problem with John Yelenic," Galloway said. If the prosecution was entitled to make inferences, so should the defense. "I am suggesting that Thomas Uss had a motive to kill, because his wife was having an affair with John Yelenic, the victim, that was witnessed by several people." The defense's inference about Tom Uss's motive should be equal to the prosecution's inference about Kevin's motive.

"No evidence here that [it was] Tom Uss, no linkage to Tom Uss," Krastek insisted.

Martin agreed: "That is correct. Do you have any evidence?"

"That Thomas Uss says he knew about [the supposed affair]? No, there is not a thing . . . I don't have any evidence that Thomas Uss made a declaration to anybody that he knew about it . . . But it was something that was happening in the neighborhood, and in the immediate vicinity of his house, with his next-door neighbor, over a period of time. And I think a jury can make a fair inference from that, that Thomas Uss would have an axe to grind with John Yelenic."

No, Martin said: whatever Bette Morris might have once said and now denied saying, there simply wasn't enough connection to Tom Uss to justify the jury hearing about it.

"Just because he had a motive—without any more, I don't believe that makes it admissible," he said. "I am going to sustain the objection . . . Unless you can tie it, where Mr. Uss said something to somebody, or if he comes in and says, 'Yeah, I knew about it.'"

He didn't have it, Galloway again admitted. He still wanted the police report of Ms. Morris's supposed statement admitted as a defense exhibit, for the purposes of appeal. But based on Judge Martin's ruling, the jury would never hear of Bette Morris.

Now it would be up to Kevin to defend himself.

29.

Galloway called his client to the witness stand shortly after 8:30 a.m. on Wednesday morning, March 18, 2009. Kevin had to know, as his defense lawyers surely did, that this was his make-or-break time. Either he could convince a jury that he had no animosity toward John and that he'd been no-where near Blairsville on the night of the murder, or he couldn't. If the jury didn't believe him, Kevin was almost certain to be convicted, even on the circumstantial evidence. And if he was convicted, he'd almost certainly spend the rest of his life in prison. For an elite Pennsylvania state trooper, such a fate was almost unthinkable.

Galloway had asked Judge Martin—begged, really—to allow him to begin his examination of his principal witness on the morning following the character witnesses and Russell States and William Bagley. The last thing Galloway wanted was for the prosecution to commence its cross-examination after the jury had had a whole night to rumi-nate on what Kevin had told them on direct examination Tuesday afternoon. He wanted a fresh start—the direct, then the cross-examination, all to occur on the same day; he wanted Kevin's own words to ring equally in the jurors' minds. He wanted to lodge reasonable doubt in one or more of the jurors' minds. Judge Martin was finally persuaded.

Galloway began by asking Kevin to define himself.

He was, Kevin said, a Pennsylvania state trooper and had been since 1994. Kevin's countenance from the witness stand radiated sincerity as well as humility. He was, his expression indicated, nothing more or less than a dedicated public servant, yet a working stiff like anyone else. To Mary Ann Clark and Tom Riley, who had attended every day of the trial, Kevin seemed confident, superior, almost smarmy, as if he was sure no jury would ever convict him, one of Pennsylvania's finest.

"Before I go any further, Trooper Foley," Galloway said, "you have heard the charges against you, that you had something to do with the homicide of John Yelenic on April 13, 2006. Did you have anything to do with the homicide of John Yelenic?"

"No, I did not," Kevin said.

After taking Kevin through his background as an adopted child in New York and his coming of age in Florida, then his law enforcement career, Galloway moved on to the more pertinent questions.

"Did you have occasion to meet John Yelenic?"

"Yes, I did."

"And where did you first meet him?"

"The first time I met John was at a T-ball game for Jamie." It was at a local YMCA in Indiana, Kevin said. Michele had introduced them.

Galloway asked Kevin to characterize Michele's ability "as a mother."

Krastek objected to this as irrelevant. Well, actually it wasn't, Galloway said: the prosecution had already made much of "what Michele did or didn't do," and while it might be irrelevant to the charge against Foley, "the door has been opened" with regard to Kevin's motive, or lack of it.

No, Judge Martin ruled, Michele's capacities as a mother weren't relevant to the murder case. Galloway moved on.

"How many times did you have a face-to-face contact with John Yelenic?"

"Three or four times."

One of these occasions, Foley said, was when John had come to the Susan Drive house to pick up Jamie—this, after John had cursed Michele over the telephone, apparently in the wake of Michele's complaint that John had sexually abused Jamie in the spring of 2005. Kevin accosted John while he was still in his car and warned him not to use bad language again with Michele. That was when John sneered at him and advised him to write him a ticket, Kevin said. He never touched John that day or threatened him, Kevin continued, although he admitted to raising his voice and cursing John.

Galloway moved on to the confrontation that had occurred outside Judge Hanna's courtroom in October 2005. Was it true that John had made a threatening gesture toward him?

Yes, Kevin said.

"Let me ask you this," Galloway said. "Did you ever wink at John Yelenic on that day, or any other day of your life?"

"No, sir, I did not."

"Did John Yelenic make a sign at you?"

"Yes, he did."

"And what kind of sign did he make?"

"He had his hand or fingers like a gun, and went like that to me," Kevin said, mimicking the finger-pointing Alexander had said John had called a *Seinfeld*.

Galloway asked Kevin if John's signal meant anything to him at the time.

"I have been in law enforcement for a number of years . . .

and made a lot of arrests in my career. And I have never had anybody do that to me, knowing the position that I hold as a state trooper. And so, that was quite disturbing. And that same day that John made that motion with his hand like he had a gun pointing toward me, he retrieved his weapons from the Indiana County Sheriff's Office . . ."

The fact that John had been awarded the return of his firearms by Judge Hanna on the same day he made the finger-pointing gesture made Kevin feel that his life had been threatened, he said.

Galloway asked Kevin to describe the traumatic meeting between John and Jamie at the Indiana police station the day before Thanksgiving 2005.

"Jamie had a look that I have never seen before," Kevin said. "He was scared to death and he was frightened. He immediately clung to Michele. He wouldn't listen to anything that John had to say. He wasn't going to go with John and he fought him."

Then it got even worse, according to Kevin.

"Jamie grabbed hold of Michele, and John was trying to remove Jamie from Michele. And Michele literally dropped her arms down by her side, and Jamie was hanging on to her hair. And John was pulling Jamie's legs, and you could see Michele's head being pulled every time Jamie's legs were being pulled by John, and that's when the police officer intervened." This was what had been on the videotape that prompted Deana Kirkland to reopen her investigation into the alleged abuse.

Galloway asked what the Indiana police officer did in response to this scene. The Indiana officer separated John from Jamie, Kevin said. The officer asked that John show a court order on the custody and, according to Kevin, John left the station, went out to his car, and returned with Judge Hanna's October order. Kevin said that John presented it to the Indiana cop, who was then in a quandary, recognizing that John had a lawful custody order but also that Jamie was terrified of him. According to Kevin, the Indiana police officer said he had no authority to force Jamie to accompany John. John insisted that Jamie was coming with him, Kevin recalled.

"And once again, they went round about, and Jamie was kicking and screaming and crying and spitting on him and swinging at him, and John just wasn't going to give up," Kevin said.

The Indiana officer separated father and son, Kevin testified. "Jamie was shaking and sweating and crying, and John said, 'Come on, Jamie, let's go.' And Jamie just ignored him and didn't do anything, and John asked him a couple more times, 'Come on, Jamie, let's go' . . . and he threw his hands up in the air and said 'Okay, you win, I'm leaving, I quit.' And John left."

Galloway took pains to ensure that Kevin appeared to be the innocent party in this horrific scene between father and son.

On that day before Thanksgiving, had Kevin tried to intimidate John? "Did you yell at him, argue with him or even talk to him?"

"No. The only thing I said was, 'John, no one is interfering with you getting Jamie, and you haven't seen him in . . .' It was a good while since John had seen Jamie. And I said, 'Maybe you should get some counseling, you and Jamie to go. Or something to that effect.'"

On this point Kevin was clearly confused or dissembling: at the October hearing, when Judge Hanna rescinded the protection-from-abuse order of April 2005, she had required both John and Jamie to attend supervised joint counseling sessions. These had been going on for more than a month, so it wasn't true that John hadn't seen his son for "a good while." And Kevin's remark "Maybe you should get some counseling" might well have been a sneer by the day before

Thanksgiving, rather than heartfelt advice—a way of Kevin telling John he was somehow defective.

Galloway moved on to the divorce agreement. While Krastek had used Effie Alexander's testimony to suggest that Michele was balking at signing the agreement, and that her unhappiness had provided Kevin with a motive to murder, Galloway wanted to paint a different picture.

"Was Michelle happy, mad, sad about signing the agreement?" Galloway asked.

Michele was happy, Kevin said, happy to finally get it over with.

Galloway went on to the subject of the shoes. Was it true that Kevin preferred ASICS running shoes?

"My favorite is Mizuno," Kevin said. He did have one or two pairs of ASICS, but wore them only as a second choice. He had purchased many ASICS shoes for other troopers, he said, because he understood how to order them and obtain a special law enforcement discount. If the ASICS people had records showing he had ordered numerous pairs of their shoes over the years, it was mostly because he was buying them for his friends in the PSP.

Galloway turned to the events of April 12 and 13, 2006. He had worked a shift from 1:00 p.m. to 9:00 p.m. on April 12, Kevin said, because he wanted to play in the hockey game that night in Delmont. After the game, Kevin said, he changed into his street clothes and then left the arena. This was shortly after midnight.

And then? Galloway asked.

"I went home," Kevin said.

Kevin now described his route back to Indiana: east on Route 22, then north on 199, off the Wayne Avenue exit, north on Wayne to Locust, then up the hill to Susan Drive and Michele. This itinerary would have passed more Sheetz stores at Blue Lick, Homer City, and the intersection of

Wayne and Locust in Indiana, all of them with video surveillance cameras. Yet, no one had bothered to collect those recordings, a point Galloway had stressed throughout the trial: it supported the defense's contention that the investigators had overlooked possible evidence to show that Kevin *hadn't* done the murder. A video showing, say, Kevin's Explorer passing the Homer City Sheetz at 12:45 a.m. would be potential evidence that Kevin couldn't have committed the murder.

"And did you at any time that evening get off Route 22 anywhere in the vicinity of Blairsville?" Galloway asked.

"No, I did not."

"Did you at any time on that morning drive into any part of Blairsville?"

"No, I did not."

"Did you go to Spring Street?"

"No, I did not."

"Did you go past a Blairsville Sheetz?"

"No, I did not."

"Did you go on Route 217 or Market Street at any time?"

"No, I did not."

"Did you, in the course of going home, get off Route 22 for any reason at any time?"

"No, sir, I did not."

"Did you get off 119, other than when you got to the Wayne Avenue exit?"

"No, I did not."

"What time did you get home?"

"It was 12:40, 12:45," Kevin said.

When he got home, Kevin said, he removed his hockey gear from the back of his Explorer. That was when his stick got hung up.

"So I pulled a little harder and it came out and the blade of the stick caught me above the eye." That was how he got the wound over his eye, he said: his hockey stick boomeranged and hit him.

It wasn't until after he had gotten off his shift at the Indiana barracks on the afternoon of April 13 that he heard about the murder of John Yelenic, Kevin said. This was when Barbara Swasy called, telling Michele that John was "gone." But Kevin's recollection of this was slightly different from Barbara's. In Kevin's version, Barbara had told Michele that John had had a heart attack.

After that, Kevin said, Barbara made a second telephone call.

"Again, she reiterated that John was dead, and she said there is crime scene tape around his house. And I said. 'Well, then. He didn't have a heart attack.' I have investigated natural deaths where you have heart attack, and you don't put up crime scene tape, so it was something other than a heart attack."

At that point, Kevin said, Barbara asked him to call the state police barracks to find out what was going on.

"And what did you tell her?"

"I said, I am not working; since it is in Blairsville Borough, they would have jurisdiction and I recommended her to call the Blairsville Borough Police."

Now Galloway inquired into Kevin's relationship with Emigh.

"Originally, it was good," Kevin said. "We had a good working relationship, but then it turned sour."

"Tell the jury about that," Galloway asked.

The friction with Emigh had begun when Kevin learned that one of his fellow troopers was dating a woman that Emigh was also dating, Kevin said. He warned the trooper that he might not want to continue seeing the woman: Emigh might hold it against him.

"Did Sergeant Emigh confront you about that?" Galloway asked.

"Yes, he did."

"What was his . . . was he happy, sad, mad?"

"He was mad."

"Was there another incident involving a car?"

There was, Kevin said. As a police supervisor, Emigh was entitled to drive a state police car to his home, in case he had to be on call. One night another trooper saw the car assigned to Emigh in the parking lot of a local bar. Troopers who took state cars home weren't allowed to drink, Kevin said. He talked about this with other troopers, Kevin said, and that was when his relationship with Emigh began to sour.

At this point, an hour and forty-five minutes into Kevin's testimony, Judge Martin ordered a recess.

When the trial resumed, Galloway turned to the testimony from others that Kevin had occasionally wished John dead, and Zenisek's recollection that Kevin had asked him he wanted to help kill John.

"There has been some testimony about remarks you made about John Yelenic; that he ought to die, or he ought to die in an accident or words to that effect; do you remember that?"

"Yes, I do."

"Did you ever intend any harm to John Yelenic by your remarks?"

"No, I did not."

"Did you admire him relative to what was going on with Jamie?"

"No, I did not."

"Did that lack of admiration at any time lead you to develop any kind of a rage against John, or anything else?"

"No, sir."

"In the barracks, is it uncommon to hear troopers talking about the fact that a suspect that they don't like, somebody ought to do him in, or words to that effect?"

"No, that is not uncommon."

He'd only been joking with Zenisek, Kevin said. You had to know him: he often made jokes like that, and Zenisek knew it.

"Trooper Foley, in any way, in any manner, at any time, with any instrumentality, did you cause or help to cause death of John Yelenic?"

"No, I did not."

"Are you innocent?"

"Yes, sir, I am innocent."

Krastek's objective in cross-examining Kevin was to force Kevin to explain all the circumstances that had led to the conclusion that Kevin was the killer. That meant probing Kevin's recollection of the "death wishing" testimony of the others, trying to get him to explain himself, and forcing him to explain the fact that he'd bought ASICS shoes, the knife-flicking habit, the coincidence that he was in Blairsville the night the murder was committed, and the damning fact that the man he wished was dead had in fact died.

Kevin told Krastek that he had made his remark to Zenisek after talking with Deana Kirkland.

"And how much longer after you talked to Deana Kirkland did you talk to Daniel Zenisek and ask his help to kill John Yelenic?"

"I was joking with Trooper Zenisek."

"The question was, how much longer?"

"I have no idea." Kevin shook his head, smiling.

"And what is funny about that? What is funny about saying, 'Trooper Zenisek, I want you to help me kill that cocksucker'? Tell me the joke. I don't get it."

Galloway objected, saying Krastek's question was argumentative.

Judge Martin overruled Galloway.

"Tell me the joke," Krastek persisted.

"There isn't any joke," Kevin said.

"What is funny about it?"

"Maybe my personality, my behavior," Kevin said.

"When you said it to Trooper Zenisek, how were you feeling about John Yelenic?"

"I don't think, I don't remember any kind of feeling I had for him."

"And you sure didn't like him; did you?"

"No, I did not like him."

"And why didn't you like him?"

"I don't think any new boyfriend or current boyfriend likes the ex-boyfriend or ex-husband," Kevin said.

Krastek tried to get Kevin to admit that his dislike for John had begun with the sex abuse allegations first raised by Michele. Kevin admitted that he believed Michele and Jamie, even after Deana Kirkland, CYS, and Judge Hanna had all found the allegations groundless. He still believed them, Kevin said. When John cursed Michele over the telephone after the allegations had been made, he began to dislike John even more, Kevin said.

"And you continued your, your expressions of ill will toward Dr. Yelenic continued; did they not?"

"What do you mean specifically?"

"Well, I mean, there were other troopers that testified here about statements that you made wishing him dead; is that correct?"

"Yes, sir."

"Okay. And in fact, that was something that you would say often, not necessarily wishing him dead, but saying disparaging remarks about him?"

"I think it was all around the same time period."

"Okay. And were they all jokes?"

"Yes, sir."

"So every time you called him a name, swear word, or wished him dead, those were all jokes?"

"Yes. I never made a threat with any intentions of carrying it out. I never made a threat to him. It was just things that I said to my fellow troopers and friends."

Krastek asked Kevin when he had first heard about John's death. It was when Barbara Swasy called and talked to Michele, Kevin said. He didn't talk to Barbara himself, Kevin said, but Michele told him that Barbara had told her that John had died of a heart attack. Some time later, Barbara called again.

"What did she say to you?"

"She said John was found dead in his house and there was crime scene tape up and I said, 'Well, Barb, that is not heart attack.'"

"And what else did she say?"

"She said, 'Can you call the barracks?' and I said no."

"And why couldn't you?"

"Because we can't interfere with investigations with other departments."

"And if you called your barracks, how is that interference in Blairsville's investigation?"

"For one thing, it was in Blairsville, so I told her that also, and I said Blairsville is investigating that crime, and you need to call Blairsville Police."

"But you didn't know that Blairsville was investigating this crime?"

"She said he was found in the house."

"So?"

"Blairsville have their own police department."

"Can't they call the state police?"

"Sure, they could."

"You made an assumption?"

"Sure."

"If you assumed that, why couldn't you call the state police?"

"I said, 'You have to call Blairsville, and if we were handling the investigation she could call the barracks, or I could have called the barracks."

"Weren't you curious as to what happened?"

"I figured I would find out soon enough."

"And John Yelenic, the bane of your existence for all of these years, is found dead and you didn't think to call anybody, or you weren't curious about it?"

"I was a little bit curious."

"A little bit curious?"

"Yeah."

"And what, if anything, did you do to find out what happened?"

"Nothing. Just like watching the news. You see something on the news and you kind of, you can look curious but I don't start making phone calls all over the place."

On redirect, to take some of the sting out of the evidence that the sexual abuse allegations were deemed unfounded, Galloway asked Kevin whether Kirkland had told him she still believed the allegations were true, but Krastek objected to this as hearsay: Kevin couldn't testify to what Kirkland had told him out of court; coming from Kevin himself, it was self-serving testimony, unverifiable. The defense should have asked Kirkland herself when she was on the witness stand.

After a few more clarifying questions by Galloway on redirect, the defense rested its case without calling Michele Yelenic as Kevin's alibi witness. The jury would have to take Kevin's word for it that he'd been at home with Michele, Nathan, and Nicole on the night of the murder.

30.

Under Pennsylvania court rules, each side could give only one closing argument, and the defense always went first. Monzo gave the argument in favor of Kevin's innocence.

He began the way he had started, accusing the commonwealth of jumping to conclusions in charging Kevin with the murder.

"This trial has been about the Commonwealth's desperate, failed attempt to build a case toward that wrong conclusion, because the evidence in the case has shown that Kevin Foley is innocent."

Monzo said that the commonwealth jumped to its conclusion because of George Emigh, the crime unit supervisor who didn't like Kevin Foley. Emigh had seized on the fact that Kevin was living with John's estranged wife as the pretext for getting the commonwealth to investigate Foley. It was personal, Monzo implied. And if the commonwealth wasn't afraid to admit that, why hadn't it called Emigh to the witness stand to say so?

Krastek objected. Another sidebar conference was held. That was an improper suggestion, Krastek said. The defense could have called Emigh themselves, but they hadn't, either. Judge Martin said he would tell the jury that Emigh was available to both sides as a witness, and that the jurors should not read anything into the fact that he wouldn't be testifying. Monzo said that was fine, and the lawyers stepped back so Monzo could resume.

It was true, Monzo said, that Kevin didn't like John.

"Mr. Krastek and the Commonwealth want you to confuse this dislike as motive to kill. And let's concentrate on that. Mr. Krastek spent about ninety percent of Kevin Foley's cross-examination talking about statements that Kevin Foley admitted he [had] said bad things about John Yelenic and [that] he did not like John Yelenic. He told you why he didn't like John Yelenic but I ask you, when you go to the jury room to deliberate, I ask you to ask yourselves one very important thing: If Kevin Foley intended to kill John Yelenic, is he going to walk around telling people that he is going to do it?

"That is what they want you to believe. Kevin sat up on that witness stand and said, 'Yes, I said things about him,' and he told you why he said things about him . . ."

Did it make any sense that if Kevin really intended to kill John, he would go around talking about it to his buddies in the Pennsylvania State Police of all people?

The commonwealth had made much of the fractious divorce as a motive for murder, but the evidence showed that the case had been settled the week before John Yelenic's death. It made no sense to murder Yelenic, because the case was over and everyone was finally happy.

Monzo said that Deana Kirkland had testified that she believed Jamie. That was a misstatement of Kirkland's testimony: it had been Kevin who'd tried to claim that Kirkland still believed the allegations but had been stopped by Krastek's objection to the hearsay. Then Monzo took Kevin's description of the Thanksgiving incident at the Indiana police station and attributed it to Kirkland.

"She . . . told you that Jamie was terrified to go with his

dad. That is why she reopened the investigation, she didn't do it as a favor to a friend. She did it because what happened at the Indiana Borough Police Station was wrong. Jamie was terrified. There is no motive to Kevin, none."

The Sheetz videos were worthless as evidence, Monzo said: they just showed some car that looked a little bit like Kevin's car but that even the FBI, with all its technical legerdemain, couldn't positively identify. As for the knives, the jury should keep in mind that despite its best efforts, the prosecution hadn't been able to link a single one of Kevin's four or five different knives to the murder. They couldn't link him with any of the shoe prints or find any bloodstains.

"And let's talk about the crime scene and the shoe print and something more troubling about it, in my opinion. The crime scene was a circus. You heard that the very first day, when Patrolman Isherwood gets to the crime scene, Craig Uss has been through the crime scene to the body, around the body and walking around the body. His uncle was in the house. His grandfather was in the house walking around . . . [D]o you remember how many people were in the house between deputies, police officers, EMTs and firefighters? Fifteen to twenty people are walking around the house the day that John Yelenic was found. You can't rely on any shoe print evidence. It should cause you to pause."

And what about the DNA evidence? Monzo asked. The police had taken only one sample of DNA—from Kevin only.

"One person was tested, but that didn't quite work out so well either, because when you send it to the FBI Crime Lab, it's a defense-oriented result. It is not enough. How is this going to play into our desperate attempt to build a case for the wrong conclusion?

"So 1 in 13,000 is just not enough. There are over a hundred thousand people just walking around Indiana County, let alone Westmoreland and Allegheny. That doesn't eliminate anybody." So the commonwealth had sent the DNA results to Drs. Cotton and Perlin, who came up with wildly inconsistent numbers that nevertheless had the effect of making it seem that Kevin Foley was the one person in the entlre galaxy who could have done the crime. The DNA evidence was simply unrellable, and the jury should just ignore it, Monzo said.

Not only that, it came from evidence that hadn't been properly stored.

"They put this man on trial for his life and they throw the evidence in a dorm refrigerator and that should cause you to pause and that should cause you reasonable doubt. And something else should because after they took it out of the dorm refrigerator and they sent it to the state police crime lab in Greensburg, what did you learn from Corporal Gardner? The state police crime lab rejected it."

Kevin had just adopted a baby, Monzo went on. It made no sense, with all that was going on in Kevin's life, that he should suddenly decide to risk it all by killing a man he had no reason to kill—and doing it just after leaving five or six other state troopers, who knew the route he would take to get home.

And what about Isaiah Brader?

"He heard the words, 'I will never loan you money again; I will never loan you money again.' There has been no evidence that Kevin Foley owed John Yelenic money. I submit to you, ladies and gentlemen, if you believe the testimony of Isaiah Brader, standing alone, and there is no reason to disbelieve him, he has nothing to gain or lose in this case, you must acquit Kevin Foley." At the very least, it all added up to reasonable doubt, he said. And if anyone on the jury had a reasonable doubt, they should not vote to convict.

Monzo reached his peroration.

"We have done all we can for Kevin Foley. The rest of his life is now in your hands. Don't let them get away with jumping to a conclusion. You own your verdict. It is your verdict.

Mr. Krastek can't do anything about it. I can't do anything about it and the judge can't do anything about it. It is your verdict. Tell them they jumped and lots of times when somebody jumps you can't stop them. You can stop them. Ladies and gentlemen of the jury, justice is not convicting the wrong person. Thank you."

Monzo had made a good effort at trying to turn the defense's deficits into assets; the very fact that so many circumstances seemingly pointed to Kevin made it unlikely that Kevin did it, he had in effect argued. Now it would be up to Krastek to pull the parts back together. Krastek would try to do so by delineating the various circumstances in terms of multiplying odds, each one narrowing the likelihood of the next circumstance. What were the odds that anyone with all those circumstances could be anything other than guilty? It was fantastic to believe that one man would be subject to such circumstantial evidence, each piece more damning than the next, and *not* be guilty.

"Mr. Monzo in his opening statement kept calling the prosecution desperate," Krastek said. "I thought after this case was concluded and with the evidence he would have stopped that. He is continuing to call us desperate. Understand it took a year and a half before charges were filed in this case, from the time that John Yelenic was brutally murdered. Is that someone jumping to a conclusion, or is that law enforcement agencies looking at this evidence in the best way they can, with the tools that they have?

"Mr. Monzo called *us* desperate, and yet you heard them bring up George Emigh and Thomas Uss and Melissa Uss and Isaiah Brader, and best of all William Bagley." Krastek shook his head at the last name: just who was really desperate, the commonwealth or the defense?

The suggestion that George Emigh had somehow orchestrated the investigation and eventual arrest of Kevin Foley to get even with him for personal reasons was ludicrous, Krastek said, and was a measurement of the defense's own desperation.

"Do you think some sergeant with the state police could call up Jerrilyn Conway, for example, and say, lie about your report?" Krastek asked. The jury had seen and heard Conway's testimony, straightforward as it was, and could see that it was a conservative evaluation of the DNA evidence.

"And you had a chance to watch this prosecution through the last week and a half. Do you think George Emigh could tell me what to do? Think about that. That didn't stop Mr. Monzo from suggesting that George Emigh somehow masterminded this, and without any evidence." Even Kevin admitted that he knew nothing of Emigh's supposed role in the investigation and his eventual arrest.

"Of all of the sophomoric, fraternity-brother, drunken, Saint Patrick's Day kind of talk, these guys suggested that because Melissa Uss and John Yelenic were neighbors and sometimes talked, appeared to be friendly, and occasionally talked on the porch together, that that must have meant something. 'It must have been *more* than just that.' Where is the evidence? I mean, let's be fair here. It is their accusation. They had Melissa Uss on the stand and they never asked her that. How fair is that? How decent is that? That didn't stop them from suggesting it to you. Why not at least ask her? But on the basis of some conversation on a porch they are going to suggest to you that it made Thomas Uss commit a crime. And there is no evidence of that to you whatsoever."

The police were obligated to check out every story, Krastek pointed out, even those that were from "whackos." Neighbors gossiped about people all the time, but when it came down to it, none took the witness stand to admit what they might have told the police. The prosecution was obliged by law to pass the raw stuff on to the defense, but that didn't mean it was true. No one had sworn an oath to tell the truth when they were telling the police their gossip.

Brader might not have been a whacko, Krastek said, but he was obviously confusing the actual time of the murder, around 1:30 a.m., with something that happened almost three hours later.

"The best one, perhaps, was when they brought William Bagley in here. You had a chance to hear William Bagley: a thief, a robber and a guy who lies to the police. And confesses to it, and is convicted of it. He is in jail and why would [the perpetrators] pick him, out of [all the] others, to come and confess? Wasn't his testimony simply laughable?" Bagley's description of what supposedly happened with Brian Ray and his accomplice didn't fit the facts of the case, as the jury could see for themselves from the crime scene photos. Had Bagley ever said a word about the broken front window? Surely, if the fabled Brian Ray had really committed the crime, he would have remembered the horrific broken window and the screams if he remembered anything at all. No, Krastek went on, William Bagley had simply read about the murder in the newspaper and tried to use it to get a get-out-of-jail-free card from the police. The police had been obligated to collect the information, and the prosecution had been obligated to turn it over to the defense, and the defense, in its own desperation, had tried to use it to throw up a smoke screen to conceal the real killer, Kevin Foley.

The desperation of the defense smoke screen was obvious by its own inconsistency, Krastek said.

"They try to suggest to you that Doctor Yelenic was both a homosexual child abuser and a heterosexual adulterer, and it doesn't matter . . . consistency is not required of them. Just throw things up, smoke screens and red herrings.

"John Yelenic provided, if not the most eloquent, but certainly the most poignant evidence in this case, because with maybe his last act, as he is fighting for his life against a man for which he was no match, he managed to reach his hand out and scratch his assailant."

The defense had tried to obscure the real meaning of the DNA results, Krastek said. Because even with the lowest match basis, Conway's 1 in 13,000, the minor donor's DNA still included Kevin. If it hadn't, the case never would have been filed. And when that inclusion was accompanied by so many other circumstances that also included Kevin—the shoes, the knife flicking, the death wishes, the timing of Kevin's journey from Delmont on the night of the murder—the likelihood of any other person having committed the crime simply got narrower and narrower and narrower, until it was beyond any reasonable doubt that Kevin was the one who had to be responsible for the crime.

The defense's suggestion that someone other than the killer had left the bloody shoeprints—say, Craig Uss, or the EMTs, or anyone else—was ridiculous, Krastek asserted. If that were so, there would have been many different shoe print types in the foyer and the bloody path to the back door documented by Gonglik. But the fact was, there was only one type of print found: an ASICS Gel Creed, the same time of shoe that the records from ASICS showed that Kevin had purchased.

The ASICS expert had testified that the company sold only fifteen thousand pairs of such shoes in the United States. What was the likelihood that another person with the same type of shoes, with the inclusive DNA, with the habit of knife flicking, with the track record of uttering threats and ill will toward John, with a relationship with his estranged wife, with the opportunity to commit the murder on the night of April 13, who drove a vehicle that was similar to the one captured by the Sheetz videos, with what almost everyone agreed was a fingernail scratch on his face, noticed by many for the first time the morning after the crime, actually existed? It was virtually nil, far beyond any reasonable doubt.

The DNA might not have perfectly matched Kevin, Krastek conceded—there just wasn't enough of it for that—but it still included Kevin, and with all the other circumstances pointing to him, "you can't walk him out that door.

"The evidence deserves a conviction, and that is what it should be. I ask [you] on behalf of the Commonwealth to find Kevin Foley guilty of first-degree murder of the killing of Doctor John Yelenic."

Judge Martin then read the jury a list of the witnesses who had testified, who they were, and on which day they had taken the stand. Then he read them instructions on the law of first-degree murder, an explanation of reasonable doubt, and an instruction on when manslaughter had occurred, as a lesser included offense—in case the jury believed that the accused hadn't intended to kill Yelenic but had acted in the heat of the moment during a fight.

At just before 4:00 p.m., the jury retired to deliberate on Kevin's fate.

All in all, it was a pretty feeble defense for Kevin, particularly in light of his lawyers' promise to the jury in the beginning that they would *prove* that Kevin could not have murdered John Yelenic. It was, it seemed, a roll-the-dice attempt at trying to establish reasonable doubt by casting shadows, and insubstantial ones at that. Virtually all of the defense's argument had come from the police investigation: Brader, who was out of sync with his neighbors in regard to times; William Bagley, the jailhouse snitch who'd claimed Brian Ray had admitted the murder; even Tom Uss—all of it was flailing and posturing. Surely, if Kevin hadn't done the crime, an independent investigation, not one that relied on just the police, might have brought out exculpatory facts: for instance, the Sheetz videos for Route 119, which had vanished into the ozone. Or an un-bloodstained knife, owned by Kevin, identified by his fellow officers as belonging to him just before the murder. Or ASICS shoes owned by Kevin on April 13 that did not match the bloody shoe prints. It was the very lack of dispositive evidence from the defense that made it difficult to believe Kevin. Surely an innocent man would have something to bolster his claim; the very lack of exculpatory facts was suspicious in itself. But Galloway and Monzo never really had much to work with other than bluster about "leap[ing] to conclusions."

In the end, if Kevin wanted to save himself, it was up to him, and to Michele, his main alibi witness, and the two Kamler kids. And they had not shown up.

The jury worked into the evening hours, deliberating. At about 8:00 p.m., they sent a note out to the judge, request a rereading of his instruction defining reasonable doubt. The jurors filed back into the courtroom, and Judge Martin read the instruction again:

" 'Although the Commonwealth has the burden of proving the defendant guilty, this does not mean that the Commonwealth must prove its case beyond all doubt or to a mathematical certainty, nor must it demonstrate the complete impossibility of innocence. A reasonable doubt is a doubt that would cause a reasonably careful and sensible person to pause, hesitate or refrain from acting upon a matter of highest importance in his or her own affairs or to his or her own interests. A reasonable doubt must fairly arise out of the evidence that was presented, or out of the lack of evidence presented, with respect to some element of each of the crimes charged. A reasonable doubt must be a real doubt. It may not be an imagined one, nor may it be a doubt manufactured to avoid carrying out an unpleasant duty.'

"All right," Judge Martin said, "I hope that helps you in your deliberations and with that I will send you back upstairs."

The jury resumed its deliberations. It seemed clear from the request that at least one juror was struggling with the reasonable-doubt concept. Galloway and Monzo knew it took only one juror to stick to his or her own reasonable doubt to have a hung jury and a mistrial. If there were several jurors with reasonable doubt, and they stuck with it, the chances of a mistrial rose considerably.

Two hours later, at 10:00 p.m., the jury sent a note to the judge: they had reached a verdict.

The jurors filed into the courtroom, taking their seats in the jury box. A paper was handed to Judge Martin. He read it to himself, then handed it to the court clerk.

"All right," the judge said. "The verdict is in the proper form. Would you inquire of the jury if this is their verdict, please."

"Members of the jury, harken unto your verdict as the court has recorded it in the case of *Commonwealth and Kevin Foley*: 'On the charge of murder in the first degree, we find the defendant guilty.' "

There was a hubbub in the courtroom as the friends of John and Kevin all began to talk at once.

"Quiet," Judge Martin ordered.

Now the judge asked Galloway if he wanted the jury polled—that is, asked individually if they agreed with the verdict. This was one way of determining if anyone had second thoughts or might have felt unduly pressured by the other jurors. All agreed that this was his or her own decision: Kevin Foley was indeed guilty of the murder of John Yelenic.

Afterward, Judge Martin permitted the jurors to exit from a rear door of the courthouse to avoid the assembled news media, if they chose to do so.

"Tears gushed Wednesday night as Yelenic's friends and family hurried to spread the word," a Pittsburgh news reporter said the following day. The reporter caught up with Mary Ann Clark, who had hounded officials from the very beginning to find out who had murdered her cousin.

"It's over now—it's over," Mary Ann said. "So John can be at peace."

Epilogue

But it wasn't over: Kevin still had to be sentenced, while Galloway and Monzo plotted an appeal. Mary Ann, meanwhile, sued Kevin, Michele, and eight Pennsylvania state troopers, including Deana Kirkland and the former commissioner of the PSP, James Miller.

"During the relationship between Michele Yelenic and Kevin Foley," the wrongful death lawsuit alleged, that while he lived with Michele Yelenic, "Foley became obsessed with killing John, and began making comments to his PSP colleagues on a daily basis about wanting to kill him. He even asked other PSP colleagues to help him kill John Yelenic. Foley was manipulated by the defendant Michele Yelenic, who intentionally fueled and encouraged his hatred and jealousy . . . Virtually none of Foley's colleagues including the defendants Bono, Fry, Zenisek, Shields, Kirkland, and Jacobs, in clear and unequivocal violation of PSP regulations to report such misconduct, ever acted to protect John Yelenic, or inhibit or discourage Kevin Foley in carrying out the plans of he and Michele Yelenic, despite being made aware by Foley himself of his intentions."

The lawsuit is still pending in federal court in Pennsylvania.

* * *

The day after the verdict was announced, according to Mary Ann Clark, Michele Yelenic packed her children and most of her household belongings into vehicles and departed the city of Indiana, walking away from the house on Susan Drive. Michele had not attended a single day of Kevin's trial, no doubt not because she didn't support Kevin but because she was a potential witness, even if she was never called to testify. Michele moved to Savannah, Georgia, where she still lives as of this writing with Jamie, the trust fund millionaire, and the child adopted by Kevin. Kevin is still listed as a mail recipient at Michele's house, even though he is in prison in Pennsylvania. Nicole Kamler eventually enrolled in college at Pittsburgh, and Nathan at UIP in Indiana. Occasionally, neighbors around Susan Drive have reported someone looking like Nathan inside the house, now foreclosed, overgrown, and abandoned. Nathan was said to be driving a truck registered to Kevin, just another tragic victim of the "Wonderful Life" in Indiana, Pennsylvania.

Blairsville police chief Donald Hess was fired by the Blairsville City Council after taking sides in a dispute over a controversial downtown redevelopment project. He raised questions about what some of the city fathers were doing with federal money and helped secrete some of the redevelopment's records pending further investigation. After being fired, Hess sued the city in federal court.

Corporal Janelle Lydic took over the position but soon was also removed. Mary Ann said she was told Lydic pulled her weapon on another police officer during a dispute and that she, too, was suing the city for wrongful dismissal. Jill Gaston took over as acting chief of the Blairsville Police Department.

George Emigh sued the Pennsylvania State Police over his own involuntary retirement, claiming that the department had violated his civil rights when it forced him out after the sexual harassment complaint lodged against him. He had the same lawyer as Mary Ann Clark.

Emigh's supervisor Fulmer likewise left the PSP early, and he, too, sued his former employer. As noted, Bob Bell lost his race for reelection as Indiana County district attorney in 2008, in part, some believed, because of the Foley-Yelenic mess.

In June of 2009, Kevin was sentenced to life in prison. He is appealing the verdict.

So—was the jury wrong when it convicted Kevin Foley of the murder of John Yelenic in less than six hours? Probably not. There was a massive amount of circumstantial evidence against Kevin, and even the disputed DNA evidence, when taken at the FBI's most conservative assessment, seemed to show he had to be the culprit. His DNA could not be eliminated, and with everything else—the imprecations wishing Yelenic dead, the habitual knife flicking, the shoe treads, the Sheetz videos—it was no wonder the jury convicted.

Yet, still one wonders: Why would Kevin sacrifice a fourteen-year career as a law enforcement officer and his relationship with a newly adopted child? By all accounts, Kevin would have been a very good father. If he did commit the murder, why did he hate Yelenic so much that he slashed him to pieces? What was to be gained? Nothing material, that was for sure. Once Michele had signed that divorce agreement, there was nothing more to be had—not the property, not the rest of the money, certainly not the life insurance. So why?

Did something happen between John and Michele on the night of April 12–13—something that had enraged Kevin? Did Kevin go to the Yelenic house to confront John with what Kevin believed to be his latest outrage? Did John, thinking perhaps of Effie Alexander's ideas about "spine," stand up to Kevin? If so, it would have been no match. And did a fight ensue, a fight in which John scratched Kevin on the forehead, inducing Kevin to produce his knife? Once John was cut, Kevin had to know he had to kill him: if John lived, Kevin's own life would be over.

Was Kevin using steroids at the time? It's hard to say. Some aspects of his behavior seem to say so, others not. Emigh, for one, was sure that wasn't the case. He would have known, Emigh said later. Still, it might be one explanation for the horrific violence inflicted on John Yelenic, but not the only one. Sometimes passion can unleash terrible cruelty. Dying for love can sometimes be the most painful death of all.

The author wishes to thank the patient staffs of the courts of Indiana County, Common Pleas, Probate, and District, who patiently assembled a great many paper court records necessary to the telling off this story. Similar thanks go to the court staffs of Armstrong and Cambria counties, who ferreted out old records. Thanks also go to Anthony Krastek and Regis Kelly of the Pennsylvania attorney general's office, who patiently answered many questions about their prosecution of Kevin Foley. The Blairsville Police Department's acting chief Jill Gaston was also very helpful.

However, special thanks are due to Mary Ann Clark and Dr. Tom Riley, who freely shared their recollections of John Yelenic. The measure of a person's true worth is often in the friendships he or she makes, and according these people and others who knew and loved John Yelenic, he was a very good man indeed. While no one deserves to die before their time, sometimes circumstances make a death particularly outrageous.

The killing of John Yelenic was one of them.

Carlton Smith
Reno, Nevada
February 2011